THE ECONOMICS OF A.R.J. TURGOT

THE ECONOMICS OF A.R.J. TURGOT

edited and translated with an introduction
by

P.D. GROENEWEGEN

MARTINUS NIJHOFF / THE HAGUE / 1977

ISBN-13: 978-90-247-1953-2 e-ISBN-13: 978-94-010-1073-3
DOI: 10.1007/ 978-94-010-1073-3

TYPESET IN GREAT BRITAIN

TABLE OF CONTENTS

Preface vii

Introduction ix

I. Letter to M. l'Abbé de Cicé on the replacing of money by paper, also known as the 'Letter on Paper Money', (1749) 1

II. Remarks on the Notes to the Translation of Josiah Child (1753–1754) 9

III. Fairs and Markets (1757) 14

IV. In Praise of Gournay (1759) 20

V. Reflections on the Formation and Distribution of Wealth (1766) 43

VI. Plan for a Paper on Taxation in General (1763) 96

VII. Observations on a Paper by Saint-Péravy (1767) 109

VIII. Observations on a Paper by Graslin (1767) 123

IX. Value and Money (1769) 133

X. Extracts from 'Paper on Lending at Interest' (1770) 149

XI. Extracts from 'Letters on the Grain Trade' (1770) 164

XII. Letter to l'Abbé Terray on the 'Marque des fers' (1773) 182

Index 189

Appendix—A Concordance to various editions of the *Reflections* 195

PREFACE

This book can be described as a development of my Masters thesis, 'The Economics of A.R.J. Turgot' written at the University of Sydney in 1961–62. It has therefore been a long time in the making and, needless to say, I incurred many an intellectual debt during this period which I would like to acknowledge here. My thanks go first to Professor J.R. Wilson, who supervised my Masters thesis and who read part of this manuscript in draft, to the late Professor Jacob Viner whose tremendous knowledge of the history of economics was put at my disposal on several occasions, and to Professor R.L. Meek with whom I discussed this work in conversation and correspondence and who has given assistance in several other ways.

I also owe a great debt of gratitude to a large number of librarians for their assistance in unearthing infrequently used material housed in the collections over which they preside. In particular, I wish to acknowledge thanks to the librarians of the Fisher Library at the University of Sydney, the Public Library of New South Wales, the Australian National Library, the British Library of Economics and Political Science, the British Museum, the Goldsmiths' Library at the University of London, the Kress Collection at the Baker Library at Harvard, the Seligman Collection at the Butler Library at Columbia University, and the Bibliothèque nationale. In connection with queries relating to unpublished material, I am indebted to the assistance provided by Mr. P. Sraffa, Professor F.A. von Hayek, Professor N. de Marchi, and Dr. K. Hennings.

The University of Sydney provided a research grant in 1968 including the provision of research assistance. For their work in checking the translations and preparing the concordance, I am indebted to the services of Ms. Ella de Rooy and Julie O'Brien. Thanks are also due to the University of London, and to Professor F.A. von Hayek for allowing me to use unpublished material in their possession.

P.D. GROENEWEGEN
Sydney, April, 1976

INTRODUCTION

Turgot, the man, needs virtually no introduction. As writer, as philosopher, and above all, as statesman and administrator, his life has been chronicled in the many short eulogies and lengthy biographies which have appeared during the two centuries after his death. A great deal of this wealth of material on Turgot[1] can be ascribed to the fact that Turgot was one of the heroes of the nineteenth century liberals in France and in England, because he, in the "dark ages of mercantilism", advocated the free-est of trade, and could therefore be regarded as one of the leading prophets of the brief interlude of laissez-faire which occurred during the nineteenth century. It was in this manner that he was re-introduced to the English reader at the end of the nineteenth century by Hodgson, by Morley, and by Stephens.[2]

Turgot the statesman also requires no introduction to the historian of the *ancien régime* in France in the eighteenth century. After the pioneering study of d'Hughes,[3] his work as intendant of Limoges has been analysed in detail. His friendship with most of the leading figures of the French enlightenment, and even more, his own political, philosophical and literary writings secure him a prominent place in the intellectual history of pre-revolutionary France. Last, but most important, his place in history is assured through his brief ministry of finance under Louis XVI, and by his measures of reform, especially the famous six Edicts, which virtually secured his downfall but which, had they been successful, might have saved the French monarchy.[4]

[1] A check of a bibliography of writings on Turgot reveals no less than twenty-one biographies written during the nineteenth century.

[2] That is, W.B. Hodgson, *Turgot: his Life, Times and Opinions,* London, 1870; John Morley, 'Turgot' in *Critical Miscellanies,* Vol. II, London, 1877; W.W. Stephens, *Life and Writings of Turgot,* London, 1895.

[3] That is, Gustave d'Hughes, *Essai sur l'administration de Turgot dans la généralité de Limoges,* Paris, 1859; a more recent study of Turgot's intendancy is in Dakin, 'Turgot: Intendant of Limoges', thesis presented for the degree of Ph.D. at the University of London, 1936, partly published in Dakin, *Turgot and the ancien régime in France,* London, 1939.

[4] On this aspect of his life, reference should be made to Foncin, *Essai sur le ministère de Turgot,* Paris, 1877; R.P. Shepherd, *Turgot and his Six Edicts,* New York, 1903, and above all, to Edgar Faure, *La disgrâce de Turgot,* Paris, 1961.

Finally, there is Turgot the economist, so frequently mentioned in the histories of economics. There he is remembered, first of all, as the great apostle of laissez-faire. Secondly, he is discussed, together with Quesnay, as the greatest of the Physiocrats and, as the man who tried to put their doctrines into practice. Finally, he is referred to as the friend and precursor of the great Adam Smith, and as the author of the most important general treatise on economics before the appearance of the *Wealth of Nations* in 1776. It would seem, therefore, that Turgot the economist also needs no introduction.

Yet such an impression would be wrong. In spite of the wealth of material on the life and writings of Turgot, including those on his economics, there is room for a study of Turgot as an economist, especially in the English language. In fact, it can be argued that Turgot the economist does need an introduction, or, at least a re-introduction, for the following reasons. First of all, most of the nineteenth century, and even some of the twentieth century studies, have given an almost unwarranted emphasis to the laissez-faire aspects of his work and have virtually ignored his contributions to economic analysis.[5] Secondly, more recent discussions of his economics have concentrated on the thought in his *Reflections* and have neglected, if not all, at least most of the other economic work.[6] Finally, and perhaps the most important reason for this comparative neglect of Turgot's economics, especially in the English speaking world: the economic writings of Turgot are relatively scarce, and apart from the *Reflections*, the article 'foundation', the extracts translated by Stephens, and more recently, the papers translated by Meek, not available in English at all.[7]

[5] This may be illustrated by quoting some remarks from Neymark's study of Turgot's economics. After briefly summarising what he considers to be the essence of Turgot's economic work, he concludes this introductory section by stating: "Ces vérités, nous les avons vues magistralement exprimées, developées, dans les écrits de Turgot: elles ont été adoptées après lui par les plus grands maîtres de la science économique: J.B. Say, Ricardo, Rossi, Bastiat, Robert Peel, Cavour, Cobden, Michel Chevalier." (Neymark, *Turgot et ses doctrines*, Paris, 1885, I, pp. 336–337). He concludes the discussion of Turgot's economics, with the following remark: "Les doctrines et les principes économiques de Turgot pourraient être résumés en un seul mot: liberté." (Ibid., I, p. 363.)

[6] This is demonstrated in P.D. Groenewegen's, 'A Reappraisal of Turgot's Theory of Value, Exchange and Price Determination', *History of Political Economy*, Vol. 2, No. 1, Spring 1970, pp. 177–196; P.D. Groenewegen, 'A Re-interpretation of Turgot's Theory of Capital and Interest', *Economic Journal*, Vol. 81, No. 2, June, 1971, pp. 327–340.

[7] The paper 'Foundation' was translated and included as an appendix to the translation of Condorcet's *Life of M. Turgot*, London, 1787, pp. 381–397. The *Reflections* was anonymously translated in the 1790's, first published in 1793, re-issued in 1795, and reprinted by J.R.McCulloch in his *A Select Collection of Scarce and Valuable Economic Tracts* in 1859. Another translation was included with the 1801 Basle edition of the *Wealth of Nations*. In 1898, W.J. Ashley published a translation in the Economic Classics series published by Macmillan. In 1973, R.L. Meek published a new translation together with translations of two other papers in his *Turgot on Progress, Economics and Sociology*, London, 1973. Meek has also translated Turgot's paper, 'Value and Money' (see R.L. Meek (editor), *Precursors of Adam Smith*, London, 1973, pp. 77–100). A selection of Turgot's writings in translation including the 'Letter on Paper Money', the 'Eloge de Gournay', and the 'Letter on the Marque des fers' was included in W.W. Stephens, op. cit.

This study of the economics of Turgot fills that gap in the literature of economics by presenting translations of all the more important economic writings, including a new translation of the *Reflections*. This, after an interval of two centuries, makes the economics of Turgot accessible to the English speaking public.

In the introduction which follows the emphasis will be on Turgot the economist. A biographical sketch of Turgot is not presented;[8] what is required is a detailed discussion of Turgot's economic work included here in translation, especially an analysis of the circumstances in which they were written. This information will supplement the editorial notes given throughout the text. Some comments on the sources of the translations will be given at the end of the introduction.

THE ECONOMIC WRITINGS

Biographies of Turgot clearly reveal that the study of theoretical economics played only a very small part in his short but crowded life. Partly as the result of the extreme pressures of work from his administrative positions, and partly because of his many other intellectual interests,[9] he devoted relatively little time to the systematic study of economics, and prepared his economic writings with only few exceptions in connection with his administrative duties. This makes his performance in economics all the more remarkable.

1. The Letter on Paper Money (1749)

Little is known about the beginning of Turgot's interest in economics,[10] except for the fact that his first piece of written work on the subject which has been preserved dates from the year 1749, when he was not quite twenty-two years of age. This is the letter to l'Abbé de Cicé on the subject of paper

[8] For details about Turgot's life the reader is referred to Dakin, *Turgot and the ancien régime in France*, which remains the best English biography. Reference should also be made to the two biographies by two close friends: Du Pont de Nemours, *Mémoires sur la vie et les ouvrages de M. Turgot*, and Condorcet, *Vie de M. Turgot*, which appeared in the decade of Turgot's death, as well as to the biographical details presented by G. Schelle, one of the editors of his works, in a separate biography published in 1909 and in the introductions to his edition of the *Oeuvres de Turgot*, Paris, 1913–1923, 5 volumes.

[9] It should not be forgotten that these interests were very wide, and included the natural sciences, the social sciences and literature. An indication of their extent is given in Condorcet's biography, *The Life of M. Turgot*, pp. 255–262. See also P.D. Groenewegen, 'Turgot and Adam Smith', *Scottish Journal of Political Economy*, Vol. XVI, No. 3, November, 1969, p. 273 and n. 14.

[10] For a detailed discussion of Turgot's early economic writings, see G. Schelle, 'Les premiers travaux économiques de Turgot d'après ses manuscrits inédits', *Revue d'histoire des doctrines économiques et sociales*, IV, 1911, pp. 1–16.

money[11] in which Turgot critically examined some arguments presented in defence of Law's system of banking and credit creation.

It seems very likely that this first excursus into economics was indirectly inspired by the publication of Montesquieu's *L'Esprit des Lois* in 1748 which, in the section on the theory of money and prices had provided an interesting account of inflation based largely on the quantity theory of money. This influential work was undoubtedly studied by Turgot on its first appearance and it must have struck him, as well as his fellow students with whom he would have discussed it, that the theory of money in *L'Esprit des Lois* could be favourably contrasted with the analysis of Law's system in Montesquieu's earlier *Lettres persanes* and in the other contemporary writings which defended the system.[12] It must have been after a thorough study of this literature that Turgot decided to put his impressions of his latest readings on this subject on paper for the benefit of his schoolfriend who had preceded him to the Sorbonne.[13]

The letter itself is interesting because it shows the development of Turgot's monetary theory, which was elaborated on and added to in his later work, but which was not substantially changed. The letter reveals him as a staunch adherent of the quantity theory of money, a convinced metallist, and an anti-inflationist who felt that the value of the currency could only be safeguarded through strict convertibility. In addition, he put forward an argument that true credit could only be granted for productive purposes since the interest payable can only be recovered from the profits of enterprise, while he also demonstrated – with the aid of some elementary algebra – the dangers of financing government expenditure by means of the printing press instead of by taxation, by showing that this policy must result in accelerating inflation.[14]

[11] See below, pp. 1–8. For a discussion of the background to, and an analysis of its contents, see D. Angelescu, *Après l'expérience de Law. La Lettre de Turgot sur le papier-monnaie,* Paris, 1928, and P. Vigreux, 'La fondement de la valeur de la monnaie d'après Turgot', *Revue d'histoire économique et sociale,* XXII, 1934, pp. 109–119.

[12] See Montesquieu, *L'Esprit des Lois,* Geneva, 1748, II, pp. 75–76, 89–93. That is, Book XXI, chapter 18, Book XXII, chapters 6–8, and *Lettres persanes*, Lettres CV and CXXXVIII in *Oeuvres de Montesquieu,* nouvelle édition, Amsterdam and Leipzig, 1758, III, pp. 209, 278–9. The other contemporary writings would have included Melon, *Essai politique sur le commerce,* n.p. 1734, esp. pp. 193–202; Du Tot, *Réflexions politiques sur les finances et le commerce*, La Haye, 1738, esp. I, chapter I, II, pp. 62–115, 338–365; and Joseph Pâris-Duverney, *Examen du livre intitulé Réflexions politiques sur les finances et le commerce*, La Haye, 1740, I, pp. 181 ff, II, pp. 1–138, which gives an excellent factual account of Law's system which is highly critical of those presented by Melon and Du Tot.

[13] Apart from Terrasson, *Lettres sur le nouveau système des finances,* which forms the basis for Turgot's critical letter on paper money, he cited Locke's monetary work, Du Tot's *Réflexions* while, most likely, he would have read Melon. (See Turgot to Caillard, January, 1771, in Schelle, *Oeuvres de Turgot*, III, pp. 499–501.) He does not appear to have studied Law's work which in any case was not listed in the catalogue of his library (see below, p. 2, n. 7, and p. 5, n. 16).

[14] In this analysis, Turgot made no allowance for the modifying influence of the presence of unemployed resources as was done, for example, in the monetary analysis of Cantillon and Hume, whose works were of course not available to him at that time.

As Du Pont noted, with the memories of the hyper-inflation of the French revolutionary period still strongly impressed on his mind, it was a very creditable performance for a student of 21 years.[15]

That Turgot maintained an interest in monetary questions can be seen from the next piece of economics which has been preserved: the fragment which Schelle has called, *Plan d'un ouvrage sur le commerce, la circulation, et l'intérêt de l'argent, la richesse des états*, and to which he has rather arbitrarily assigned the date 1753–54.[16] This fragment indicates that Turgot's thoughts on the scope of economics at the time were still fairly orthodox and did not go beyond questions connected with trade, money and credit, as well as definitions of wealth, and were as yet not concerned with the production and distribution of wealth.[17] On the other hand, he already showed himself to be a strong anti-mercantilist, he criticised confusions between wealth and money, stressed the necessity of security and private property for trade, and included a section with a fairly well developed argument on the impediments to free trade of indirect taxation.[18] It can therefore be presumed that at this time, he was already acquainted with Gournay's economic thought, but not as yet with the ideas of Quesnay.[19]

2. *Remarks on the Notes to the Translation of Child* (*1753–54*)

The other piece of economics of this period, and the second to be included in this volume, is associated with the French translation of Josiah Child's *New Discourse of Trade* which was published in 1754 under the title *Traité sur le commerce et les avantages qui resultent de la réduction de l'intérêt de l'argent*.[20] This translation was to have been accompanied by notes written by one of the translators, Vincent de Gournay who apparently showed his work to his friend, Turgot, for comments. It is the comments by Turgot on Gournay's notes which are included here. Unfortunately, Gournay's notes themselves were not allowed to be published with the translation by the censor, so that Turgot's notes on notes are sometimes difficult to follow.

[15] Du Pont, *Oeuvres de Turgot*, II, p. 1, n. 1.

[16] See Schelle, *Oeuvres*, I, pp. 376–387. This fragment has not been included in this volume.

[17] Ibid., pp. 376–378.

[18] Ibid., pp. 382–386.

[19] Turgot probably met Gournay not long after leaving the Sorbonne; Quesnay he did not meet till several years later at least. See Dakin, *Turgot and the ancien régime in France*, p. 18. As Schelle has shown, Gournay exerted considerable influence on Turgot's economics. See G. Schelle, *Vincent de Gournay*, Paris, 1897, e.g. pp. 131–132 on the question of the desirability of suppressing the guilds. Gournay probably also introduced Turgot to the writings of some English economists such as Child and Gee. See below, p. 9, n. 1 and the reference to this in the 'Eloge de Gournay', below, pp. 22, 33. It is interesting to note that Du Pont (*Oeuvres de Turgot*, 1, p. 45) states that it was the translation of Tucker's work (see below, p. XIV) which "le lié plus intiment avec MM. *Trudaine*, père et fils, et avec M. de Gournay . . .", so that they may have induced him to publish it in 1755.

[20] See below, pp. 9–13.

Nevertheless, it is this work, rather than the previously discussed fragment which has been included here, since the notes on the translation of Child have a greater bearing on the later development of Turgot's economics: they present his early views on the regulation of interest rates and on the grain trade, topics on which he later wrote extensively.[21]

Another small economic work, written prior to the preparation of the *Encyclopédie* articles may also be mentioned at this stage. Once again, this work was a set of notes on a translation, but this time the translation was by Turgot himself. In 1755 it appeared anonymously as Turgot's first published piece on economics under the title *Questions importantes sur le commerce, à l'occassion des oppositions au dernier Bill de Naturalisations*, translated from the English of Josiah Tucker[22] to which the translator had appended some eight notes. This work deserves mention for several reasons. In the first place, because several of these notes once more reveal at this still early stage of Turgot's career, the tremendous importance of free competition and free trade in the development of Turgot's economic thought. Further, they reveal the fact that thanks to Gournay Turgot's economics came under the influence of English economics to a far greater extent than that of his French contemporaries who were followers of Quesnay.[23]

3. The article 'Fair' for the Encyclopédie (1757)

The appearance of the *Dictionnaire raisonée des sciences, des arts, et des métiers*, the first two volumes of which were published in 1751, provided the place for Turgot's next published work. As he was acquainted with one of the editors, d'Alembert, and also because he already at that stage had a considerable reputation as an intellectual, he was invited if not pressed to give his support to this project. This he did after securing a promise of complete anonymity for his contributions from the editors, by giving five articles to the

[21] That is, 'Paper on Lending at Interest', below pp. 149–163, and his 'Letters on the grain Trade', below pp. 164–181.

[22] Included in Schelle, *Oeuvres*, I, pp. 442–70. It is a translation of Part II of Josiah Tucker's *Reflections on the Expediency of a Law for the Naturalisation of Foreign Protestants* which was published in London in 1751. At this time, Turgot is also supposed to have translated Hume's essay 'Of the Jealousy of Trade', according to Du Pont (in *Oeuvres*, I, p. 45). No trace of this translation has been found, while Du Pont's anecdote that Turgot translated this essay at the same time as he translated Tucker cannot be true since the 'Jealousy of Trade' was first published in 1758 in Hume's *Essays and Treatises on Several Subjects*, three years after Turgot's Tucker translation was published. Hume's other economic essays had, however, first appeared in 1752.

[23] Cf. note 19, above. For the importance of this, see my 'Turgot and Adam Smith', op. cit., pp. 286–287. Morellet, who was also acquainted with Gournay, states that Gournay was one of the few Frenchmen acquainted with English economic writings at the time, and that he was instrumental in having many of them translated. See *Mémoires de Morellet*, Paris, 1821, I, pp. 56–57

Encyclopédie altogether. Three of these *Etymologie, Existence*, and *Expansibilité* appeared in 1756; the other two *Foire* and *Fondations* in 1757.[24]

In this connection, it may be pointed out that Turgot was most loath to appear in print under his own name and auspices, even though he was quite willing to have his material used by others. Gournay probably persuaded him to publish his translation of Tucker's pamphlet as part of the group of English works on trade which appeared in translation in the first half of the 1750's.[25] Strong persuasion similarly appears to have been necessary for the *Encyclopédie* articles, which were invariably well received.[26] According to Du Pont,[27] Turgot was to have contributed many more articles; while Diderot, with whom Turgot was not particularly on friendly terms, tried to persuade him by letter as late as 1759 to provide eight articles on subjects of which some must have been most tempting to Turgot.[28] Furthermore, one of the five articles he wrote and which was printed appears to have been an accidental contribution, if Morellet's anecdote on the subject can be believed.[29]

The last two of these five articles for the *Encyclopédie* have economic content. *'Fondation'*, which is not included in this volume, relatively little since it deals mainly with endowments. In section 5 of this article there is, however, a small discussion of the "wants of society" which entails a comparison of private and public wants, the latter being seen as suitable objectives for en-

[24] See *Encyclopédie ou dictionnaire raisonné des sciences, des arts et des métiers*, Paris, 1756, Vol. VI, pp. 98–111, 260–267, 274–285; 1757, Vol. VII, pp. 38–41, 72–75.

[25] See G. Schelle, *Vincent de Gournay*, p. 271; cf. *Mémoires de Morellet*, I, pp. 56–57.

[26] Voltaire, for example, after having received a visit from Turgot at his home in 1760 at the suggestion of d'Alembert, wrote back to the latter: "Je suis encore tout plein de M. Turgot. Je ne savais pas qu'il eut fait l'article Existence; je n'ai guerre vu d'homme plus aimable ni plus instruit et, ce qui est rare chez metaphysiciens, il a le goût le plus sûr". (Cited by Leon Say, *Turgot*, Paris, 1887, p. 35.)

[27] Du Pont, *Oeuvres*, I, p. 43, III, p. 136. Titles mentioned by Du Pont include: Grammaire générale, Hôpital, Humide et Humidité, Immatérialité, Inspecteurs, Origine des langues, Mendicité, Probabilité, and Sensations.

[28] Diderot to Turgot, 21/1/1759, cited in Schelle, *Oeuvres*, I, p. 594. The titles of the eight requested articles were: Humiditée, Idée, Idéalisme, Intérêt de l'argent, Impôt, Immatérialisme, Inspecteur and Intendant de province. In connection with taxation and interest, it should be noted that Quesnay also prepared articles on these subjects, which he showed to Turgot and on which the latter made notes. Turgot's notes on Quesnay's 'Impôt' have been preserved (see *François Quesnay et la Physiocratie*, Paris, 1958, II, pp. 579–617) but those on 'Intérêt de l'argent' have been lost. See Turgot to Du Pont (20/12/1766 in Schelle *Oeuvres*, II, p. 512), where reference is made to them. For the author of the actual article 'Impôt' in the *Encyclopédie* see 'Fairs and Markets' below p. 17, n. 4.

[29] *Mémoires de Morellet*, I, p. 40. The gist of this anecdote is as follows: Morellet was apparently given the task to prepare the article *Etymologie* for the *Encyclopédie*, and when he had completed a draft, Morellet showed it to his friend Turgot for comment. Turgot claimed that this was not the article *Etymologie* however, but the article *Onomatopée*, stated further that he had collected many notes on the subject of etymology, and so his article "was substituted for mine" in the first edition of the *Encyclopédie*.

dowments.[30] *'Foire'*, on the other hand, which is included,[31] contains more economic material.

In an interesting argument using the method of conjectural history, Turgot linked the development of markets as a natural consequence of the growth of economic society, with the unnatural development of the great European fairs, whose establishment resulted from the privileges granted to them during the Middle Ages. The grandeur of these fairs is ascribed to the fact that participating traders were exempt from all duties and other barriers to trade for the duration of the fair. From this experience Turgot argued that the best method of ensuring a general growth in commerce was the complete removal of all barriers to trade. The article on the privileged trade of fairs is turned into a plea for free trade in general.

4. In Praise of Gournay (Eloge de Gournay) (1759)

The theme of free trade is further pursued in Turgot's next economic work, the famous biographical essay, 'In Praise of Gournay'.[32] On 27 June, 1759 Turgot's friend and teacher, Vincent de Gournay died after a long illness and, as is usually the case with public figures, an obituary was required. Marmontel, who was entrusted with this task, was acquainted with Turgot and requested his help in providing material for the preparation of the official eulogy.[33] This material was abundantly provided by Turgot in the work now known as the *'Eloge de Gournay'*, so that Marmontel could simply complete his task by editing extracts from Turgot's manuscript, which were published as the obituary in the August issue of the *Mercure*. The work as a whole was not published till the nineteenth century when Du Pont de Nemours included it in his edition of Turgot's works.[34]

The essay can easily be described as one of Turgot's more important works since it provides the only systematic exposition of his general views on

[30] Included in *Oeuvres de Turgot* (Schelle edition), I, pp. 584–593. It is interesting to note that this article was translated into English in the eighteenth century, and published as an appendix to the English translation of Condorcet's *Life of M. Turgot*. For bibliographical details see n. 7 above.

[31] This is included here (below pp. 14–19) under the title, 'Fairs and Markets', the title which Turgot used in a letter to Du Pont (29/11/1769 in Schelle, *Oeuvres*, III, p. 72). Although the proper translation of the *Encyclopédie* article would be 'Fair', I have followed Du Pont and Daire in using the longer title, since it also seems more appropriate as a description of the contents of the article.

[32] This is included here (below pp. 20–42) under the title under which extracts from it were translated and published in W.W. Stephens, *Life and Writings of Turgot*. This seems to be a most appropriate manner of translating the French title, 'Eloge de Gournay'.

[33] Turgot to Marmontel, 22/7/1759, below p. 20.

[34] Du Pont de Nemours, *Oeuvres*, III, pp. 321–375. As was so frequently the case, Du Pont "improved" on the manuscript by making changes and additions. These have been indicated in the translated text, see below p. 30, n. 16 and p. 39, n. 28.

economic policy. It attempts an explanation, in the words of Schelle[35] of "one of the most important problems of mankind, that of knowing the proper objectives of government in society". Turgot's answer to this problem in the *Eloge* is limited to the economic sphere, and he discussed in turn the methods and consequences of government intervention in manufacturing and trade in general and, more particularly, in the manufacture of cloth, in the grain trade, in the money market, in the labour market, in colonial trade and in the imposition of taxation. His conclusion, a qualified laissez-faire position, is worth quoting:

> ... M. de Gournay did not pretend to limit the duties of government towards commerce strictly to that of maintaining its free course and removing the obstacles that oppose the improvement of industry. He was also quite convinced of the usefulness of the encouragements that could be given to industry either by recompensing the authors of useful inventions or by encouraging, by prizes and gratuities, a competition among artists to attain perfection.[36]

The *Eloge* is also the last work on economics completed during Turgot's formative years when he was still able to command considerable periods of leisure. The remainder of his economic work, with only a few exceptions, was concerned with matters related to the administrative tasks which occupied the bulk of his time when he was appointed, first as an intendant, and later as Contrôleur-général.

5. *Reflections on the Formation and Distribution of Wealth (1766)*

One of these exceptions, and Turgot's most important work, is the *Reflections on the Formation and Distribution of Wealth*, which is the next item included in this volume.[37] This work was completed in November 1766, the date given in the earliest known edition[38] for reasons explained by Turgot in a letter to Du Pont in the following month, which may be quoted in full:

> I have scribbled on a great deal of paper since I last saw you.... I have completed some *Questions* for the two Chinese of whom I have Spoken, and in order to clarify their objective and meaning, I have preceded them with a type of outline of the analysis of the working of society and the distribution of wealth. I did not want to include any algebra in it, and there is only the metaphysical part of the *Tableau économique*; moreover, I have left out many questions which should be treated to render the work complete, but I have treated rather thoroughly questions relating to

[35] See Schelle, *Vincent de Gournay*, p. 7. Following the quoted remarks (my translation), Schelle raises the pertinent question that it is often difficult in the *Eloge* to distinguish the ideas of the subject of the praise from those of the author.

[36] 'In Praise of Gournay', below pp. 31–32.

[37] Below, pp. 43–95.

[38] That is, the *tirage-à-part*, presumably printed in 1770. The date, Novembre 1766, occurs on the last page of the text, before the errata.

the formation and the movement of capitals, the interest of money, etc. It is a brief outline.[39]

The issue of the origin of what has frequently been described as the most important treatise on economics prior to Adam Smith's *Wealth of Nations*[40] must be further discussed since it has appeared ludicrous to some commentators[41] that such an important work should have been written as an aid to a catechism on China to be answered by two Chinese students visiting Paris in order to provide more information about this largely unknown country which fascinated the intellectuals of the eighteenth century. Yet all the evidence seems to point in that direction so that economics appears to owe the existence of the *Reflections* to the accident of a visit to Paris of MM. Ko and Yang as guests of the Jesuits.

This evidence is both direct and indirect. Apart from the letter quoted above, Turgot ascribed the existence of the *Reflections* to the two Chinese on other occasions and to other persons. In a letter written to Du Pont over three years later,[42] Turgot repeated that the *Reflections* was written "without a plan and with no other object than to explain the questions which I put to some Chinese about their country". The same explanation is given in a letter to Josiah Tucker in September, 1770 when Turgot sent him a copy of the book; and, four years later, in a letter to Caillard when the matter of a German translation was raised.[43] It seems most unlikely that Turgot would have lied about this matter to three different people on various occasions over a period of nearly eight years.

The indirect evidence is perhaps even more convincing. The fact that the *Reflections* was written with such a trivial objective in mind fits in neatly with the facts surrounding the writing of many of Turgot's works. To take two examples. The *Eloge de Gournay* was written at what was probably a rather casual request by Marmontel for material for Gournay's obituary; while secondly, Morellet's anecdote about the accidental nature of the origin of the *Encyclopédie* article, *Etymologie*, seems also characteristic.[44] This discussion of the reason for writing the *Reflections* has one implication which needs to be further discussed. The fact that the work was not published till three years after its completion, suggests the possibility that Turgot may have considerably revised the work in that period. The description of the contents

[39] Turgot to Du Pont, 9/12/1766, in Schelle, *Oeuvres*, II, p. 519 (my translation). The questions referred to are Turgot's 'Questions sur le Chine' (in Schelle, *Oeuvres*, II, pp. 523ff.).

[40] For example, Batbie, *Turgot*, Paris, 1861, pp. 11, 162–163; W.B. Hodgson, *Turgot*, pp. 64–65; J. A. Schumpeter, *History of Economic Analysis*, pp. 247–249; Neymark, I, pp. 330–332.

[41] See for example, R.L. Meek, *Turgot on Progress, Economics and Sociology*, pp. 18–19.

[42] Turgot to Du Pont, 6/2/1770 in Schelle, *Oeuvres*, III, p. 375.

[43] Turgot to Tucker, 12/9/1770 in Schelle, *Oeuvres*, III, pp. 421–422; and Turgot to Caillard, 5/5/1774, in Schelle, *Oeuvres*, III, pp. 675–676.

[44] See above, pp. XV–XVI, n. 29.

given in 1766 in the letter to Du Pont just quoted, indicates that such changes, if they were made, were probably minimal.

The story of the publication, and possibly, the preservation of this work, also contain peculiarities which must be examined.[45] As indicated earlier, the work was not published until three years after it was written, when Turgot offered it to his friend, Du Pont, for publication in the journal, *Ephémérides du Citoyen*, in serial form. Presumably in reply to a request from Du Pont for material for the journal which was running behind schedule for lack of copy, Turgot promised to send a "piece on *wealth*, very incomplete and in need of development, but it will give you eighty pages".[46] The piece itself was sent a few days later with the apology that it was "not very good, but . . . long, even though also too short. It contains 101 paragraphs, marginal summaries which could be used as titles to fill even more space and a little preface".[47] In January 1770 Turgot asked Du Pont to delete "the theological part of the manuscript" on interest, since by then he was completing his 'Paper on Lending at Interest' which contained similar material,[48] while at the end of the month he wondered whether Du Pont had received his manuscript.[49] This last query was answered when Turgot received his copy of the *Ephémérides* for November 1769 which contained the first instalment of his *Reflections* and which had been passed by the censor at the end of January 1770.[50]

The history of Turgot's arguments with Du Pont over the alterations he had made to the manuscript in the published version in the *Ephémérides* need not be discussed, since they have been commented on elsewhere.[51] Only the

[45] Good, but not quite complete accounts of the publication and the various editions of the *Reflections* are contained in the following: G. Schelle, 'Pouquoi les "Refléxions" de Turgot sur la formation et la distribution des richesses ne sont-elles pas exactement connues', *Journal des économistes*, XLIII, July 1888, Part II, pp. 2–16; W. Ashley, introduction to *Reflections on the Formation and Distribution of Riches*, New York, 1963, pp. viii–xiii; and I.C. Lundberg, pp. 8–18, 85–97.

[46] Turgot to Du Pont, 1/12/1769, in Schelle, *Oeuvres*, III, p. 72.

[47] Turgot to Du Pont, 2/12/1769, ibid., pp. 73–74. In this letter Turgot also sent instructions to Du Pont for the preparation of offprints for distribution to his friends, and he also disclosed his intentions, not to be realised, of making "something passable of this piece one day".

[48] Turgot to Du Pont, 12/1/1770 in Schelle, *Oeuvres*, III, pp. 370–371. The 'Paper on Lending at Interest' was completed on the 27th January 1770 and was presumably sent off to Terray shortly afterwards. (See below p. XXVIII). One reason for the deletion of this paragraph may have been a desire for anonymity (cf. Turgot to Du Pont, 2/12/1769 in Schelle, *Oeuvres*, III, pp. 73–74) which would be jeopardised by the appearance of similar arguments in both works.

[49] Turgot to Du Pont, 30/1/1770, in Schelle, *Oeuvres*, III, pp. 372–373.

[50] Turgot to Du Pont, 2/2/1770, in Schelle, *Oeuvres*, III, p. 373, and note (b).

[51] Turgot to Du Pont 2/2/1770, 6/2/1770, 20/2/1770, 2/3/1770 and 23/3/1770 in Schelle, *Oeuvres*, III, pp. 373–384. The textual variations made by Du Pont have been indicated in notes to the text of the *Reflections* below. The incorrectness of Du Pont's text was first discovered by Schelle, and the first corrected text of the *Reflections*, which, however, still contains some inaccuracies, was published by him in the Robineau edition of a selection of Turgot's economic works in 1889. (That is, G. Robineau (ed.), *Turgot: Administration et oeuvres économiques*, Petite libraire économique, Paris, 1889.) Schelle presented a detailed discussion of the quarrel in 1888 in his article, 'Pourquoi les "Réflexions" de Turgot . . .', op. cit.

final result of the argument need be noted. This was the preparation and printing of an edition conforming to the original manuscript – the 1770 *tirage-à-part* with its errata – which Turgot had Du Pont circulate among his friends.[52] Two associated questions do, however, require some discussion. The first is why Du Pont used his own, incorrect version of the *Reflections* in the edition of Turgot's works which he published four decades later, thereby ensuring the circulation of the wrong text for nearly the whole of the nineteenth century. The second relates to the publication of a corrected text of the *Reflections* in 1788, drawn from the *tirage-à-part*, the publisher of which being therefore responsible for the preservation of what appears to be Turgot's authentic text.

The first of these questions can be easily answered. The basic reason for Du Pont's alterations of the text of the *Reflections* was doctrinal, and this doctrinal position does not appear to have altered much between the 1770's and the first decades of the nineteenth century. As Schelle has argued, all these changes and additions were designed to give the *Reflections* a greater Physiocratic flavour and to remove conflicts between Turgot's economics and Physiocratic thought. As shown by his correspondence with J.B. Say, Du Pont remained a convinced Physiocrat till his death – hence the text of the *Reflections* was not only left uncorrected but was in fact even further "improved" by the insertion of additional notes by Du Pont in the edition of Turgot's works which he prepared.[53]

The responsibility for the publication of the 1788 edition of the *Reflections* is less easy to ascertain. From internal evidence it is clear that this edition was virtually a reproduction of the *tirage-à-part*, which indicates that it must have been published by a relatively close friend of Turgot. Schelle's suggestion[54] that Du Pont was responsible for its publication seems odd in view of the text of the *Reflections* which he later published in his edition of Turgot's works,

[52] See Turgot to Du Pont, 23/3/1770, in Schelle, *Oeuvres,* III, pp. 383–384. The number of copies which Turgot originally requested was 100 or 150 (see Turgot to Du Pont 2/12/1769, ibid., III, 73–74), but it is not certain how many were actually produced. Only three of the corrected copies appear to have survived, two of which are at present in the Bibliothèque nationale in Paris; the third is in the Seligman Collection, Butler Library at Columbia University in New York. This copy contains the Errata which Turgot had asked Du Pont to print in his letter of 23 March 1770. I am indebted to the librarian of the Butler Library for providing me with a photocopy of their copy of the *Reflections* known as the *tirage-à-part.*

[53] See Schelle, 'Pourquoi les "Réflexions" de Turgot . . .', op. cit., esp. pp. 14–16. Du Pont also edited other parts of Turgot's works in this fashion – as shown in the text below – generally to remove criticisms of Physiocracy but also for political and stylistic reasons. See, for example, 'Observations on a Paper by Saint-Péravy', below pp. 109–110, n. 5, and cf. Meek, *Turgot on Progress, Sociology and Economics*, pp. 6–7 and n. 1. (The textual change noted there was undoubtedly inspired by fear of giving offence to Napoleon, the "great law giver".) Even Du Pont's own biography of Turgot was changed by him for the edition of the *Oeuvres*; for example, the reference to the *tirage-à-part* was suppressed in the later edition. Cf. Schelle, 'Pourquoi les "Reflexions" . . .', op. cit., p. 16, n. 1.

[54] Schelle, 'Pourquoi . . .', op. cit., p. 16. This seems to contradict his arguments in the following paragraph.

and must therefore be discounted. In my opinion, the more probable candidates in this connection are Caillard, Turgot's secretary, or his close personal friend, Condorcet. Both had access to Turgot's manuscripts, and Caillard had assisted with the German translation of the *Reflections* made during Turgot's life time.[55] Both, moreover, could easily have inserted the quotation from Virgil – placed by Voltaire at the base of Houdon's bust of Turgot[56] – on the title page of the *Reflections*, which differentiates it from other contemporary publications of Turgot's works. Other evidence suggests Condorcet as the most likely candidate. He appears to have been responsible for the publication of several other of Turgot's works in 1789 and 1790 and these show greater textual accuracy than Du Pont's later editions of the same works. It can therefore easily be conjectured that Condorcet, after publishing his successful biography of Turgot in 1786 followed up this publication by reprinting the more important of his friend's works, which, in addition, were highly relevant in the changing political situation which was developing in the last few years of the *ancien régime*. At the same time, he therefore seems to have been responsible for preserving the accurate text of these works, including that of the *Reflections*.[57]

6. *Plan for a Paper on Taxation in General* (*1763*)

More characteristic of Turgot's work on economics written while he was intendant at Limoges are the various papers on taxation. Some of these, such as the annual reports to the Contrôleur-général in connection with the levying of the taille in his province were the direct consequence of his administrative responsibilities. Other, more theoretical pieces, owed their existence to his strong interest in taxation theory and policy. One of these is the 'Plan for a Paper on Taxation in General' written in 1763 in response to a questionnaire circulated by Bertin, then Contrôleur-général, on the subject of land taxes, of a land register, and on corporations. Turgot's characteristic response to this request consisted of the intention of preparing a lengthy paper in which the matter would be "resolved in a satisfactory and practical manner" by the development of answers to the question from first principles of taxation theory. This project appears to have been carried no further than the preparation of a detailed plan, itself not finished, but which nevertheless forms the

[55] Turgot to Du Pont, 23/3/1770, in Schelle, *Oeuvres*, III, pp. 383–384; Turgot to Caillard, 5/5/1774, ibid., III, pp. 675–676.

[56] See Lundberg, op. cit., p. 22. Apart from the English translations of the *Reflections* (published in 1793, reprinted in 1795) this is the only published work of Turgot which carries the epigram.

[57] For a discussion of Condorcet as the publisher of Turgot's writings see my review of Meek's *Turgot on Progress, Sociology and Economics* in *History of Political Economy*, Vol. 6, No. 4, Winter 1974, pp. 478–481.

clearest account of Turgot's taxation theory, and which therefore has been included in this collection.[58]

The first part of this paper provides a plan for the various chapters, frequently indicating their proposed contents by no more than a single sentence or phrase; it dwells mainly on the classification of taxes into direct or indirect taxation and on the proposition that "all these different types of taxation ultimately fall entirely on the proprietors of the soil". This is followed by a more detailed elaboration of the nature of direct and indirect taxation, and of the revenue of the land. This last section is the most fully developed. Starting from Quesnay's analysis of the revenue of landed property which is therein sharply distinguished from profit and wages – the necessary costs of production – Turgot then demonstrates why taxes should be levied on the revenue of land and not on those other forms of income. This is followed by an extensive critique of other forms of land tax: including Vauban's project of a "Dîme royale" or royal tithe, the ecclesiastical tithe, and the proportional tax on the net product of land as proposed by Mirabeau in his *Théorie de l'impôt* in 1760, and in the *Philosophie rurale* in 1763. In passing, Turgot also makes some interesting criticisms of the English land tax, and of the role of taxation in a constitutional monarchy of the British type. Mirabeau's proposals are finally rejected on administrative grounds, but Turgot's own alternative solution to the problem of land tax administration is only mentioned and not elaborated before the manuscript breaks off.

Although incomplete, the paper is an important one. It demonstrates Turgot's critical acceptance of Physiocratic taxation policy, it sheds some light on Turgot's ambivalent attitude to profit, but above all it reveals his highly developed sense of theory in the well ordered presentation of his ideas. The basic form of these ideas were not to change during his life time, as is shown, for example, when Turgot later argued in correspondence with Hume on the subject of indirect taxation. Hume's various arguments could not shake Turgot's views on the nature of indirect taxation, its inefficiency and inequity.[59]

The firmness of Turgot's views on taxation is further illustrated in the prospectus for an essay competition on the subject of indirect taxation organised under the auspices of the Royal Agricultural Society of Limoges. In this prospectus, direct taxation is defined as that imposed directly on the landlord's net revenue, all other taxes being classified as indirect.[60] The aim of the competition was to elicit more factual information about the effects of in-

[58] See 'Plan for a Paper on Taxation in General', below, pp. 96–108 and n. 1. Bertin's departure from the post of Contrôleur-général at the end of 1763 was probably the reason why Turgot did not complete this project.

[59] Turgot to Hume, 7/9/1766, in J.H. Burton (editor), *Letters of Eminent Persons addressed to David Hume*, London and Edinburgh, 1849, pp. 147–148.

[60] See La Société d'Agriculture du Limousin, 'Programme d'un Concours sur la Impôt (sic) Indirect', in Schelle, *Oeuvres*, II, pp. 430–433, esp. p. 431.

direct taxation, as Turgot explained to Hume, and although Turgot felt that his theoretical position on the subject would not be affected by the arguments presented, he welcomed contributions by people whose views differed from his own.[61] The results of the competition were rather disappointing,[62] and the prize winners selected – Saint-Péravy and Graslin – were to please neither the Physiocrats nor their opponents.[63] Indeed, Turgot's personal satisfaction from organising the contest came mainly from "inspiring the contestants" and thereby having served the public good,[64] while the most important result of the competition for the later development of economics came in the form of comments which Turgot himself wrote on the efforts of the two prize winners.

7. *Observations on a Paper by Saint-Péravy* (1767)

The prize winning essay was Saint-Péravy's *Mémoire sur les effets de l'impôt indirect* which was published in 1768. Turgot was not very happy with this award; the paper was not well written, it depended heavily on the analysis presented by Quesnay and Mirabeau in the *Philosophie rurale*, and although it did contain some new material, it also contained many errors.[65] It was presumably to justify his decision of awarding the prize, that Turgot penned a series of comments on Saint-Péravy's contribution in which apart from criticising Saint-Péravy's opinions on several subjects, he himself contributed important theoretical points.[66]

Only five different comments are presented, or, what is also possible, have been preserved. Three of them are short – only a few paragraphs in all – and deal with the question of the taxation of interest, that of taxes on house rent, and those on luxury goods, all subjects on which Turgot disagreed with Physiocratic opinion.[67] The other two comments are much longer.

The first of these deals with the assumption about the laws of returns made in the *Tableau économique* and utilised by Saint-Péravy in his analysis, which states that the "proportion between the annual advances in agricultural production and its total product is as two to five". Although Turgot admitted that this proportion had some empirical foundations, he argued that there was therefore no need for this proportion to be fixed but that in fact it was more aptly described as a variable proportion. In the argument that follows, Turgot

[61] Turgot to Hume, 7/9/1766, in J.H. Burton, op. cit., p. 148.

[62] Turgot to Hume, 8/3/1768, in J.H. Burton, op. cit., p. 162.

[63] Turgot to Du Pont, 13/10/1767, in Schelle, *Oeuvres*, II, pp. 672–673, where Turgot wrote: "As for me, I would have liked to have seen a paper which truly deserved the prize". (My translation.)

[64] Turgot to Hume, 8/3/1768, in J.H. Burton, op. cit., p. 162.

[65] Turgot to Du Pont, 13/10/1767, in Schelle, *Oeuvres*, II, pp. 672–673.

[66] 'Observations on a Paper by Saint-Péravy', below pp. 109–122. It would perhaps have been better if Turgot himself had written a book on this question, thereby deserving his own prize as he suggested to Hume (in a letter, dated 25/3/1767, in J.H. Burton, op. cit., p. 154).

[67] 'Observations on a Paper by Saint-Péravy', below, pp. 113–115.

sets out the law of variable proportions including a statement of diminishing returns which, as Schumpeter has argued, "was not surpassed till Edgeworth took the matter in hand."[68]

Turgot's second major comment deals with the problem of monetary leakages from the circular flow and contains the essence of Turgot's account of what became later known as "Say's Law".[69] In response to Saint-Péravy's complaint that the profits of the tax-farm were spent in the capital, and this hindered the circulation of agricultural production, Turgot argued that no such loss to the circular flow incurred in fact, either through the saving-investment process, or through international trade, two forms of leakage from the circular flow referred to by Saint-Péravy in this connection. In developing his argument against this view, Turgot put forward his version of the automatic specie mechanism, his analysis of hoarding and the role of money in saving and in investment, and, in a footnote, his theory of competitive equilibrium.[70] These, together with his analysis of diminishing returns, constitute some of his more important contributions to economic analysis, and thereby make this paper an especially interesting part of his economic writings.

8. Observations on a Paper by Graslin (1767)

The work which won second prize was Graslin's *Essai analytique sur la richesse et sur l'impôt*, which Turgot regarded as much better written than the prize winning effort of Saint-Péravy. Although he strongly disagreed with Graslin's position on indirect taxation, he felt that the author had presented many "ingenious" ideas which would force the Physiocrats to explain themselves more fully and thereby help them to approach more closely to an elucidation "of the truth" in this matter.[71] More recently, Graslin's work has been praised, especially for the theory of value which it contains and to which, according to one commentator, Turgot himself may have been indebted in his contribution to value theory written a few years later.[72]

As he did with Saint-Péravy's paper, Turgot also wrote a series of observations on the work of Graslin which are included in this collection. These

[68] Schumpeter, *History of Economic Analysis*, p. 260; 'Observations on a Paper by Saint-Péravy', below pp. 111–113. Edgeworth's formulation to which Schumpeter referred in the above quotation, is the paper on the laws of returns published in the *Economic Journal* in 1911. See F.Y. Edgeworth, *Papers relating to Political Economy*, London, 1925, I, pp. 63–90.

[69] See my 'A Re-interpretation of Turgot's Theory of Capital and Interest', op. cit., pp. 334–336.

[70] 'Observations on a Paper by Saint-Péravy', below, pp. 115–122.

[71] See Turgot to Du Pont, 13/10/1767, in Schelle, *Oeuvres*, II, pp. 672–673, cf. Turgot to Hume, 8/3/1768, in J.H. Burton, op. cit., p. 162.

[72] That is, Yoshio Yomakawa, 'The Transition of Turgot's Theory of Value', *Waseda Economic Papers*, III, 1959, esp. pp. 31, 47; and see E. Vattierlle, 'La pensée fiscale de J.J.L. Graslin (1727–1790)', *Revue d'histoire économique et sociale*, XLIX, 1971.

comments are much more extensive, and cover observations on seven different topics raised by Graslin. A great deal of space is devoted to the meaning and definition of wealth, and to the special role of the net product in the economy. The first comment therefore concentrates on the Physiocratic notion of national income accounting, the second on the distinction between productive and unproductive labour, the third on the notion of disposable income, while the fourth comment presents a few concise definitions of wealth, value and revenue and their interrelationship.[73] The last three comments are longer, and get to the heart of the difference of opinion between Graslin and Turgot on the subject of indirect taxation.

The first of these longer comments explains Turgot's theory of distribution in a little more detail by showing the relationship between the net product and the expenses of agricultural production. These expenses are in fact resolved into the income shares of two other classes in society, the agricultural entrepreneurs and the farm labourers. In this context, Turgot also expanded his theory of wages.[74] The next note discusses the relationship between exchange value and cost of production, and presents some material on the theory of money, subjects which Graslin had treated in a confused manner according to Turgot.[75]

Finally, there is a lengthy reply to Graslin's proposition that the example of industrial and commercial nations such as Holland is a telling argument against the Physiocratic theory of taxation since the governments of such countries can thrive without a large net product from which to obtain tax revenues. Turgot's answer depends on a distinction he draws between a 'nation' and a 'state' and on the fact that trading states rely on the net product of other states for the effective payment of their taxation, the burden of which is transferred in the form of higher prices through trade.[76] The view that indirect taxation is inefficient and ruinous to agriculture is strongly maintained by Turgot.

9. *Value and Money* (*circa 1769*)

This paper is quite different from the three works discussed previously and, apart from the *Reflections*, is the only theoretical work produced by Turgot while intendant which was not inspired by the needs of administration. The paper was probably written in 1769, though possibly a little earlier,[77] and

[73] 'Observations on a Paper by Graslin', below, pp. 123–125.

[74] Ibid., pp. 126–127. The only wage theory presented by Turgot so far was a single section in the *Reflections* (below, pp. 45–46). Turgot's wage theory was further elaborated in one of his letters on the grain trade (below, pp. 167–169).

[75] 'Observations on a Paper by Graslin', below, pp. 127–128.

[76] 'Observations on a Paper by Graslin', below, pp. 129–132.

[77] The direct evidence for the date of writing is a reference to Galiani's *Della Moneta* (published in 1750) which is as follows: "It is this truth which l'Abbé Galiani stated twenty

was, it is generally assumed, intended as a contribution to Morellet's venture of a *Dictionnaire de Commerce*, a project never completed.[78] A prospectus for the project was, however, finished and was published in 1769. This prospectus contains, as a specimen article, a paper on the subject of money which in part is very similar to Turgot's views expressed in 'Value and Money', thereby raising the possibility that it was written to aid Morellet in his preparation of the prospectus, rather than for the dictionary itself.[79]

This last point is not unimportant,[80] and should be further explored. The first few pages of Morellet's article are very similar to the preliminary parts on value of Turgot's paper; they give similar definitions and use similar examples.[81] The order of the argument also follows Turgot's paper closely. In the analysis of exchange, Morellet starts with the case of isolated exchange, which like Turgot's analysis is extended to a four individual case.[82] Morellet's conclusions on the subject of the measure of value read as if they were an elaboration of Turgot's paper and the analysis of the *Reflections*. The same

---

years ago in his Treatise *Della Moneta*". (Below, p. 140.) The issue of dating the paper is, however, confused by a series of comments by Du Pont in his edition of the works, where the article is placed immediately behind Turgot's *Encyclopédie* contributions, though with the warning that "cet ouvrage est cependant d'une époque plus récente..." (*Ouvres*, III, p. 256). In his biographical introduction to the works (ibid., I, pp. 43–44), Du Pont wrote that "nous ne savons pas avec exactitude à quelle époque il a été écrit". From the similarities between 'Value and Money' and Morellet's paper on money in the *Prospectus* – which are discussed below – it is possible that the paper may have been prepared in early 1769 or even 1768. The reference to Graslin's *Essai* (below, p. 140), suggests a date after 1767.

[78] See Du Pont, *Mémoires*, I, pp. 107–109, and *Oeuvres*, I, pp. 43–44. It is interesting to note that Morellet in his *Mémoires* (I, pp. 175–176) makes no reference to Turgot's proposed contribution to his project when he refers to his plan for a *Nouveau dictionnaire de commerce*, which is surprising in view of the many other anecdotes about Turgot which he included. Schelle, *Oeuvres de Turgot*, III, p. 79, accepts Du Pont's evidence and gives 1769 as the most likely date, with the warning that it is open to doubt. He makes no reference to either Morellet's *Mémoires* or to the *Prospectus* of 1769.

[79] See Morellet, *Prospectus d'un nouveau dictionnaire de commerce*, Paris, 1769. The paper on money, which includes a digression on value theory, is printed as a "Digression pour servir à l'intelligence de la partie du Plan du nouveau *Dictionnaire de Commerce*, relative aux monnaies, &c." (Ibid., pp. 98–183.)

[80] For example, it shows a possibility in which Turgot's views on value could have spread to other writers well before the publication of his works in 1808–10. It would also have given Smith access to these views, since he owned a presentation copy of the *Prospectus*. See Mizuta, *Adam Smith's Library*, Cambridge, 1967, p. 122. It also raises the possibility that Turgot did in fact complete the paper 'Value and Money' and that the versions printed by Du Pont and by Schelle are only a manuscript version of an incomplete draft.

[81] Morellet, *Prospectus*, pp. 98–102; 'Value and Money', below, pp. 137–138. The common examples include references to food, which being bad for the health and ill-tasting is worthless, and to hides, to keep out the cold.

[82] *Prospectus*, pp. 105–106, 110–114, 126ff; these models also occur in 'Value and Money' below, pp. 141–143, 147–148. The example used by Morellet of the exchange of wine for corn is that used in the *Reflections* (below, pp. 57–58). It should be remembered that the latter by this time, had not been published, so that Turgot probably lent Morellet a manuscript copy. See also Turgot to Du Pont, 6/2/1770, in Schelle, *Oeuvres*, III, p. 375, which indicates that Turgot had sent Du Pont his last copy of the *Reflections*.

applies to his general, competitive model of price determination in the market.[83] Only in the discussion of the relationship between value, time, and space is new ground covered in Morellet's paper, which has no counterpart in Turgot's writings on value which have been mentioned so far in this connection.[84]

In the case of the monetary theory, similar observations can be made. Here again, a great deal of the analysis, the ordering of the argument, and even some of the examples used, are those of Turgot in both the *Reflections*, and in 'Value and Money'. A similar conclusion applies to Morellet's treatment of bimetallism, his discussion of the concept of money of account, and his evaluation of the methods of making international comparisons of the value of money.[85] The one difference between the authors is that Morellet's treatment of these monetary subjects is more detailed than the rather brief accounts offered by Turgot.[86] In the final part of the article, Morellet breaks new ground in his discussion of banking and credit, but not in the analysis of capital and interest which largely follows that of Turgot.

The comparison given above should not be taken as implying plagiarism on the part of Morellet. The hypothesis that it indicates Turgot's assistance to his friend implies a great deal less, and has mainly been raised here because it sheds further light on the dating, and possible motivation for this important paper by Turgot, which has remained in doubt.[87]

10. Paper on Lending at Interest (1770)

Not long after completing 'Value and Money', Turgot turned to a further elaboration of his theory of interest in a paper which was inspired by practical rather than theoretical issues. This is the 'Paper on Lending at Interest', extracts of which are included below. The paper was written in connection with a law suit in Angoulême, one of the major towns in Turgot's province,

[83] *Prospectus*, pp. 111–113, 117ff; *Reflections* below pp. 57–58, 'Value and Money' below, pp. 144–147.

[84] *Prospectus*, pp. 128–131. The relationship between value and time was analysed by Turgot at the end of 1769 in his 'Paper on Lending at Interest' (below pp. 154, 157). See also my 'Reappraisal of Turgot's Theory of Value, Exchange and Price Determination', op. cit., pp. 192–193. These considerations may reinforce the opinion (expressed in note 80 above) that Morellet may have had access to a more complete discussion of Turgot on value and money than that subsequently published in the editions of his *Works* by Du Pont and Schelle.

[85] *Prospectus*, pp. 131–183; *Reflections*, below, pp. 58–64, 'Value and Money', below, pp. 134–136. One of the common examples used by Morellet and Turgot is the reference to 'Vin du Cap' and 'Vin de France'. (*Prospectus*, p. 137, *Reflections*, below, p. 59).

[86] The brevity of Turgot's account of monetary theory can be explained by the nature of the *Reflections* (see above, pp. XVIII–XIX), and by the fact that the preserved version of 'Value and Money' may have only been an incomplete draft.

[87] For a discussion of Turgot's theory of value and money, see P.B. Vigreux, 'Le fondement de la valeur de la monnaie d'après Turgot', op. cit., and my 'Reappraisal of Turgot's Theory of Value, Exchange and Price Determination', op. cit.

between two debtors and their creditor. The former had charged the latter with demanding an illegally high interest rate, despite the fact that the rate actually charged was the customary rate on loan transactions in the district. While the hearing was in progress, all dealings involving credit were suspended until the verdict was known, since prospective lenders did not wish to enter the loan market in the climate of uncertainty created by the lawsuit.[88]

These circumstances, and the resulting disruptions of credit in his province prompted Turgot to write to the Royal Council on the facts of the case, the gravity of its consequences, and to present a general solution to the problem which would prevent further occurrences of this nature. After a general discussion of the harmful effects of the matter on the trade and industry of his district, and a recommendation to the Council to clarify the legal position on interest rates, Turgot presented a series of arguments against legal interference in loan transactions which are partly theological but mainly economic. Loan transactions and the provision of credit are described as a commercial necessity, and best results in this type of exchange, as in all others, are obtained through a policy of laissez-faire. This brief for free trade in the loan market is written with elegance and force and is a good example of Turgot's ability of stating a case with great clarity. Since the theoretical contents of this paper have been analysed elsewhere,[89] no further discussion of this aspect of the paper is required.

A manuscript version, written by an amanuensis, gives the date of completion of the paper as 27 January 1770, so that the bulk of it must have been drafted towards the end of 1769.[90] The first reference to the paper by Turgot is slightly earlier than the date of completion, and occurs in a letter to Du Pont in which Turgot asked his friend to remove the theological part on interest from the *Reflections* as he had made use of it in another paper on the subject.[91] A few weeks later, Turgot again wrote to Du Pont that he had produced a piece on interest which would be useful for publication in the *Ephémérides*, except for the fact that Du Pont would not be allowed to print it.[92]

Although it could not be published at the time, Turgot was happy to circulate his piece on interest in manuscript form, as is shown by his correspondence. In a letter to Du Pont, Turgot asked his friend whether he had received the manuscript copy which "Mme Blondel tells me she has sent

[88] 'Paper on Lending at Interest', below pp. 149–150, the full text is in Schelle, *Oeuvres*, III, pp. 154–156, and see his note (a) on pp. 154–155. These references give the details of the law suit and thus provide the background to the paper.

[89] See my 'A Re-interpretation of Turgot's Theory of Capital and Interest', op. cit.

[90] 'Paper on Lending at Interest', below, p. 149, n. 1.

[91] Turgot to Du Pont, 12/1/1770, in Schelle, *Oeuvres*, III, p. 371. The theological part in the *Reflections* referred to is either sections 73 *and* 75, or section 75 only. See *Reflections*, below, pp. 78–81, and n. 51.

[92] Turgot to Du Pont, 30/1/1770, in Schelle, *Oeuvres*, III, p. 372.

you", because he wanted it back as soon as Du Pont had read it, "for I have no other neat copy of it".[93] Furthermore, extracts from the paper were published during Turgot's life time in a work entitled *Théorie de l'intérêt*, first published in 1780 and in a revised edition in 1782.[94]

Full publication did not occur till the year of the French revolution when a complete version, the only one conforming to the text of the 1770 manuscript was published together with Turgot's paper on the *'Marque des fers'*, possibly by Condorcet.[95] It was included in the three editions of Turgot's works in slightly different versions which may indicate that Du Pont had a copy made of Turgot's manuscript in 1770 in which, as usual, he embodied some alterations.[96]

The paper became one of Turgot's most influential works. It was approvingly referred to by Bentham in the second edition of his *defence of Usury*[97] and was reprinted with this work on two occasions during the nineteenth century.[98] It seems also to have exerted a profound influence on the young Böhm-Bawerk.[99] It is here printed for the first time in English translation.

[93] Turgot to Du Pont, 13/11/1770, in Schelle, *Oeuvres*, III, p. 398. A further reference to this work is contained in Turgot to Du Pont, ibid., III, p. 484, which implies that Du Pont by then had read it.

[94] *Théorie de l'intérêt de l'argent, tirée des principes du droit naturel, de la théologie et de la politique, contre l'abus de l'imputation de l'usure*, Paris, 1780. A second, revised edition was published in 1782. In the 1780 edition, quotations from Turgot's 'Paper on Lending at Interest' appear on pp. 42–49, 72–74, 74–86, 170–174, 194–198, 208–214, 217–219. It can be presumed that Turgot was acqainted with the author, since use is also made of the *tirage-à-part*, which Turgot had only circulated among his friends. Barbier, *Dictionnaire des ouvrages anonymes*, third edition, Paris, 1882, attributes the work to l'Abbé J.L. Gouttes and Turgot, an attribution followed by the catalogue of the Bibliothèque nationale.

[95] Turgot, *Mémoires sur le prêt à intérêt, et sur le commerce des fers*, Paris [1789]. H. Higgs (*Bibliography of Economics 1751–1775*, Cambridge, 1935, item 6698) and Schelle, *Oeuvres*, III, p. 154 give a slightly different title and give 1789 as the publication date. Du Pont (*Oeuvres*, V, p. 262) wrote in the introduction to this work, "Ce mémoire a déjà imprimé *deux* foix" (my italics); presumably a reference to the 1789 edition, and the work listed in note 94 above.

[96] See below, 'Paper on Lending at Interest', p. 149, n. 1. The variations in text in the *Works* as edited by Schelle and Du Pont are indicated in footnotes throughout the text. It should be noted that Schelle attempted to correct Du Pont's text through a comparison with the extracts given in *Théorie de l'Intérêt* (see note 94 above).

[97] W. Stark (editor), *Jeremy Bentham's Economic Writings*, London, 1952, I, pp. 188, 190. Bentham's knowledge of the piece was derived from the summary of it given in Condorcet's *Life of Turgot* which reveals that Condorcet must have had access to the manuscript at one time or another, thereby strengthening the possibility that he was responsible for its publication in 1789. In the second edition of *Defence of Usury*, Bentham appended the passage from Condorcet mentioned.

[98] Turgot's Paper was included with a French translation of Bentham (*Défence de l'usure*, Paris, 1828) and with a Spanish translation (*Defence de la usura*, Paris, 1828).

[99] In 1876, Böhm-Bawerk presented a paper at Knies' seminar in Heidelberg, the subject of which was a critical evaluation of Turgot's theory of interest as contained in the 'Paper on Lending at Interest' and the *Reflections*. This paper, as yet unpublished, shows the great indebtedness of Böhm-Bawerk's studies on capital and interest to Turgot. I am indebted to

11. Letters on the Grain Trade (1770)

Turgot's correspondence for the whole of 1770 reveals a growing concern with the important question of freedom for the internal and external grain trade. This concern was partly aroused by the economic situation within his own province which, after a succession of poor harvests from 1765 to 1768, suffered a further poor harvest in 1769, an experience this time shared with neighbouring provinces as well. As usually happened, the rising price of food produced riots in several of the major towns, some of which had to be put down with force. The disturbances in his own province, and those in others, started a pamphlet agitation for a renewal of the restrictions on the internal trade in grain, thereby reversing the freer trade policy introduced by Laverdy in 1764.[100]

The most influential item in this pamphlet literature was undoubtedly Galiani's *Dialogues sur le commerce des blėds*, published in early 1770 and in Turgot's own words, a book all the more dangerous to the cause of free trade because it upheld the case for restrictions in the grain trade with "wit, gracefulness, skill, humour, ingenuity even, and detailed discussion".[101] Despite this praise for the author, or rather, because of it, Turgot felt that the book had to be attacked. Unfortunately, he himself did not have the time, and he doubted whether his friends – such as Morellet and Du Pont – who had the required skill to make a devastating critique of the work, would have the time either.[102] These last fears proved to be wrong. A month later, he could write to Du Pont that he was "very glad that so many people have taken up the cudgels with l'Abbé Galiani".[103]

Despite his earlier pleading of lack of time, Turgot was to write himself on the question of the grain trade before the end of the year, although not in direct response to Galiani. This was due to the fact that the limited free trade granted in 1764 was under attack at the official level from early 1770 as well. Already in February, the Parlement in Bordeaux, not far from Turgot's own jurisdiction, had published an *arrêt* interfering with the grain trade, which gave Turgot cause for alarm.[104] During March, April and May, his cor-

Professor F.A. von Hayek and Dr. Klaus Hennings for providing me with a copy of this paper, which was presented to Professor von Hayek by Böhm-Bawerk's widow in 1922–23. For a discussion of Böhm-Bawerk's critique of Turgot's theory, see my 'Re-interpretation of Turgot's Theory of Capital and Interest', op. cit., and the correspondence between Marshall and Wicksell reprinted in T. Gardlund, *Life of Knut Wicksell*, Stockholm, 1958, pp. 339–345.

[100] 'Letters on the Grain Trade', below, pp. 164–165, notes 1–3; Dakin, *Turgot and the ancien régime in France*, chapter VIII.

[101] Turgot to Morellet, 17/1/1770, in Schelle, *Oeuvres*, III, pp. 419–420.

[102] Turgot to Mlle de Lespinasse, 26/1/1770 in Schelle, *Oeuvres*, III, 420–421. Turgot to Du Pont, 30/1/1770, ibid., III, p. 373.

[103] Turgot to Du Pont, 2/3/1770, ibid., III, p. 381.

[104] Turgot to Du Pont, 16/2/1770, ibid., III, pp. 376–377.

respondence reveals mounting concern with the famine and hardship in his own province and expresses fears that the mistaken opinions published on the subject would probably lead to undesirable action from Terray, who had just then been appointed to the position of Contrôleur-général.[105] During the summer, the position in his province worsened due to a further harvest failure, and although he tried with heroic measures to increase the supply of grain in his province, the situation continued to deteriorate. At the same time, his correspondence with Terray over his measures to deal with the famine problem increased his suspicions that Terray would remove the freedom granted by the 1764 Edict.[106] The matter came to a head in October when Terray demanded at very short notice opinions from the intendants concerning his proposal for new regulations for the grain trade. It was on this occasion that Turgot started to write his letters on the question, notwithstanding the pressures of work in his administration.[107]

The letters themselves were written under the most difficult circumstances while Turgot was on tour in his province, organising relief work and food supplies for the approaching winter months. This is clearly indicated from the places in which the letters were written: the first was written at Limoges on October 30, the second at Tulle is dated 8 November, the third at Egletons is dated 10 November, the fourth was started at Egletons a day later, 11 November but was finished at Bort on the thirteenth, the fifth letter was completed at Saint-Angel on the fourteenth, the sixth at Angoulême on the twenty-seventh, while the seventh and last letter was produced back at Limoges and is dated 2 December.[108] In the middle of November, just prior to completing the fifth letter, Turgot described his labours to Du Pont in the following terms:

> Unfortunately, I am a lazy fellow. I have been forced through lack of time to limit myself to five letters, hastily rushed from the pen and containing only 53 quarto pages in my small handwriting. All the sound reasons are contained in them, and expressed without reserve, but they are not as well developed as I would have wished. I will redraft all of it so that it will be suitable for publication . . ..[109]

As the dating of these letters shows, time became available for a further two letters, which are considerably longer than the other five. By early December, the task was, however, completed and by the middle of the month he at last had sufficient leisure to write to Du Pont at greater length.[110]

[105] Turgot to Du Pont, 23/3/1770, 29/3/1770, 4/5/1770 in Schelle, ibid., III, pp. 382–386; Turgot to Condorcet, 6/4/1770, ibid., pp. 418–419.

[106] Dakin, *Turgot and the ancien régime in France*, pp. 105–111.

[107] Turgot to Du Pont, 20/10/1770, in Schelle, *Oeuvres*, III, p. 390 and n. (a).

[108] See ibid., III, pp. 266–354. The distances between these towns were not inconsiderable and travelling in the eighteenth century entailed considerable hardship on the bad roads. This makes the letters an even more remarkable performance.

[109] Turgot to Du Pont, 13/11/1770, in Schelle, *Oeuvres*, III, p. 392 (my translation).

[110] Turgot to Du Pont, 14/12/1770 in Schelle, *Oeuvres*, III, p. 394. In the interval between this letter and the letter cited previously, Turgot added the last two letters on the grain trade of nearly one hundred pages in his endeavour to convert the Contrôleur-Général to free trade.

As indicated earlier, the letters on the grain trade are long, especially the last three. "From beginning to end, my seven letters contain 150 pages in my small handwriting.... The last three alone contain a hundred pages."[111] Although they were written in haste, they contain considerable evidence of the thoroughness with which Turgot had investigated the grain trade question.[112] The letters cover all aspects of this trade: production, marketing, prices, while the last three give an excellent account of the effects of the policy of free trade on the welfare of the proprietors, of the farmers, and of the consumers. These letters also provide a further elaboration of Turgot's theory of distribution as sketched in the *Reflections*, and for this reason form a most important part of his economic writing.[113]

As Turgot had feared, his letters had no immediate effect on the policy to be followed by Terray. Shortly after Turgot had finished writing his last letter, Terray rescinded the provisions for free trade in grain and established a grain administration to organise and regulate the trade.[114] As Turgot wrote to Caillard at the beginning of 1771:

> I have just written 150 quarto pages, in very small handwriting on the grain trade question, in order to convert the Contrôleur-général if I can do this ... I am afraid that I have wasted all the time that I spent on it ... for the government is becoming more and more prohibitive in every way, and the events of the day will contribute thereto ....[115]

A few years later, Turgot, was, however, able to use his arguments presented in the letters more effectively, when he himself took Terray's place as Contrôleur-général in 1774. In September of that year he was able to restore the internal free trade in grain for the whole of France with the exception of Paris. The preamble to the Edict which announced this measure explained the new policy to the people in a manner similar to that in which Turgot had tried to influence his predecessor's opinion four years earlier.[116]

Although Turgot had himself indicated a desire to publish the letters, they were in fact not published till after his death, though their precise date of publication is not known.[117] They were re-published, together with Du Pont's

[111] Turgot to Du Pont, 14/12/1770, in Schelle, *Oeuvres*, III, p. 394.

[112] Turgot's interest in obtaining information on this question is revealed, for example, in a letter to Josiah Tucker (10/12/1773) in which he requested information on, and gave criticism of English statistical series of grain prices at various markets. (See Schelle, *Oeuvres*, III, pp. 614–617.)

[113] See below, pp. 166–170, 177–179.

[114] See Schelle, *Oeuvres*, III, pp. 355–357, which reproduces Terray's *arrêt* on the grain trade, which is dated 23 December 1770.

[115] Turgot to Caillard, January 1771, in Schelle, *Oeuvres*, III, p. 501.

[116] See Dakin, op. cit., pp. 117–119.

[117] That is, *Lettres sur les Grains, écrites à M. l'Abbé Terray, Contrôleur-Général, par M. Turgot, Intendant de Limoges*, n.p.n.d. Higgs (*Bibliography*, item 4945) gives 1770 as the publication date, Schelle (*Oeuvres*, III, p. 265) says 1788. Internal evidence in the preface of

summary of the missing second, third and fourth letters in the various editions of Turgot's works. Extracts from the important last three letters are included here for the first time in English translation.

12. Letter on the 'Marque des fers' (1773)

A further letter to l'Abbé Terray, this time a plea for freer trade for the iron industry in his province, constitutes the last major work Turgot wrote while intendant of Limoges. It is also the last piece included in this selection of his economic writings. The letter, dated 24 December 1773, was inspired by a rumour that Terray wanted to increase the duties of iron and that for this reason, he wanted an account of the state of the iron works from those intendants in whose provinces such works were situated.[118]

Turgot, as he had done on other occasions, turned this request of the Contrôleur-général into a plea for free trade in general, and for the iron industry in particular. Like the preceding 'Letters on the Grain Trade' this part of his economic writings is important as an elaboration of the general case for laissez-faire which was stated in the 'Eloge de Gournay'. The different background from which the topic is broached – manufacturers rather than agriculture – provides new insights which allowed Turgot to present the arguments against protection in a different manner. New theoretical arguments are also introduced, including one that comes close to an enunciation of the principle of comparative advantage.[119]

Little is known of the consequences of Turgot's letter or indeed about what happened to Terray's project of increasing iron duties.[120] When Turgot succeeded Terray to the finance ministry, he himself wanted to reform the 'marque des fers' and to abolish the anlogous 'marque des cuirs' but like so many other of his proposed reforms, "these remained mere projects at the time of his dismissal".[121]

The letter itself was first published in 1789, together with the 'Paper on Lending at Interest' when times had become more propitious for stating the case for freer trade.[122] Du Pont included the letter in his edition of the *Works*,

---

this publication suggests after 1783, possibly after 1786, since it refers to recent 'mémoires sur la vie' of Turgot, presumably those by Du Pont and Condorecet which were published in 1782 and 1786 respectively.

[118] Below, pp. 182–188 and n. 1. Schelle, *Oeuvres*, III, p. 617, note (a), gives details of the history of these iron duties which were first established as a protective device in 1608.

[119] See below, p. 187.

[120] See Schelle, *Oeuvres*, III, p. 617, note (a) where it is indicated that no trace of the relevant documents can be found in the Archives of Haute-Vienne.

[121] See Dakin, op. cit., p. 203.

[122] Details of this publication are given in note 95 above.

from where it was reproduced in the later editions of Daire and Schelle. Extracts from the letter in English translation appeared in 1895.[123]

SOURCES OF THE TRANSLATIONS

It is not intended to provide detailed notes on the way in which Turgot's economics has been translated and on the manner in which his economic vocabularly has been rendered into English. Those interested can easily check this for themselves by comparing the English text here presented with the French original, a comparison which is facilitated by the fact that page references to that original are provided in the margins. The general rule in translation that was followed was to preserve Turgot's style as much as possible, and to use eighteenth century English terminology in rendering the French economic terms into English. However, some comments on the various sources of the translations are required.

It has already been indicated in this introduction that there are difficulties relating to the authenticity of the text of Turgot's works which arise from Du Pont's habit of making alterations to Turgot's text in the edition of his works. For this reason, a variety of sources had to be utilised in order to prepare the translations from as accurate a text as possible.

Although Daire virtually reprinted the Du Pont text, many of the translations have nevertheless been prepared from this source. However, in all cases the text has been compared with that given in Schelle and textual differences have been indicated in footnotes. This is the case with the 'Letter on Paper Money', the article 'Fairs and Markets' which was also checked with the original as it appeared in the *Encyclopédie*, 'In Praise of Gournay', the papers on taxation, the paper 'Value and Money',[124] and the 'Letter on the Marque des fers', which was also checked with the 1789 edition.

Three of the items were directly translated from Schelle's text. These are 'Remarks on the Notes to the Translation of Josiah Child' which is only available in the Schelle edition, and the extracts from the 'Paper on Lending at Interest' and the 'Letters on the Grain trade'. These last two were further checked for textual alterations against other available sources: the 'Paper on Lending at Interest' with the 1770 manuscript (Goldsmiths' Library, London, MS 131) and with the text of the 1789 edition; the 'Letters on the Grain

[123] In W.W. Stephens, op. cit., where these extracts are presented under the title 'On Protection of Native Manufactures'.

[124] This paper provided the only case where it was felt desirable to examine the original manuscript in the Turgot archives at Lantheuil. An attempt was made to secure a photocopy of the manuscript in question – for which I am grateful for the assistance of Professor R.L. Meek and Mme Jacqueline Hecht – from the present owner, Madame la Marquise de Naurois-Turgot who, for a variety of reasons, felt unable to oblige.

Trade' with the version published at the end of the 1780's. Again, textual differences were recorded in footnotes.

Turgot's major economic work, the *Reflections*, posed the greatest difficulty since here none of the texts presented in the editions of Turgot's *Works* proved to be completely satisfactory. The text ultimately selected for translation was the 1788 edition, itself a reprint from the 1770 *tirage-à-part* and incorporating the corrections made in the Errata to that work, as well as some other minor corrections. It is felt that this text would conform most closely to the original manuscript that Turgot had written.[125] The footnotes indicating textual differences involving so many varying editions became rather complicated so that some further explanations are in order.

The policy adopted for the translation of the *Reflections* is then as follows. The text is translated from the 1788 edition, the only changes made being to correct obvious misprints including those in the numbering of the various sections. In the footnotes, all textual differences have been noted as between this version, and those in the 1770 *tirage-à-part*, the first English version in the anonymous 1793 translation as to omissions and differences in paragraphing; the Du Pont edition in the *Works*, the Daire edition which follows Du Pont closely, and finally, Schelle's version in his edition of the *Works*. Du Pont's own footnotes first inserted in the *Ephémérides*, and added to in his edition of the *Works* have been omitted; footnotes indicate where they were added and provide a summary of their contents. Finally, cross-references to Turgot's extensive correspondence on the *Reflections*, have been provided at the relevant points.

In the case of the *Reflections*, the identification of textual and other differences between editions is especially important in order to correct errors in Lundberg's *Turgot's Unknown Translator*, the argument of which relies heavily on a comparison between the early French editions of the *Reflections* and the 1793 English translation. These errors are revealed by a comparison of the textual differences between the 1788 text and that of the *tirage-à-part*, as well as by comparing her arguments on paragraphing with the information contained in the Table of Concordance of the major editions of the *Reflections* included below.[126]

Finally, a comment on the abbreviations used in connection with the three editions of Turgot's *Works* referred to throughout the text. In footnotes these are indicated as follows: Du Pont, *Oeuvres* followed by a Roman numeral indicating volume and a page reference, this refers to the edition by Du Pont de

[125] I was further encouraged in pursuing this policy by the fact that I was able to persuade Professor Meek of its merits for the purpose of his translation of the *Reflections* for his *Turgot on Progress, Sociology and Economics*.

[126] See Appendix below, p. 195; cf. my 'Turgot and Adam Smith', op. cit., p. 276 and n. 39 for reasons why Lundberg's hypothesis cannot be treated seriously.

Nemours published in the first decades of the nineteenth century;[127] Daire, *Oeuvres*, followed by a Roman numeral indicating volume and a page reference refers to the edition of Turgot's *Works* prepared by Eugene Daire and Hippolyte Dussard for the Guillaumin collection des principaux économistes in 1844;[128] Schelle *Oeuvres*, followed by a Roman numeral indicating volume, and a page reference, refers to the definitive edition of Turgot's *Works* edited by Gustave Schelle in the early twentieth century.[129] A different form of abbreviation is used at the beginning of each of the items translated, D.D. stands here for Daire edition, S. for the Schelle edition. As indicated earlier, to facilitate comparison between the translation and the originals, the margin gives the page reference to the original for each new page.

[127] That is, *Oeuvres de Turgot, précédées et accompagnées de mémoires et de notes sur sa vie, son administration et ses ouvrages*, edited by Pierre Samuel Du Pont de Nemours, 9 Volumes, Paris, 1808–1811.

[128] *Oeuvres de Turgot, nouvelle édition, classé par ordre de matières avec les notes de Du Pont de Nemours, augmentée de lettres inédites, des questions sur le commerce et d'observations et de notes nouvelles*, edited by Eugene Daire and Hippolyte Dussard, *et précedé d'une notice sur la vie et les ouvrages de Turgot par M. Eugene Daire.* 2 volumes, Paris, 1844. (These two volumes form volumes III and IV of the *Guillaumin Collection des principaux économistes.*)

[129] *Oeuvres de Turgot et Documents le concernant*, edited by Gustave Schelle, *avec biographie et notes par Gustave Schelle*, 5 volumes, Paris, 1913–1923.

CHAPTER I

1749

LETTER TO L'ABBÉ DE CICÉ, SINCE THEN BISHOP OF AUXERRE, ON THE REPLACING OF MONEY BY PAPER. ALSO KNOWN AS THE 'LETTER ON PAPER-MONEY'.

D.D. 94–102

Paris, the 7th of April, 1749

I avail myself of the first free time which has come along to write to you.[1]

You are well aware that the seminary is not a place of comfort,[2] and you know also that it is not one which can compensate me for the pleasure of seeing you.

Here we are already reduced to conversing from a distance. I have by no means forgotten my promises, and, to start immediately on some matters which merit our attention, I shall tell you that I have read the three letters, published by l'Abbé Terrasson in favour of Law's system, some days before the famous decree of the 21st of May, 1720, which, as you know, covered it with ridicule.[3] p. 95

Part of these writings deals with 'rentes constituées',[4] which, he maintains,

[1] This passage was apparently changed by Du Pont de Nemours, and should read as follows:

"The duties with which we are burdened have prevented me to write until today, my dear friend, and I avail myself of the first free time available. Undoubtedly, you yourself are also very busy, as much with the duties of holy week as with your visits to town. At least, I've seen a letter from l'Abbé Véri where he indicated that his company at Bourges was good as well as numerous; I request you to give my regards to all, but especially to him; that could alleviate the boredom caused by being away from Paris and refresh you after the hardships of study and the important matters you would like to discuss. As for me, my dear friend, you fancy that the seminary isn't a place of comfort, but you know also that there is nothing which can compensate me for the pleasure of seeing you, and of embracing you as frequently as my affection desires."

[2] Little is known of Turgot's sojourn at the Seminary of Saint-Sulpice, and his biographers are virtually silent on this matter.

[3] L'Abbé Jean Terrasson (1670–1750) in 1720 published three letters in the *Mercury* in which he defended John Law's financial system against the criticism of D'Aguesseau. See Schelle, *Oeuvres de Turgot*, I, p. 28. Two of these letters were later published in pamphlet form under the title, *Lettres sur le Nouveau Système des Finances*, Paris, 1720.

The Edict of 21 May, 1720 to which Turgot refers, legally devalued the shares of Law's India Company. As a contemporary described it, "Enfin, l'arrêt du 21 May, qui reduisoit le papier a sa moitié, *tourna tout le monde contre l'auteur du Système . . .*". (Cited in Du Tot, *Réflexions politiques sur les finances et le commerce*, La Haye, 1738, Vol. I, p. 293.)

[4] *Rentes constituées*: annuities in the National Debt. As Turgot pointed out, nearly the whole of Terrasson's first letter is devoted to this subject. See Terrasson, *Lettres sur le Nouveau Système des Finances*, Letter I, pp. 2–8.

are usurious. His reasoning contains some truth, some falsity, and nothing profound. He knows nothing of the origin of interest on money, nor of the way in which this is produced through labour and circulation, but he shows quite clearly that the Parliament,[5] in its remonstrances about the falling value of the funds, was even more ignorant than he himself.

The remainder of the work deals with credit and its nature, and as this is the foundation of the *system*, or rather, is *the whole* system,[6] I will give you an account of the reflections that occurred to me while reading it. I believe that the principles which he expounds are those of Law himself, since he was undoubtedly writing in harmony with him; and consequently I cannot help thinking that Law had neither a sufficiently certain nor a sufficiently extensive insight for the work which he had undertaken.[7]

"Firstly", says l'Abbé Terrasson at the beginning of his second letter, "it is an accepted commercial axiom that the credit of a well-managed merchant amounts to ten times his capital".[8] But this credit is not a credit of banknotes as that of Law's bank. A merchant who desires to purchase merchandise worth ten times his capital, and who pays in bills payable to the bearer, would soon be ruined. The true meaning of this statement is as follows. A merchant borrows a sum of money in order to invest it to good account, and not only does he derive from this sum enough to pay the agreed interest and to repay the principal at the end of a certain period, but also considerable profits for himself. This credit is not founded on the property of this merchant, but on
p. 96 his integrity and industry, and it necessarily assumes an exchange for a fixed term, arranged in advance; for if these bills were payable at sight, the merchant would never be able to invest the money which he borrowed. It is therefore inconsistent that a bill payable at sight should bear interest, and a credit of this nature could not exceed the capital of the borrower. Thus the profit which the merchant makes through his credit, and which is claimed to be ten times what he would make with his own funds, comes solely from his industry; it is a profit which he draws from the money which passes through his hands by means of the confidence caused by his punctuality in repaying it, and it is ridiculous to conclude from this, as I believe I read in Du Tot,[9] that he is able to draw bills for ten times the money or assets he owns.

[5] This could refer to the remonstrances in 1709 and 1718 by the Parliament of Paris relating to the public debt and changing the value of money. See Terrasson, op. cit., Letter I, pp. 5–8, who criticised this attempt by the judiciary to interfere with interest rates; and Voltaire, *Siècle de Louis XIV*, Paris, 1910, pp. 591, 593.

[6] I.e. Law's system of banking, credit and public finance which operated in France from 1716–1720. Law described the theory behind his system of credit in his *Money and Trade Considered with a Proposal for Supplying the Nation with Money*, 1705; a French edition with some notes on the system in practice had appeared in 1720.

[7] It appears from this passage that Turgot had not read Law's pamphlet at this stage. Cf. note 16 below.

[8] Terrasson, op. cit., Letter II, p. 4.

[9] I.e. Du Tot, *Réflexions politiques sur les finances et le commerce*, La Haye, 1738. The

Observe, that the king derives no interest from the money he borrows: he needs it either to pay his debts, or for the expenses of the kingdom; consequently he is able to refund it only by taking from his domain, and it follows that he ruins himself if he borrows more than he owns. His credit resembles that of the clergy. In short, all credit is a loan and has a necessary relationship to its repayment. The merchant can borrow more than he owns, because it is not from what he owns that he pays both interest and principal, but from the merchandise which he buys with the borrowed money, and which, instead of dwindling in his hands, increases in price through his industry.

The state, the king, the clergy, the provincial estates, whose needs consume their loans, necessarily ruin themselves if, every year, their revenue is not sufficient to pay, besides their current expenses, the interest and part of the principal of what they have borrowed in times of exceptional needs.

L'Abbé Terrasson thinks very differently. According to him "*the king can greatly exceed the proportion of tenfold to which merchants and private persons are bound*". "The bill of a merchant", he says, "since it can be refused in commerce, does not circulate like money and consequently returns quickly to its source; its drawer finds himself obliged to honour it, and is deprived of the benefit of the credit. It is different with the king: since everybody is obliged to accept his bill, and since it circulates like money, *he validly pays with his own promise*".[10] This doctrine is obviously an illusion.

If the bill is worth money, why promise to pay? If the bill takes the place of money, it is no longer credit. Law was conscious of this, and he states that his circulating paper is really a type of money; he maintains that it is as good as that of gold and silver.[11] "These two metals", says l'Abbé Terrasson, "are only the tokens which stand for real wealth, i.e. commodities. *An écu is a bill conceived in these terms: Any seller will give the bearer the produce or commodity which he needs to the amount of three livres, for that same value of another commodity which has been given up to me, and the effigy of the prince takes the place of a signature.* Now what does it matter whether the token is silver or paper? Wouldn't it be better to choose a material which costs nothing, which does not have to be taken out of commerce where it is used as merchandise, which is indeed manufactured in the kingdom and which does not necessarily make us dependent on the foreigners and proprietors of mines *who profit greedily from the enticement which the glitter of gold and silver holds for the other nations*; a material which one can increase according to need, without ever fearing its deficiency, which, indeed, one would never be p. 97

passage to which Turgot refers is presumably the following: "Un crédit bien gouverné monte au décuple du fonds d'un Marchand; & il gagne autant avec ce crédit, que s'il avoit dix fois son fonds. Cette maxime est généralement reçu chez tous les Négocians" (Vol. I, p. 226).

[10] This passage presumably refers to remarks made by Terrasson in his second letter. See Terrasson, op. cit., Letter II, pp. 4–5.

[11] John Law, *Money and Trade Considered with a Proposal for Supplying the Nation with Money*, p. 89.

tempted to put to any use other than circulation? Paper has all these advantages, which make it preferable to silver".[12] If all these reasonings were correct, this would be as good as the Philosophers' Stone; for there would never be any shortage of either gold or silver to buy all sorts of goods. But was it permissible for Law to ignore that gold, like everything else, lowers its price by its increase? If he had read and studied Locke,[13] who had written twenty years before him, he would have known that all the commodities of a State are always balanced among themselves and with gold and silver, in accordance with the proportion of their quantity and their vent; he would have learned that gold has no intrinsic value which always corresponds to a fixed quantity of merchandise; but that, when there is more gold, it is cheaper, and more of it is given for a fixed quantity of merchandise; that gold, therefore, when it circulates freely, is always sufficient to meet the needs of the State, and that it matters little whether there are 100 million marks or one million, if all commodities are purchased more dearly in the same proportion. It would. be ridiculous to imagine that money is only token wealth, the repute of which is based on the stamp of a prince.

This stamp is only there to certify its weight and standard. In their respec-
p. 98 tive relation with commodities, uncoined silver is at the same price as coined silver, the legal value is purely a name. This is what Law ignored when he established the bank.

It is thus as merchandise that silver is, not the token, but the common measure of other commodities, and this is not by an arbitrary convention based on the glitter of this metal, but because its value may always be ascertained, since it can be used in various shapes as merchandise, since it has, on account of this property, an exchange value, which is slightly raised by its use as money as well, and since it is, moreover, convertible to the same standard, and accurately divisible.

Thus gold draws its value from its scarcity, and far from it being an evil that it is used both as ordinary merchandise and as a measure at the same time, these two uses maintain its price.[14]

I assume that the king can establish a system of paper money, although this would not be easy in spite of all his authority: let us examine what will be gained thereby. Firstly, if he increases its quantity he will debase it thereby; and as he reserves the power to increase it, it is impossible that the people would consent to give their wares at a nominal price, for a bill which a stroke of the pen can lower in value. "But", says l'Abbé Terrasson, "the king, in

[12] This passage presumably refers to remarks made by Terrasson in his second letter. See Terrasson, op. cit., Letter II, pp. 11–13. This argument is also stressed by John Law, op. cit., pp. 60–62, 93–95, 100.

[13] I.e. John Locke, *Some Considerations on the Consequences of the Lowering of Interest and Raising the Value of Money* which was first published in London in 1691.

[14] John Locke, *Some Considerations* . . ., London, 1870, pp. 239–243. John Law was aware of all these points, see *Money and Trade Considered*, pp. 9–10, 92–95.

order to keep his credit, has an interest in restricting the paper within just bounds, and this interest of the prince is sufficient to build up confidence".[15] What will these just bounds be, and how are they to be determined? Let us follow the system in all the different assumptions which can be made, and see what will be its soundness relative to its usefulness in each case.

At first I observe that it is absolutely impossible that the king should substitute the use of paper for that of gold and silver. The actual gold and silver, to consider them simply as tokens, are in fact distributed among the people by their very circulation, according to the proportion of commodities, industry, land and real wealth of each private person, or rather of the income derived from his wealth compared with his expenditure. Now this proportion can never be known, as it is hidden, and varies continually through new circulation. The king is not going to distribute his paper-money to each according to his possessions of gold money simply by prohibiting the use of the latter in commerce; it is essential that he draws the gold and silver from his subjects to himself, giving them his paper in place of it, and he is able to do this only by p. 99
giving them his paper as representative of money. To make this clear, you only have to substitute a commodity for money, and see if the prince would be able to give paper for grain, if it would be accepted if he were never obliged to give anything else. Certainly not, then the people would not take it; and if attempts were made to force them, they would justly say that their grain is taken without payment. Thus the bank-notes used to announce their value in terms of silver; by their nature they were subject to repayment; and all credit is repayable, because people are loath to give silver for paper. That would be to put their fortune at the mercy of the prince as I will show below.

It is a point of theory and experience alike that the people will never receive paper other than as representative of, and therefore, convertible into, silver.

One of the ways, and perhaps the only one, in which the king would be able to draw the silver to himself through exchange, would be to receive his bills conjointly with silver, and to give out only bills while keeping the silver. Then he would choose between these two things: either to have this silver melted for use as merchandise and to reduce his subjects to the use of paper; or to allow silver and paper to circulate conjointly, both representative of one another.

I begin by examining this last hypothesis. Well then, I assume that the king puts a certain quantity of paper into commerce, equal to that of silver (Law wanted to put in ten times more):[16] as the total quantity of tokens must always balance with the total quantity of commodities, which is always the

[15] This passage presumably refers to remarks made by Terrasson in his second letter. See Terrasson, op. cit., Letter II, pp. 6–7.

[16] I can find no justification for this assertion by Turgot in Law's *Money and Trade Considered*, and cf. note 7 above. In fact, Law proposed several regulations to insure against overissue of paper money. See ibid., pp. 86–87. This assertion may have derived from Terrasson, who argued that the King's credit was more than ten times his assets, see Terrasson, op. cit., Letter II, pp. 4–5.

same, it is evident that the tokens would halve in value; or, what is the same thing, that the commodities would double. But independently of their capacity as tokens of value, gold and silver have a real value as merchandise; a value which is also balanced with the other commodities proportionally to the quantity of these metals, and which, on the contrary, they do not lose through their capacity as money. That is to say, their value, as metals, will balance with more merchandise than the paper with which they are balanced as money. And since, as I will show below, the king is continually obliged to increase the number of his bills, if he does not wish to render them useless, this disproportion will increase to the point where the specie will no longer be reciprocally convertible with paper, which will be discredited daily, while
p. 100 silver maintains its value always, and will balance itself with the same quantity of goods. Now, as soon as the bills are no longer reciprocally convertible into silver, they have no longer any value, and this is what I am going to prove by examining the other assumption, which is that the king completely reduces his subjects to the use of paper-money.

I have already remarked that this has a general inconvenience, which is, that, since the quantity is arbitrary, there can never be any sure basis for its balance with commodities. While the legal value of money changes with its weight, it is always in the same proportion. But in the case of paper as sole legal tender, nothing is fixed, nothing ensures that the bills are of the same legal sum, neither greater nor smaller, as all the silver which used to be in the kingdom. And even if, by assumption, they were given all the confidence imaginable, if the bills were doubled, the commodities would rise proportionately etc.

Firstly, it is therefore not true that the system is, as l'Abbé Terrasson puts forward, a means of always having enough tokens of the commodities for the expenses which are made,[17] since it is equally contradictory that there should not be enough silver to counterbalance the commodities, and that it should be possible to have too much of it, since the price of the commodities is related to the relative scarcity of silver, and is simply the expression of that scarcity.

In the second place, the benefit which the king will derive from the system will be only a transient one during the creation of the bills, or rather, during their increase, but it will vanish very quickly, since the commodities will increase in price in proportion to the number of bills.

I can see what the retort will be: "There is", it will be said, "a difference with the pure increase of legal values by which specie increases in the hands of all the private persons among whom it circulates, and which affects nothing but the debts fixed in legal value. But when it is a question of the bills of the State, the increase is left entirely in the hands of the king who thereby creates wealth for himself according to his needs, and who, by putting the bills into

[17] This passage presumably refers to remarks made by Terrasson in his second letter. See Terrasson, op. cit., Letter II, pp. 13–14.

circulation only while depreciating them, has already drawn from them all the profit when, through their circulation, these bills begin to raise the price of commodities".[18]

What happens next? The king will be able, by thus creating bills for his needs, to exempt his people entirely from taxes, and to incur much more considerable expenses. It will be enough simply to know (and this is easily calculated) in what progression the number of bills must be increased each year; for it is evident that since those of the preceding year will have increased the price of commodities and balanced themselves with them, it will be necessary, in order to incur the same expenses, to make many more of them in the second year, following a progression which will again increase as the expenses take on a higher nominal value. In general, it is necessary always to keep the same proportion between the total sum of old bills and that of new bills, a quarter, for example. p. 101

Let us follow this hypothesis and consider its advantages and disadvantages. We will then draw some conclusions.

1. I acknowledge that, by this means, the king, while giving bills to his subjects for their commodities, bills which are not equivalent to goods, which would in any case be making use of their welfare, would at least save them the charges and vexations which increase the quantity and burden of taxation.

2. I am not very sure how one would be able to know if this aid which the king draws from his subjects would be paid by all in proportion to their wealth. It is evident that if the merchant, who has received the king's bill, obtains for it only the price which it must have in its circulation with the total of bills whose number it has increased, then in this case, those with whom the king deals directly would alone carry the burden of the tax.

The answer to this question depends on a fairly complicated problem, which is as follows: *when and how, through circulation, does a new sum of silver come to balance itself with the total mass of commodities?* – It is clear that it is only through being successively offered for the purchase of various commodities, that it comes to raise the price for the public and to lower its own price. When those who have received the silver of the king, spend it, it has not yet circulated and thus the commodities are not yet raised in price; it is only by passing through several hands that it succeeds in raising the price of all of them. It appears from this, that although nothing very precise can be said about this, it is, all the same, likely that the loss would spread itself fairly uniformly over all private persons, i.e. that they would all be discontented, and not unreasonably so.

It is known, through the money registers, that since the general recoinage[19] p. 102

[18] This argument does not occur in Terrasson's *Lettres sur le Nouveau Système des Finances*, but it may have occurred in the third letter which was not printed in that edition. It does not occur in Law's pamphlet.

[19] A declaration of 15 June 1726 stabilised the coinage of France by making 1 marc in gold

of 1726, 1200 million worth of coin has been manufactured in France; what the foreigners have manufactured balances itself with what has left the kingdom due to the needs of the State. 1200 million may thus be taken as a rough estimate. The revenue of the king is approximately 300, or a quarter. The king, therefore in order to provide for his necessary expenditure, needs a quarter of the total mass of legal value existing in the state and distributed in the circulation. In the case where the king creates all his revenue for himself, as in the case of the Philosophers' Stone or of the bills which are increased arbitrarily, since at the moment of multiplication the commodities have not yet increased in price, he would not be forced to make a greater increase. In the first year the total of bills will then be:

$$a + \frac{a}{4} = 1200 + 300 = 1500$$

The second year:

$$a + \frac{a}{4} + \frac{a + \frac{a}{4}}{4} = 1500 + \frac{1500}{4} = 1975$$

and so on.

...

(It is unfortunate that the remainder of this letter has been lost, but what has just been read of its shows that the young seminarist, at less than 22 years of age, had some very sound ideas on political economy in 1749. Note by Du Pont de Nemours.)

---

the equivalent of 740 livres, 9 sols, 1 denier, and 1 marc in silver the equivalent of 51 livres, 3 sols, 3 deniers. This value lasted till 1785 when the coinage was further debased. See P. Hanotaux (editor), *Histoire de la Nation française*, Paris, 1927, Vol. X, p. 259.

CHAPTER II

1753–1754

REMARKS ON THE NOTES TO THE TRANSLATION OF CHILD[1]

S.I. 372–376

1. (*Effects of high interest.*)[2] I am not sure whether it is correct to say that *a high rate of interest impedes the circulation of money* and that *by making it liable to a charge, it compels us as it were to bury it by converting it into hoards or into plate.* On the contrary, it appears at first glance that the higher is the rate of interest on money, the less of an encumbrance it should be for people, because it is a good's low price that renders it troublesome to the owner. Thus if the opulent rentier invests his money in plate and jewels, it is not because opportunities for lending are wanting, but rather because they are on too easy terms, because people grow rich in too little time, because they p. 373
soon prefer the pleasure of spending what they have acquired to that of increasing their wealth. Thrift lasting for some years is sufficient to restore a family's fortune; this is followed by dissipation and by the enormous extension of luxury. Luxury is the fruit of the excessive inequality of wealth and idleness. Now, the high rate of interest of money causes the inequality of wealth because money attracts money and absorbs all the profits of industry. It produces idleness because it offers an easy means of growing rich without working.

The high rate of interest of money therefore increases the opportunities for lending, but it produces luxury and luxury causes these opportunities to be scorned.

[1] This translation is the one that was published with the title: *Traité sur le commerce et les avantages qui resultent de la réduction de l'intérêt de l'argent,* by Josiah Child, bart., *avec un petit traité contre l'usure* by Sir Thomas Culpeper (the Elder), translated from the English, Amsterdam and Berlin, 1754. This translation was the work of Vincent de Gournay and Butel-Dumont, and was to be accompanied by extensive notes of which Gournay, in the autumn of 1752, had already edited the greater part, but the Contrôleur-général did not permit their publication. See below, 'In Praise of Gournay', pp. 22, 33. These notes have unfortunately been lost.

[2] Child refers to the effects of high interest rates several times; for example: "... for while we that are *Merchants* can so easily turn *Gentlemen* by buying Lands for less than twenty years purchase. Let no Man expect that if we thrive, we will drudge all our days in Trade; or if we would, to be sure our Sons will not." *New Discourse of Trade,* London 1693, p. 158.

2. (*The grain trade.*)[3] The examples of Holland, Genoa, and Venice, where the State is without power and poor, even though the private citizens are rich, are not at all applicable to the question of the interest of money, since it is lower in these republics than in any other state of Europe.

Genoa and Venice are weak states relative to the more powerful states which surround them. I do not know whether the proportion between public revenue and military power and the extent of their territory and the state of their commerce is the same as in the majority of other states in Europe. If this proportion is smaller, I believe that it is proper to praise their governments for it; for apart from the fact that it has not been decided that it is too considerable in many of the more powerful states, no matter how much these republics would burden their subjects with taxes, they would be no more capable of resisting their neighbours because of it, and the people would be unhappy to no purpose.

With regard to Holland, it is far from true that the State is poor or weak relative to its size; it is true that the resilience of the government is weakened at present by the enormity of the public debt and by the changes which have occurred in the constitution of the State, but the Dutch have only their own imprudence to blame, and the wars in which they have involved themselves when blinded by their prosperity. The weakening of Holland is, moreover, a necessary consequence of the increase in the commerce of other states.

p. 374 I should be sorry if the difference in the rate of interest between France and England is the cause of the difference in thinking on the subject of the grain trade; for it would be certain to be made into an argument against the freedom of this trade, on the pretext that the foreigners would profit from this difference by taking all our grain in times of abundance in order to sell it back to us in times of famine, with a profit of which the nation would be deprived.

3. (*The rate of interest.*) I. In truth, I believe that our prejudices in this matter have a different origin. In the setting up of all the legislation dealing with corn, the cries of the consumers have been heeded to the exclusion of the needs of the cultivators. This manner of thinking has arisen in the republics where the sovereignty resides with the people of the cities, because the city dwellers are consumers only. The fear of sedition and the influence of the people's clamouring on timid magistrates who always observe the towns more intimately than the country side, has perpetuated it in nearly all the cities of Italy: corporations have the exclusive charter in corn and oil, which they supply to the people at a price fixed by the government and invariable. Our legislators have adopted the dispositions of Roman Law in this matter, and conform in this to popular demands. The same prejudices have held sway in all of Europe and even in England. The latter country had abandoned these

[3] The discussion on the grain trade and its relationship with the rate of interest in various countries, in this note and part of the next one, seems to be based on a note by Gournay rather than Child's work; there is little if any reference to this in the *New Discourse* ....

ways sooner than we, not so much because the rate of interest is lower there than it is among us, but rather because they have been enlightened by the principles of commerce before us.

II. When the English changed their manner of thinking about the regulation of corn, they were as much at a disadvantage relative to the Dutch through the difference in interest rates as they are at present at an advantage relative to us. The Dutch did not find sufficient profit in removing their grain in order to discourage the English from establishing warehouses for themselves, and the latter have found a sufficiently strong interest to destroy all their prejudices.

III. I believe that it would be the same with us. It is true that in England the dispositions of the Act of Navigation[4] were able to avert the competition of the Dutch and to counterbalance the effects of the different prices of money. But are we not capable of making up for this in part? Government inspection of the importation and exportation of corn, attention to lowering or raising duties at the right moment, would these not be adequate to avert the competition of foreigners and to assure our storehouse keepers a fair profit? p. 375
But I doubt whether even these would be necessary.

IV. To prohibit interest as Moses[5] did, is to prohibit lending, for people will not lend for nothing, above all when it is possible to borrow from foreigners. It is giving a monopoly of usury to the latter and to the evaders of the law, and consequently raising interest. The agrarian laws among the Jews compensated for what might be hurtful to the cultivation of the soil in the laws dealing with lending.

The Frenchman who is willing to lend to me on my bill, does not compel me to make my property over to him, but he makes his over to me; he gives up his right to demand reimbursement, but I do not renounce my duty to repay him. Besides, neither the French nor the Dutch practise usury; the price of money, like that of any other thing, must be settled by the relation between the supply and the demand and not by laws.[6]

V. I do not know if five per cent at present is so very disadvantageous for us with respect to the English and the Dutch. The difference in the interest of money has some absolute and some relative aspects.

[4] Navigation Act, *Statutes,* 12 *Charles II*, c. 18 (1660). Child refers to this Act in the following terms: "For my own part, I am of Opinion that in relation to *Trade, Shipping, Profit* and *Power* it is one of the choicest and most prudent *Acts* that ever was made in *England*, . . .", op. cit., p. 91.

[5] Child refers to Moses as follows: "This makes me conclude that *Moses* (that Wise Legislator) in his forbidding the Jews to lend Money at use to one another, and permitting them to lend their Money to *Strangers*, ordained that Law as much to a *Political* as a *Religious intent*; knowing that by the latter, they should enrich their own Nation, and by the former no public Goods could issue; the consequence being only to Impoverish one *Jew* to make another Rich", ibid., p. 28. Cf. Deut. 24:20, "Unto a stranger though mayest lend upon usury; but unto thy brother thou shalt not lend upon usury . . .".

[6] Cf. Locke, *Some Considerations on the Consequences of the Lowering of Interest and Raising the Value of Money*, London, 1870, pp. 221, 223–225.

VI. I shall not dwell on the exceedingly vast subject of public credit, but I should wish to examine the usefulness of the transfer of debts in itself, and the advantages which result therefrom, and the means of making it more favourable.[7]

VII. If all the sums paid by apprentices and at receptions[8] were used to repay the debts of the corporations and not for feasts, edifices, and law suits, the evil, if it were left to exist for a while, would perhaps bring with it its own remedy. Would there be no means of setting up a bureau of administration to deal with this?[9]

VIII. This regulation which Child proposes[10] to be imposed on the manufacturer is not unjust, but what purpose does it serve? It would give facilities for selling by the piece, but is not the declaration of the manufacturer
p. 376 enough? If he is dishonest, would he not be equally punished by the loss of his reputation, whether he had marked his piece or not.

IX. I doubt strongly that the regulations would be useful even for the original establishment of manufactures. Some examples and some prices would be more useful.

X. On the gain of the State when the merchant loses.[11]

XI. It is not the lack of opportunities, but the too large quantity on the one hand, and the kind of discredit attached to commerce on the other, which draw the money away from it, and raise interest.[12]

[7] Child states regarding the transfer of debts: "The great Advantage that would accrue to this *Kingdom by a Law for Transferring Bills of Debt*, from one person to another, is sufficiently understood by most Men, especially by *Merchants*", op. cit., p. 106.

[8] I.e. into the guilds. See Henri Sée, *Economic and Social Conditions in France during the Eighteenth Century*, New York, 1931, pp. 123–126, 132–133.

[9] Turgot's comment here would seem to refer to Gournay's notes rather than Child, although the latter does devote a chapter to this subject, arguing for the abolition of privilege; see chap. III, 'Concerning Companies of Merchants', op. cit., pp. 80–90.

[10] The regulations referred to would seem to be certain exceptions to the general rule of freedom which Child proposes; see ibid., pp. 132–134:

"But some may then ask me, whether I think it would be for the advantage of the Trade of *England*, to leave all men at liberty to make what *Cloth* and *Stuffs* they please, how they will, where and when they will, or any lengths or sizes?

"I answer: Yes, certainly in my judgment it would be so, except such Species only as his *Majesty* and the *Parliament* shall think fit to make *Staples* . . . to be allowed the honour of a *publick Seal*. . .; and where-ever such Seal is allowed . . . I would desire the Commodity should be exactly made according to the Institution . . ..

"For all *Cloth* and *Stuffs* not being made *Staples*, I think it would be of very great use that the Makers did weave in their Marks, and affix their own Seals, containing the length and breadth of the Pieces . . .".

[11] This may refer to Child's chapter on the balance of trade, where he states: ". . . *if our Trade and Shiping encrease*, how small or low soever the profits are to private men, it is an infallible Indication that the Nation in general thrives" (ibid., p. 148). Cf. ". . . for where a great Trade is driven, especially where much Shiping is employed, whatever becomes of the poor Merchant, that drives the Trade, Multitudes of People will be certain gainers . . . which indeed more or less the whole Kingdom doth" (ibid., p. 150).

[12] These remarks obviously refer to Gournay's notes.

XII. If the Kings had truly desired it, the nobility would enter commerce; it was necessary to set examples and worthy examples at that.[13]

[13] Ibid.

CHAPTER III

1757

FAIRS AND MARKETS[1]

D.D. I 291–298

The word *fair*, which is derived from *forum*, a public square, was originally synonymous with that of *market*, and is still so in certain respects. Both signify a gathering of *sellers* and *buyers* at a set time and place, but the word
p. 292 *fair* seems to present the idea of a more numerous, more solemn, and consequently, less common gathering. The use of these two words in ordinary language appears to be determined by this distinction, which is immediately perceptible, but which itself arises from a less obvious, and as it were, more radical difference between these two things. This will be developed further.

It stands to reason that sellers and buyers cannot gather together at certain times and places without an attraction or an interest which compensates for, or which even exceeds the expenses of the journey and of the transportation of the produce and merchandise. Without this attraction, each would remain at home. The stronger it is, the longer the transportation which the produce can support, the more numerous and solemn the gathering of merchants and customers will be, and the more the district which has this gathering as its centre, can be extended. The natural course of trade in itself is enough to fashion this gathering and to increase it up to a certain point. The competition of the sellers limits the price of the produce, and the price of the produce in turn limits the number of sellers. Indeed, since all trade must support the person who undertakes it, it is essential that the number of sales compensates the merchant for the low profit which he makes on each sale, and that, consequently, the number of merchants is proportioned to the current number of consumers, so that each merchant is matched by a certain number of the

[1] The article in the *Encyclopédie* on which this paper is based was titled simply 'Foire'; see *L'Encyclopédie ou Dictionnaire Raisonné des Sciences, des Arts et des Métiers*, ed. Diderot, vol. 7, Paris 1757, pp. 39–41. Some minor changes in punctuation and italics, one textual change, and one alteration in paragraphing were noted; apart from these the two versions are the same. Turgot refers to this paper in his correspondence with Du Pont. See Turgot to Du Pont, 1/12/1769 in Schelle, *Oeuvres*, III, p. 72. For a discussion of the change in title of this paper, see 'Introduction', above p. XVI, n. 31.

latter. Recognising this, I assume that the price of a commodity is such that in order to support the trade in it, it has to be sold in a market of three hundred families. It is obvious that three villages, each containing only one hundred families, will be able to support only a single merchant of this commodity. This merchant will probably live in that village of the three where the largest number can gather most conveniently and at the least expense, because this curtailment of expenses will give the merchant who is established in this p. 293
village an advantage over those who would be tempted to set up business in any of the others. But several types of commodities would probably be in the same category and the merchant of each of these commodities would set up in the same place because of the curtailment of the expenses and because someone who needs two types of commodities prefers making one journey to making two; it is really as if he were paying less for each piece of merchandise. Once a place has become notable because of this self-same gathering together of different trades, it becomes more and more important, because all artisans who are not confined to the country side by the nature of their work, and all those whose wealth permits them to be idle, assemble there to obtain the conveniences of life. The competition of buyers draws the merchants in the hope of sales, and several of them set up business to deal in the same commodities. The competition of the merchants draws buyers in the hope of a good bargain, and both of them continue to increase in turn up to the point where for the remote buyers, the disadvantage of the distance offsets the cheapness of the commodities caused by competition, and even what custom and force of habit add to the attraction of a good bargain. In this manner different centres of commerce, or *markets*, are naturally formed, to which correspond an equal number of districts or departments of various sizes, according to the nature of the commodities, the relative ease of communications and the condition and relative size of the population. And such is, by the way, the most important and the most common origin of *small market towns* and *cities*.

The same reason of convenience which settles the gathering of buyers and sellers at certain places, also confines it to certain days, when the commodities are too paltry to support long transportation and when the district is not sufficiently populous to provide an adequate, daily market. These days are settled on through a form of silent agreement, for which the smallest circumstances provide a reason. The number of days' journey between the most important places in the neighbourhood, together with certain dates which give rise to the departure of travellers, such as the proximity of certain feastdays, certain days hallowed by usage for the payments of rents, all types of recurring solemnities, in short, all the types of occasions which bring together a group of people on specific days, become the principle for the establishment p. 294
of a market on these same days, because traders have an interest in searching out buyers and vice versa.

But it takes only a fairly short distance for this interest, and the low prices resulting from competition, to be offset by the expenses of travel and of the transportation of the produce. Therefore it is not to the natural course of a commerce animated by freedom that one should attribute these splendid fairs, where the products of part of Europe are assembled at great expense and which appear to be the *rendez-vous* of nations. The gain which must compensate for these exorbitant expenses does not arise from the natural order of things but results from the privileges and franchises granted to trade at certain times and places while everywhere else it is overburdened with taxes and duties. It is not surprising that the lack of freedom and the customary obstructions with which commerce has been burdened for so long in all of Europe, has forcibly directed it to those places where it was granted a little more freedom. This is how princes, by granting exemptions from duty, have created so many fairs in the various parts of Europe, and it stands to reason that these fairs are all the more important as the trade is more overburdened with duties in normal times.

A fair and a market are therefore both a gathering of merchants and customers at a set time and place; but in the case of markets the merchants and buyers are brought together by the mutual interest they have in seeking each other; while in the case of fairs it is the desire to enjoy certain privileges: from which it follows that this gathering is inevitably much more numerous and solemn at fairs. Although the natural course of commerce is sufficient to establish markets, as a result of the unfortunate principle which in nearly all governments has infected the administration of commerce, I mean, the mania of directing all, regulating all, and of never relying on the self-interest of man, it has happened, that in order to establish markets, the police[2] has been made to interfere; that the number of markets has been limited on the pretext of preventing them from becoming harmful to each other; that the sale of certain goods has been prohibited except at certain appointed places, either for the convenience of the clerks charged with receiving the duty with which they are burdened, or because the goods were required to be subjected to the for-
p. 295 malities of testing and marking,[3] while offices cannot be established everywhere. The opportunity cannot be grasped too often to attack this

[2] 'Police' is used here in the sense of a branch of civil government, as defined by Adam Smith in his *Lectures on Justice, Police, Revenue and Arms*, ed. E. Cannan, New York, 1964, p. 155, as "the regulation of the inferior parts of government", that is, "cleanliness, security, cheapness or plenty". Cannan adds a definition from Johnson's Dictionary, 1755, "regulation and government of a city or country as regards the inhabitants", op. cit. Cf. the article 'Police' in the *Encyclopédie*, XII, 904–912.

[3] The testing and marking of manufactures of various kinds was current in various countries; for a description of these formalities in France, see for example E.F. Heckscher, *Mercantilism*, 2nd ed., London, 1955, I, 160–164. See also below, Letter to l'Abbé Terray on 'le marque des fers', pp. 182–188 in which Turgot attacks this custom of trade marking and testing as a constraint on trade.

system so fatal to industry; it can be found more than once in the *Encyclopédie.*[4] The most celebrated fairs in France are those of Lyons, Bordeaux, Beaucaire, etc.; in Germany, those of Leipzig, Frankfurt, etc. My objective here is neither to list them nor to give a detailed exposition of the privileges granted by various sovereigns either to fairs in general or to any one fair in particular. I shall limit myself to some reflection against the common enough illusion which makes some people cite the importance and the extent of the trade at certain fairs as a proof of the greatness of the commerce of a State.

Undoubtedly, a fair must enrich the place where it is held, and bring about the importance of a particular town; and when the whole of Europe was groaning under the manifold shackles of feudal government, when each village was, as it were, an independent and sovereign state, when the lords enclosed in their castles envisaged commerce only as an opportunity of increasing their revenue by subjecting all those who were forced of necessity to cross their territory to a tax or to an exorbitant toll, there is no doubt that those who were the first to be sufficiently enlightened to feel that in slightly relaxing the severity of their duties, they would be more than compensated by the increase of commerce and consumption, soon observed the enrichment, the growth, and the improvement of their places of residence. It is certain that when kings and emperors had sufficiently increased their authority to remove the taxes levied by their vassals from the merchandise destined for the fairs of certain towns which they wished to favour, these towns necessarily became the centres of an exceedingly large commerce and saw the increase of their p. 296
power as well as of their wealth. But since all these small sovereign states have been united into a single State, under a single prince, is it not strange that, if negligence, force of habit, the difficulty of redressing abuses even if desired, and the difficulty of desiring it, if these things have combined to keep the constraints in existence, namely these local duties and privileges which were established when each province and each village owed allegiance to a different sovereign, is it not strange, I repeat, that this haphazard result has not only been praised, but even imitated as if it were the act of rational policy? Is it not strange that with very good intentions, and with a view to making trade flourishing, new fairs have again been established, the privileges and exemptions of certain towns have yet again been increased, that certain branches of commerce have even been prevented from settling in the midst of

[4] In the volumes of the *Encyclopédie* preceding that in which Turgot's article 'Foire' appeared, similar views are expressed in such articles as 'Communauté', III, 724, 'Concurrence', ibid., p. 832, 'Compagnie', ibid., pp. 739–743, all of which are signed M.V.D.F. (presumably Forbonnais); see also 'Economie', IV, 337–348, by Rousseau, and of course Quesnay's 'Fermier', VI, 528–540.

A more detailed criticism of the financial and commercial policies of the time occurs in the article 'Impôt', VIII, 601–604, by D(e) J(aucourt); however, this volume was not published until 1765.

the poor provinces for fear of hurting some other towns which for a long time have been enriched by these same branches of commerce? And what does it matter whether Peter or Jack, Maine or Brittany manufacture this or that commodity, provided that the state is enriched and Frenchmen are earning their living? What does it matter whether a piece of cloth is sold at Beaucaire or in its place of manufacture, provided that the labourer receives the value of his work? An enormous mass of trade, gathered together in one place and lumped closely together, will attract the attention of shallow politicians in a much more obvious manner. Water artificially brought together in lakes and canals amuses the traveller as a display of frivolous luxury, but the water which the rain uniformly diffuses over the fields, and which is only guided by the incline of the terrain and distributed through all the valleys, forming pools there, carries wealth and fecundity everywhere. What does it signify that a great deal of trading takes place in a certain spot on certain occasions, if this momentary trade is large only through the same causes which obstruct trade and which tend to decrease it at all other times and over the whole extent of the State? "Is it necessary", said the civic magistrate to whom we owe the translation of Child (M. de Gournay)[5] and to whom France will one day perhaps owe the destruction of the obstacles which have been placed in the way of commerce in the desire to promote it – "is it necessary to fast all year in order to live sumptuously on certain days? In Holland there are no fairs at
p. 297 all, but the whole extent of the State and the whole year are, as it were, a continuous fair, because commerce in that country is always and everywhere equally flourishing."

It is said: "The State cannot do without the revenue; in order to provide for its needs it must burden commodities with various taxes. However, it is no less necessary to facilitate the sale of our products, above all abroad, which cannot be done without lowering their prices as much as possible. Now these two objectives are reconciled by appointing places and times of immunity from duty, where the low price of the commodity attracts the foreigner and causes an extraordinary consumption, while the everyday consumption of necessaries sufficiently supplies the public revenue. The very desire to profit from these occasions of grace give sellers and buyers an eagerness which the solemnity of these *great* fairs enhances even more by a type of enticement, from which an increase in the whole of commerce results." Such are the pretexts which are alleged to uphold the usefulness of the great *fairs*. But it is not difficult to be convinced that it is possible, by general agreement, and while favouring equally all members of the State, to reconcile much more advantageously the two objectives which the government may have in view. Indeed, since the prince agrees to lose part of his duties and consents to sacrifice them in the interest of commerce, nothing prevents him, in making the duties uniform, from diminishing the total of what he agrees to forego.

[5] Cf. 'In Praise of Gournay', below, pp. 37–38.

The objective of exempting the sales abroad from duty while letting them survive only on domestic consumption would be even more easily carried out by exempting from duty all the goods which leave the country, for after all, it cannot be denied that our *fairs* supply a large part of our domestic consumption. Under this arrangement, the extraordinary consumption which occurs at the time of fairs would greatly diminish; but it stands to reason that the reduction of the duties in ordinary times, would make the general consumption a great deal more abundant; with this difference that in the case of a uniform but moderate duty, commerce would gain all that the prince is willing to sacrifice to it; whereas in the case of a general and heavier duty, with local and temporary exemptions, the king may sacrifice much, and commerce gain almost nothing; or, what is the same thing, the commodities and merchandise can be lowered in price to a much lesser extent than the duties are lowered, and this because it is necessary to subtract from the advantages which this p. 298
decrease yields, the costs of transportation of the produce and merchandise to the place designated for the *fair*, the change of abode, the rents of the marketplace increased yet again through the monopoly of the proprietors, and finally the risk of not selling in a rather short time, and of having made a long journey to no avail. Now, it is always necessary that the merchandise pay for all these expenses and these risks. It is far from true, therefore, that the sacrifice of duties by the prince is as useful to commerce in the form of temporary and local exemptions as it would be in the form of a slight reduction over the whole of the duties; it is far from true therefore, that the extraordinary consumption increases by special exemptions as much as the daily consumption is diminished through customary overtaxing. Add to this that there are no special exemptions which do not give rise to frauds in order to profit by them, to new constraints, to increases in the number of clerks and inspectors to prevent these frauds, and to the trouble of punishing them. This is another loss of men and money to the State.

Let us conclude that the *great* fairs are never as useful as the constraints which they imply are harmful; and that far from being the proof of the flourishing condition of commerce, they can only exist, on the contrary, in States where commerce is restricted, burdened with duties, and consequently, indifferent.

CHAPTER IV

1759

IN PRAISE OF GOURNAY (ELOGE DE GOURNAY)

D.D. I 262–291

LETTER FROM TURGOT TO MARMONTEL[1]

Paris, 22 July, 1759

I have certainly not forgotten, sir, the note on the late M. de Gournay, which I promised you. I even counted on giving it to you last Monday, at Mme. Geoffrin's,[2] but, not having found you there, and believing you to be in no great hurry, moreover, I took it back home, with the idea that perhaps I would have the time to complete the draft of the eulogy which I would like to make of this excellent citizen.

Since you can wait no longer, I am sending you an outline of it, sketched in great haste, which may yet be able to help you write it, and which you will undoubtedly use in a manner which does much greater justice to his glory than my efforts.

You are aware of my affection.

* * *

Jean Claude Marie Vincent, Seigneur de Gournay, honorary councillor of the Grand Council, and honorary Intendant of Commerce, died at Paris, June 27 (1759) at the age of forty-seven.[3]

[1] Jean François Marmontel (1723–1799), French writer and contributor to the *Encyclopédie.* He prepared the official eulogy of Gournay by having extracts of Turgot's eulogy printed in *Le Mercure,* August, 1759, No. 8; the first full edition of this work did not appear till the 19th century when it was included in Du Pont's edition of Turgot's works. (See III, pp. 321–375.)

[2] Marie Thérèse Rodet Geoffrin (1699–1777), famous for her salon, which Turgot frequented.

[3] Turgot made two errors in this official description. Gournay's name was Jacques Claude Marie and not Jean Claude Marie, and his title was M. le Marquis de Gournay and not simply Sieur de Gournay. See G. Schelle, *Vincent de Gournay,* pp. 17, 24 which remains the standard biography.

He was born in St. Malo in May 1712. His father was Claude Vincent, one of the most important merchants of that town, and Secretary Royal.

His parents destined him for a commercial life, and sent him to Cadiz in 1729, when he was only just seventeen.

Left to his own devices at this early age, he was yet able to avoid the perils and frivolity which are but too common at that age, and, during his entire stay in Cadiz, his life was divided between study, the work of his business, and the numerous connections which his business required and which his personal merit soon procured him.

Through diligence and alertness he found time to enrich his mind with a mass of useful knowledge, without yet neglecting that higher literature, but it p. 263 was, above all, to the science of commerce that he felt himself drawn and to which he directed his mind in all its vigour. To compare the products of nature and those of the arts in man in different climes, to arrive at the value of these different products, or, in other words, their relationship with the needs and wealth of people at home and abroad, the costs of transport which vary according to the nature of the commodities and the diversity of the routes, the many duties to which they are subject, etc., etc.; in short, to comprehend in its full scope, and to follow in its continual upheavals, the condition of natural production, of industry, of population, of wealth, of finance, of the needs and even the vagaries of fashion in all the nations that are united by commerce, in order to theorise profitably on the basis of a thorough study of all these details – this is to be concerned with the science of trade, as a merchant and constitutes only a part of the science of commerce. But to discover the causes and effects of that multitude of upheavals in all their diversity, to search out the elemental forces whose action, always in combination with, and sometimes disguised by, local circumstances, directs all the transactions of commerce; to recognise those special and basic laws, founded in Nature itself, by which all the values existent in commerce are balanced against each other and settle at a certain value, just as bodies left to themselves take their place, unaided, according to their specific gravity; to discern those complicated relations which link commerce with all the branches of political economy; to perceive the interdependence of commerce and agriculture, the influence of the one and the other on the wealth, the population, and the strength of states, their intimate connection with the laws and customs, and with all the processes of the government, especially with the distribution of its finances; to weigh the assistance which commerce receives from the Navy and that which it renders to it in return, the changes it produces in the respective interests of States, and the weight it places in the political balance of nations; in fine, to select, from among chance events and principles of administration adopted by the different nations of Europe, the true causes of their progress or of their decline in commerce – this is to approach the subject as a philosopher and a statesman.

p. 264 If his position in life caused M. Vincent to concern himself with the science of commerce as under the first of these two points of view, his vast and penetrating intellect did not allow him to confine himself to this.

To the enlightenment which he drew from his own experience and his reflections, he added a reading of the best works on this subject produced by the different nations of Europe, and particularly by the English nation – the richest of all in such works, and with whose language he familiarised himself for this reason. The works which he read with most pleasure, and whose doctrine he most appreciated, were the Treatises of the famous Josiah Child[4] (which he afterwards translated into French) and the Memoirs of the Grand Pensionary, Johan de Witt.[5] We know that these two great men are considered (the one in England, the other in Holland) as the legislators of commerce; that their principles have become national principles, and that the observance of these principles is regarded as one of the sources of the vast superiority in commerce which these two nations have acquired over all the other powers. M. Vincent constantly found verification of these simple and enlightened principles in the practice of an extensive business. He made them his own, without foreseeing that he was destined one day to spread their light through France, and to merit from his own country the same tribute of gratitude which England and Holland pay to those two benefactors of their nation and humanity. His talents and knowledge, together with the most perfect integrity, assured M. Vincent the admiration and the confidence of that multitude of merchants that commerce brings together at Cadiz from all parts of Europe, while at the same time his charming manners procured him their friendship. He soon enjoyed there an esteem unusual for his age, and which the natives of the country, his own compatriots, and the foreigners there, were equally eager to bestow upon him.

During his stay in Cadiz he had paid several visits to the Court of Spain, and to the various provinces of that kingdom.

In 1744, some commercial enterprises which had to be arranged with the Government brought him to France, and in contact with the Comte de Maurepas,[6] then Minister of Navy, who soon discovered M. Vincent's worth.

p. 265 After leaving Spain, M. Vincent resolved to spend some years travelling through the different parts of Europe in order to increase his knowledge, as

[4] Sir Josiah Child (1630–1699), English merchant and economist. The treatise to which Turgot refers is his *Discourse Upon Trade* (1690) which Gournay had translated into French. See above, 'Remarks on the Notes to the Translation of Child', p. 9, n. 1.

[5] Johan de Witt (1623–1672), prominent Dutch statesman. The treatise to which Turgot refers is the *Political Maxims of the State of Holland ... by John de Witt, pensionary of Holland*; first Dutch edition in 1662, first English edition in 1702, the first French edition was published in 1709 under the title *Mémoires de Jean de Witt.*

[6] Jean Fréderic Phélypeaux, Comte de Maurepas (1701–1781), Minister for the Navy and Colonies (1723–1749). On the accession of Louis XVI he became First Minister, and on the advice of his wife and Abbé de Véri invited Turgot to the ministry, first of the Navy, then of Finances.

well as to extend his correspondences and to form connections favourable to the business he intended to pursue. He visited Hamburg and travelled through Holland and England. Everywhere he made observations and collected notes on the state of commerce and shipping, and on the principles of administration adopted by the different nations in respect to those great objects. During his travels, he maintained an uninterrupted correspondence with M. de Maurepas, whom he acquainted with the knowledge which he was gathering. Everywhere, he made a favourable impression, and attracted the goodwill of the most considerable merchants, of men of great distinction in all walks of life, and of the ministers of foreign powers who were resident in the places through which he travelled. The Court of Vienna, as well as that of Berlin sought to procure his services, and made him very enticing proposals, but he rejected them. He had no other intention than to continue in business and to return to Spain, after having again seen Germany and Italy, when an unforeseen event interrupted his projects and brought him back to his own country.

M. Jametz de Villebarre, his business partner and friend, died in 1746, and being without children, made M. Vincent his sole heir. The latter was in England when he received this news; he returned to France. The amount of his fortune was sufficient for his modest needs; he felt he should settle in his own country and he gave up commerce in 1748. He then took his name from his estate of Gournay, which was included in the legacy he received from M. de Villebarre. The minister[7] was aware how useful his knowledge of commerce might prove to the administration of that important sector. The court had planned to send him to the general peace discussions being held at Breda,[8] not unlike M. Ménager, who in 1711, had been sent to the conferences which preceded the Treaty of Utrecht, in order to discuss the commercial aspects of our interests. The changes which occurred in the conferences did not permit this wise project to be executed, but M. de Maurepas adhered to his original desire to make the talents of M. de Gournay useful to the government; he advised him to consider the prospects of a position as Intendant of Commerce, and to enter, in the meantime, one of the higher Courts. Consequently, in 1749, M. de Gournay purchased the office of coun- p. 266
cillor in the Grand Council. When an Intendancy of Commerce fell vacant in 1751, M. de Machault,[9] who was also most familiar with the merits of M. de Gournay, had that office conferred on him. From this time onwards, his life was devoted to public affairs: his entry into the Ministry of Commerce appears to have marked the beginning of a period of profound change. During twenty years of experience in a wide and varied trade, in his frequent

[7] I.e. de Maurepas, see above, p. 22, n. 6.

[8] In 1748, at the end of the War of Austrian Succession. The peace treaty itself was signed at Aix-la-Chapelle in the same year.

[9] M. de Machault d'Arnouville (1701–1794). Intendant of Hainaut (1743–1745), President of the Ministry of Commerce (1745), Contrôleur-Général des finances (1745–1750).

visits to the most competent merchants of Holland and England, in the reading of the most highly esteemed authors of these two nations, in his careful observation of the causes of their prosperity, M. de Gournay had formulated principles which appeared to be new to some of the magistrates of whom the Ministry of Commerce was composed – M. de Gournay was of the opinion that every man who works deserves the gratitude of the public. He was astonished to find that a citizen could neither manufacture nor sell anything without having bought the right to do so by entering a corporation or guild at great expense, and that, after having bought this right, it was still sometimes necessary to have a law suit, to determine whether by entering this or that corporation he had acquired the right to manufacture precisely this or that article. He thought that a workman who had manufactured a piece of
p. 267 cloth had made a real addition to the stock of wealth in the State; that if this cloth happened to be inferior to others, there might yet be found among his customers somebody to whom this inferiority would be more suitable than a
p. 268 more expensive perfection. He could not see why this piece of cloth, for failing to conform to certain regulations, should be cut up into fragments of three ells in length, and why the unfortunate man who had made it should be ordered to pay a penalty, enough to reduce him and his family to poverty.[10] He could not conceive why a workman, when making a piece of cloth, should be exposed to risks and expenses from which an idle man was exempt. He could not see of what use it might be that a manufactured piece of cloth should involve legal procedures and tedious discussions in order to establish whether it conformed to an extensive system of regulation, often difficult to understand, nor did he think that such discussions ought to be held between a manufacturer who cannot read and an inspector who cannot manufacture, nor that that inspector should yet be the final judge of the fortune of the unlucky man, etc.

M. de Gournay found it equally strange that, in a kingdom in which the order of succession was determined simply by custom, and in which the question of applying the death sentence to certain crimes was still left to the discretion of the courts, the government should have deigned to regulate by special legislation the length and breadth of each piece of cloth,[11] the number of threads it was to contain, and to hallow with the seal of the legislature four volumes in quarto filled with these important details, and in addition in-
p. 269 numerable statutes, dictated by the spirit of monopoly, the whole purpose of which were to discourage industry, to concentrate trade within the hands of a few people by multiplying formalities and charges, by subjecting industry to apprenticeships and journeymanships (*compagnonnages*) of ten years in some

[10] For a full description of some of these regulations, see E.F. Heckscher, *Mercantilism*, second edition, London, 1955, I, pp. 157–166.

[11] E.F. Heckscher, *Mercantilism*, I, pp. 160–161, where the first five rules in the regulations for the weaving of woollen cloth are quoted.

trades which can be learned in ten days, by excluding those who were not sons of masters, or those born outside a certain class, and by prohibiting the employment of women in the manufacture of cloth, etc., etc.

He had not imagined that in a kingdom subject to the same prince, all towns looked on each other as enemies, that they would assume the right to prohibit work within their precincts to other Frenchmen, classifying them as *foreigners*, to oppose the sale or the free transit of commodities of a neighbouring province – and thereby for the sake of some fleeting interest, to contend against the general interest of the State, etc., etc.

He was no less astonished to see the government concern itself in regulating the circulation of each commodity, in prescribing one kind of industry in order to encourage another, in subjecting to special constraints the sale of the provisions most necessary to life, in forbidding the setting up of stores of a product whose crop varies from year to year and whose consumption is nearly always the same, in forbidding the exportation of an article subject to depreciation, and to see the government expect to secure the abundance of corn by making the condition of the farm labourer more uncertain and more unhappy than that of all other men, etc.

M. de Gournay was well aware that several of the abuses to which he was opposed had existed in former times in a large part of Europe, and that vestiges of them still remained even in England; but he also knew that the p. 270
English government had abolished part of them; that, if some still remained, far from adopting them as useful institutions, that government tried to restrict them, and to prevent them from spreading, and continued to tolerate them only because the republican constitution sometimes places obstacles in the path of reform of certain abuses when these abuses can be corrected only by an authority which is always mistrusted by the people, even if it is used to their own advantage. Finally, he knew that for more than a century, all enlightened minds, whether in Holland or in England, had regarded these abuses as remnants of mediæval barbarism and of the weakness of all the governments which had known neither the importance of public liberty, nor how to protect it against the invasions of the spirit of monopoly and of particular interests.

For twenty years, M. de Gournay had himself carried out, and had seen carried out, the greatest commerce on earth without having had occasion to learn, other than from books, of the existence of all those laws to which he saw so much importance attached, and therefore he did not believe that he would be taken for an *innovator* and a *man of systems*, when all he did was to develop those principles which experience had taught him, and which he saw unanimously recognised by the most enlightened merchants with whom he was associated.

These principles, which others styled as a *new system*, to him appeared to be no more than the maxims of the plainest common sense. This whole so-called *system* was founded on this maxim, that in general every man knows his own interest better than another to whom it is of no concern.

Hence he concluded that when the interest of individuals is precisely the same as the general interest, every man ought best to be left at liberty to do what he likes. Now, in the case of unrestrained commerce, M. de Gournay thought it impossible for the individual interest not to concur with the general interest.[12]

p. 271 Commerce can be connected with the general interest, or, what is the same thing, the State can interest itself in commerce, in two respects only. As protector of the individuals who compose it, it is in its interest that no one should be able to inflict any great injustice on another, against which the latter has no protection. Next in its capacity as a political unit forced to defend itself against foreign invasions, it is in the interest of the State that the stock of its wealth and the annual product of the soil and of industry should be as great as possible. In both respects, the State has a special interest in protecting the value of the necessities of life from those sudden shocks which, by plunging the people into the horrors of famine, may endanger public tranquility and the safety of citizens and magistrates. Now, it is clear that the interest of all the individuals, kept free from restraint of any kind, necessarily fulfils all these conditions of general usefulness.

As for the first object, that in trade no one should injure another, it is evidently sufficient that the government should always protect the natural liberty of the buyer to buy, and of the seller to sell. For if the buyer is always the one who decides whether to buy or not, it is certain that he will select among all the sellers the man who will give him at the best price the merchandise that suits him best. It is no less certain that every seller, it being his chief interest to gain preference over his competitors, will sell in general the best merchandise at the lowest possible price, in order to attract customers. It is not true therefore that a merchant may be interested in deception – unless he has some exclusive privilege.

But if the government limits the number of sellers by exclusive privileges or otherwise, it is certain that the consumer will be wronged and that the seller, certain of selling, will compel him to buy bad articles at a high price.

p. 272 If, on the contrary, it is the number of buyers which is diminished, by the exclusion of foreigners or of certain other persons, then the seller is wronged, and, if the injury is carried to the point where the price does not compensate him, with profit, for the costs and risk, he will cease to produce the commodity in such abundance, and scarcity will result.

The general freedom of buying and selling is therefore the only means of assuring, on the one hand, the seller of a price sufficient to encourage production, and on the other hand, the consumer, of the best merchandise at the

[12] Cf. Charles Davenant, *Discourses on the Publick Revenues* (1698) in *Works* (edited by Charles Whitworth), London, 1771, I, p. 146.

lowest price. This is not to say that in particular instances we may not find a cheating merchant and a duped consumer; but the cheated consumer will learn by experience and will cease to frequent the cheating merchant, who will fall into discredit and thus will be punished for his fraudulence; and this will never happen very often, because generally men will be enlightened upon their evident self-interest.

To expect the government to prevent such fraud from ever occurring would be like wanting it to provide cushions for all the children who might fall. To p. 273 assume it to be possible to prevent successfully, by regulation, all possible malpractices of this kind, is to sacrifice to a chimerical perfection the whole progress of industry; it is to restrict the imagination of artificers to the narrow limits of the familiar; it is to forbid them all new experiments; to renounce even the hope of competing with the foreigners in the making of the new products which they invent daily, since, as they do not conform to our regulations, our workmen cannot imitate these articles without first having obtained permission from the government, that is to say, often after the foreign factories, having profited by the first eagerness of the consumer for this novelty, have already replaced it with something else. It means forgetting that the execution of these regulations is always entrusted to men who may have all the more interest in fraud or in conniving at fraud since the fraud which they might commit would be covered in some way by the seal of public authority and by the confidence which this seal inspires, in the consumers. It is also to forget that these regulations, these inspectors, these offices for inspection and marking, always involve expenses, and that these expenses are always a tax on the merchandise, and as a result overcharge the domestic consumer and discourage the foreign buyer. Thus, with obvious injustice, commerce, and consequently the nation, are charged with a heavy burden to save a few idle people the trouble of instructing themselves or of making enquiries to avoid being cheated. To suppose all consumers to be dupes, and all merchants and manufacturers to be cheats, has the effect of authorising them to be so, and of degrading all the working members of the community.

As for the second object for the Government in this connection, which is to procure for the nation the greatest possible stock of wealth, is it not evident that since the only real wealth of the State is the annual output of its land and of the industry of its inhabitants, its wealth will be at its greatest when the p. 274 produce of each acre of land, and of the industry of each individual is carried to the highest possible level? And is it not evident that each proprietor has more interest than any other person in drawing from his land the greatest possible return? That every individual has the same interest in gaining by his work as much money as possible? It is equally obvious that the employment of the soil or of industry which yields the greatest revenue to each proprietor or to each inhabitant will always be the one that is of the greatest advantage to the State, because the sum which the State can use annually for its needs is always an aliquot part of the total revenue which is annually produced in the State, and because the sum of these revenues is composed of the net revenue of each estate and of the product of the industry of each individual – if then, instead of leaving all this to private interests, the government takes it upon itself to prescribe to each what he must do, clearly all the benefits individuals lose because of the constraints imposed upon them, will represent an equal deduction from the total net revenue produced in the State each year.

To imagine that the State should encourage the earth to bring forth one kind of produce rather than another, that it ought to establish certain types of manufactures rather than some others; that consequently it ought to prohibit the production of some goods and order that of others; to forbid certain kinds of industry for fear of injuring other kinds; to claim to sustain manufacturing, when it is at the expense of agriculture by forcibly maintaining the price of provisions below their natural level; to establish certain manufactures at the expense of the Treasury; to heap privileges on them, favours, exclusions of all manufactures of the same kind for the purpose of procuring for the manufacturers a profit which it is assumed they could not obtain by the natural sale of their products: all this is to misunderstand greatly the true advantages of commerce; it is to forget that no commercial transaction can be anything other than reciprocal, and that, therefore, the desire to sell everything to the foreigners and to buy nothing from them, is absurd.

p. 275 There is no need to prove that each individual is the only competent judge of this most advantageous use of his lands and of his labour. He alone has the particular knowledge without which the most enlightened man could only argue blindly. He alone has an experience which is all the more reliable since it is limited to a single object. He learns by repeated trials, by his successes, by his losses, and he acquires a feeling for it which is much more ingenious than the theoretical knowledge of the indifferent observer because it is stimulated by want.

If the objection is raised that apart from exchange value, the State may also be interested in being as little dependent as possible on other states for the commodities of prime necessity; firstly, all that this proves is that, although both freedom of industry and freedom of trade in the produce of the soil, are very precious, freedom of trade in the produce of the soil is yet the more essential; secondly, it will always be true that greater wealth and a larger population will give the State in question the means of ensuring its independence in a much more reliable manner. Besides, that suggestion is purely speculative; a large State always produces everything and with regard to a smaller one, a bad harvest would soon wreck this fine scheme of independence.

As for the third object, which may interest the State in two respects, both as protector of the individuals whom it must put in the way of earning a comfortable living by their own labour, and as a political body interested in preventing the domestic troubles which a famine could cause, this matter has been developed so clearly in the work of M. Herbert,[13] and in the article *Corn* by M. Quesnay,[14] that I refrain from discussing it here, since M. Marmontel knows these two works thoroughly.

It follows from this discussion that, in all respects in which commerce may p. 276
interest the State, unrestrained individual interest will always produce the public welfare more surely than the operations of government, which are always faulty and of necessity directed by a hazy and dubious theory.

M. de Gournay concluded that the only aim the administration should set for itself was: firstly, to restore to all branches of commerce that precious liberty they had lost through the prejudices of ages of ignorance, through the ease with which the Government fell in with particular interests, and the desire for a misplaced perfection; secondly to grant the right to work to all members of the State, for the purpose of exciting the greatest competition in the market, which will infallibly produce the greatest perfection in manufacture, and the most advantageous price to the buyers; thirdly, to give at the same time as many competitors as possible to the buyer by opening for the seller all the outlets for his commodity, which is the only means of assuring labour its reward, and of perpetuating production, which has this reward as its sole object.

Besides this, the government should plan to remove those obstacles which retard the progress of industry by diminishing the extent and the certainty of its profits. M. de Gournay considered the chief of these obstacles to be the high interest of money,[15] which, by offering to all owners of capital the means of spending their lives without working, encourages luxury and idleness and withdraws from commerce the riches and industry of a multitude of citizens, rendering them unproductive to the State; which excludes the nation from all branches of commerce not yielding one or two per cent more than the current rate of interest; which consequently gives foreigners the exclusive privilege of all these branches of commerce, and enables them to gain preference over us in almost all other countries by lowering the price more than we would afford to do; which gives the inhabitants of our colonies a powerful reason to engage in smuggling, and in this way weakens the natural affection they ought to have for the mother country; which alone would secure for the Dutch and the Hanse towns the carrying trade of all of Europe including even France itself; which, every year, makes us tributaries to the foreigners by the high rates we p. 277
pay on their loans to us; which, finally, withdraws from cultivation all those lands which would not yield more than five per cent, since it is possible, to ob-

[13] Claude-Jacques Herbert, *Essai sur la police des grains, sur leur prix, et sur les effets de l'agriculture*, Londres, 1753.

[14] François Quesnay, 'Grains', first published in the *Encyclopédie* in 1757. See *Quesnay et la Physiocratie*, II, pp. 459–510.

[15] Cf. Turgot, 'Remarks on the Notes to the Translation of Child', section 1, above, pp. 9, 10–11.

tain the same return with the same capital, without working. But similarly, he believed that the dealings in capital itself, which have this rate of interest as their price, can be made to regulate this price equitably and with all necessary economy only, as in the case of all commerce, by competition and by mutual liberty, and that the government could best bring this about by, on the one hand abstaining from making laws whenever agreements can serve this purpose, and on the other hand, by not swelling the number of debtors and consumers of capital whether by borrowing or by not repaying punctually.[16]

Another kind of obstacle to the progress of industry which M. de Gournay considered could not be cleared away too soon was that multiplicity of taxes which, owing to the necessity of meeting the requirements of the State, had been imposed upon labour of every kind, entailing vexatious modes of collection which were often more onerous than the taxes themselves; the arbitrary nature of the *taille,* the multiplicity of dues on every sort of merchandise, the complexity of tariffs, the inequality of these dues in the different provinces, the innumerable customs houses at the frontier of these provinces, the frequency of inspections and the importunity of enquiries necessary to provide against fraud, the necessity of relying on the solitary testimony of mercenary men of low character for proof of these frauds; the interminable disputes, so fatal to commerce that almost any merchant would prefer, in this respect, a disadvantageous arrangement to a law suit, no matter how obvious the justice of his case. Finally, he condemned the impenetrable obscurity and mystery resulting from this complexity of local dues and regulations published at different dates, an obscurity which is always interpreted in favour of revenue and against commerce. He condemned the excessive duties, the evils of smuggling, the loss of a multitude of citizens which this entails, etc., etc., etc.

p. 278 Public finance is necessary, since the State needs revenue; but agriculture and commerce, or rather agriculture animated by commerce, is the ultimate source of these revenues. Thus public finance should not be prejudicial to commerce, since it would at the same time harm itself. These two interests are of necessity united, and if a conflict of interests seems to exist, it is perhaps because we have confused the interests of finance as related to the State and the monarchy, which are eternal, with the interests of the financiers, who, being charged with the collection of the revenues for a certain period only, prefer to increase present revenue rather than to conserve the source which produces this revenue. Add to this the dubious and fortuitous way in which this hydra of all types of duties has taken shape, i.e. by the successive gathering together of a multitude of fiefs and sovereignties, and the conservation of the taxes which each individual sovereign used to enjoy, while the urgency of the kingdom's needs has never left time to reform this chaos by establishing a uniform system of duties. Finally, there are the facilities which

[16] The last sentence of this paragraph is not in the original manuscript but was included by Du Pont in his edition of Turgot's works. (Note by G. Schelle.)

public finance has had at all times of making its voice heard, to the prejudice of commerce.

The fiscal authority consists of a body of accredited men, whose prestige varies with the urgency of the needs of the State. They are always occupied with a single object, never distracted nor negligent, resident in the capital and in constant touch with the government. The merchants, on the other hand, occupied each with his individual objective, dispersed in the provinces, without fame or protection, without a central meeting place, are only able to raise a feeble and solitary voice in any given case, a voice that is inevitably stifled both by the number and the prestige of their adversaries, and by the opportunities the latter have of engaging skilled writers in the defence of their interests. If the merchant agrees to abandon the care of his affairs in order to hold a litigation rather than to surrender his rights, the odds are high against him, and even if he wins, he still remains at the mercy of a powerful body which has, through the rigour of the laws which it has suggested to the ministry, an easy means of crushing the merchant; for (and this is not one of the least abuses), there exist several laws of this type which are impossible to execute and which the tax farmers only use to ensure the submission of individuals, by threatening a rigorous application of them.

M. de Gournay thought that the Board of Trade would be of much greater use if, rather than managing commerce, which ought to go its own way, it p. 279
protected commerce against the activities of the public revenue. He would have liked the needs of the State to be such that they would allow commerce to be delivered from all kinds of duties. He believed that a nation fortunate enough to have reached this point would necessarily draw to itself the greater part of the commerce of Europe. He believed that all taxes, of whatever kind they may be, are, in the final analysis, paid by the landowner, who sells by so much the less the produce of his land, and that if all the taxes were assessed on landed property, the proprietors and the kingdom would thereby gain all that was now absorbed in the cost of administration, the unproductive employment of men now wasted in tax collection, in smuggling, or in preventing it, without even counting the immense gain from the increase in riches and value that would result from the increase in commerce.

There exist also some obstacles to the progress of industry that arise from our customs, from our prejudices, from some of our civil laws, but the two which are most disastrous I have already discussed, and the others would entail too much detail. Besides, M. de Gournay did not pretend to limit the duties of the government towards commerce strictly to that of maintaining its free course and removing the obstacles that oppose the improvement of industry. He was also quite convinced of the usefulness of the encouragements that could be given to industry[17] either by recompensing the authors of useful

[17] Cf. Turgot 'Remarks on the Notes to the Translation of Child', where he argued in section

inventions, or by encouraging, by prizes or gratuities, a competition among artisans to attain perfection. He knew that even when industry enjoyed the most complete freedom, these measures are often useful in hastening its natural progress, and that they are essential above all when the fear of constraints has not been completely dispelled and still slows down its development. But he could not give his approval when these encouragements could conceivably stand in the way of new progress through prohibitions and exclusive advantages. It was only with great reservations that he supported loans by the government, and he preferred other encouragements: rewards in proportion to production, and prizes designed to attain perfection in work, in
p. 280 short, marks of distinction and all measures which encourage competition among a greater number of men.

This, more or less, expresses M. de Gournay's attitude towards the administration of commerce; these are the principles which he constantly applied to all the matters discussed at the Board of Trade from the moment he entered it. As he had no idea of creating a new system, he was satisfied to develop only what was necessary to support his opinions in regard to each particular affair; but it was not long before the consistency and fruitfulness of his principles were recognised, and soon he had to countenance a mass of challenges.

He gave himself with pleasure to these discussions which could only elucidate the subject and in one way or another produce a knowledge of the truth. Free from all selfish interest, from all personal ambition, he lacked even that slavery to his opinions which self-love might have induced. All he lived for, and aspired to, was the public welfare; thus his opinions were expressed with a much modesty as courage. Equally incapable of taking an overbearing tone, and of speaking against his opinion, he delivered his sentiments in a straightforward manner which derived all its power from the strength of his reasoning. He skilfully put his ideas within the grasp of all minds, stating his principles with a kind of luminous precision, and emphasising them by a sensible use of some well chosen examples. When he was contradicted, he listened with patience; however sharp the attack might be, he never discarded his customary politeness and gentleness, nor did he lose anything of the presence of mind and composure necessary to fathom completely the artful reasoning advanced against him.

His simple eloquence, animated by that engaging earnestness which pervades the discourse of a virtuous man who is deeply persuaded that he is upholding the cause of the public welfare, never detracted from the soundness of the discussion; sometimes it was seasoned with a harmless jest which was all the more pleasant since it was never pointless.

IX: "I doubt strongly that the regulations would be useful even for the original establishment of manufacturers". See above, p. 12.

His zeal was gentle because it was purged of all self-esteem; but it was not therefore any the less earnest, for love of the public welfare gripped him.

He was convincing without being excessively attached to his opinions; his mind, always without bias, was constantly ready to receive fresh enlighten- p. 281 ment; sometimes he did change his mind on important matters, and there was nothing to suggest that his previous opinion had in the least delayed that sudden impression which the proffered truth makes on one as fairminded as he.

He had the good fortune to find in M. Trudaine,[18] who was even then at the head of the administration of commerce, the same love of truth and of the public welfare that motivated himself. Since at that stage he had developed his ideas only as occasion arose during business discussion or in conversation, M. Trudaine urged him to give as it were an outline of his doctrine. It was with this in mind that he translated in 1752 the treatises on trade and the interest of money by Sir Josiah Child and Sir Thomas Culpeper. He added a great many interesting remarks in which he thoroughly examined and discussed the principles of the text, and clarified them by applying them to the most important questions of commerce. These remarks formed a work as considerable as that of the English authors, and M. de Gournay counted on having them printed together. He printed only the text however, in 1754: reasons, which no longer exist, then prevented the printing of the commentary.[19]

His reputation became well established, and his zeal communicated itself to others. It is to the ardour with which he sought to direct all men of talent with whom he was acquainted to the study of commerce and political economy, and to the ease with which he communicated all the knowledge he acquired, that we owe that propitious fermentation of thought on these important questions that has taken place these last few years, and which sprang up two or three years after M. de Gournay had been Intendant of Commerce. Since then, it has already presented us with several works[20] filled with laborious

[18] Daniel Charles Trudaine (1703–1769), Intendant of Reom (1730–43), Director of Roads and Bridges (1743–69). His son, Jean Charles Trudaine (1733–1777) was Intendant-Général des Finances in 1769. Both were friends of Turgot.

[19] Together with Butel-Dumont and published in 1754 under the title *Traité sur le commerce et les avantages qui résultent de la réduction de l'intérêt d'argent*, par Josiah Child bart., *avec un petit traité contre l'usure* par Sir Thomas Culpeper. The notes and explanations by Gournay were not published at the time for reasons explained by Turgot and appear to have been lost. See Palgrave, *Dictionary of Political Economy*, II, p. 236. See also above, 'Introduction', pp. XIII–XIV.

[20] These "several works" to which Turgot refers would presumably include: Forbonnais, *Elémens du Commerce* published in 1754; Forbonnais, *Divers mémoires sur le commerce* published in 1756 (Ange Goudar), *Les Intérêts de la France mal entendus, dans les branches de l'agriculture, de la population, des finances, du commerce, de la marine & de l'industrie*, published in 1756; Simon Cliquot de Blervache, *Considérations sur le commerce, et en particulier sur les compagnées, sociétés, et maîtrises*, published in 1758. This last work is reputed to have been written with Gournay's advice and guidance. Turgot may also have referred to

research and profound views, works that have cleared our nation of the charge of frivolity which it had not failed to incur by its indifference to those studies which are the most truly useful.

In spite of the opposition which he had to endure, M. de Gournay often tasted the satisfaction of succeeding in eradicating part of the abuses which he was attacking, and above all, of weakening the authority of those archaic
p. 282 principles which even then had to be relaxed as to the rigour and the extent of their application in order to withstand his attacks. However difficult people may have found it to embrace his principles to their full extent, his insight, his experience, the general esteem of the merchants for him personally, the unimpeachable purity of his views, these things inevitably earned him the confidence of the minister and the respect even of those who yet fought against his ideas.

His zeal induced him to make plans to tour the kingdom in order to see for himself the state of commerce and of manufactures, and to discover the reason for the rise or decay of each branch of trade,[21] the abuses, the needs, the resources of each type. He started the execution of his plan in 1753 and departed in July. From that time up to December he traversed Bourgogne, Lyonnais, Dauphiné, Provence, upper and lower Languedoc, and returned finally by way of Lyon.

In 1754, he was unable to travel because of a tumour situated on his back, which he had cut out twice, and which had to be burned out the third time with the help of caustics, at the beginning of 1755. He resumed his travels in 1755 and made a tour of inspection of La Rochelle, Bordeaux, Montauban, the remainder of Guyenne and Bayonne. In 1756 he followed the course of the Loire from Orléans to Nantes, travelled through Maine, Anjou, the coast of Bretagne from Nantes to Saint-Malo, and returned to Rennes for the sitting of the States in 1756. The deterioration of his health did not permit him to make any further journeys.

At each step he found further reasons to confirm him in his principles, and new arguments against the restriction of commerce against which he was fighting. He took up the complaints of the friendless, poor manufacturer who, unable to write and to present his claims in plausible arguments, and having no representative at the Court, has always been the victim of a government misguided by interested men to whom he was forced to appeal. M. de Gournay applied himself to uncovering the hidden interests which had called for those allegedly useful rules whose sole object it was to put the poor more and more at the mercy of the rich. The fruits of his travels were the reform of an infinite number of abuses of this kind; a knowledge of the true state of the

---

the articles appearing in the *Journal économique* whose first series appeared from 1751 to 1757, while the second series started in 1758 and finished in 1772.

[21] Turgot accompanied Gournay on several of these tours of inspection. See Dakin, *Turgot and the Ancien Régime in France*, p. 18.

provinces giving more certainty and better direction to the operations of the Ministry; a more exact appreciation of complaints and requests; the facility p. 283
which was afforded to the people and to the simple artisans of making known their own complaints; finally, a fresh spirit of emulation in all branches of commerce which M. de Gournay was able to spread by his persuasive eloquence, by the exactness with which he stated his ideas and by the happy contagion of his patriotic zeal.

He sought to inspire in the magistrates and notable persons in the places he visited a zeal for the prosperity of their town or their district; he interviewed men of letters, suggested subjects for treatment, and urged them to direct their studies towards questions of commerce, agriculture and all economic matters.

It is partly to his suggestions and to the zeal which he had inspired at the sittings of the States of Bretagne during his stay at Rennes in 1756 that the Society[22] for the Perfection of Agriculture, Commerce and Industry, established in Bretagne under the protection of the States and the auspices of the Duke d'Auguillon,[22] owes its existence. This society was the first of its kind to be formed in France. Its programme, which is connected with the municipal administration of the province, was drawn up by M. de Montaudouin, a merchant from Nantes.

M. de Gournay knew how to adapt himself to the degree of intelligence of his audience, and he answered the absurd objections – dictated by ignorance – with the same suavity and exactness with which he answered the bitter opposition, dictated by quite different principles, in Paris.

Full of respect for all those persons charged with the administration of the provinces which he visited, he gave them no occasion to think that his mission could cast the least shadow on their authority. Always forgetting himself, sacrificing himself without effort for the benefit of the objective, it was as far as possible through them and with them that he acted; he seemed only to supplement their zeal, and he often credited them in the presence of the minister with his own ideas. By this conduct, if he did not always succeed in convincing them of his principles, he at least always won their friendship.

The life of M. de Gournay does not offer any other outstanding event during the time that he continued as Intendant of Commerce. Ever occupied with the functions of his office, never missing any opportunity to put forward some useful ideas, or to spread light among the public, there is hardly an important question on commerce or political economy on which he has not p. 284
written several notes or reasoned letters. He devoted himself to this sort of work with a type of prodigality, producing nearly always, on every occasion, new papers, without referring his audience to the earlier ones he had written.

[22] *Société d'Agriculture de Bretagne*; for further details of Gournay's association with this society see Palgrave, *Dictionary of Political Economy*, II, p. 236.

[23] Duc d'Aiguillon (1720–1788), Administrator of Bretagne (1753–1770), Foreign Minister in the Maupeou government (1770–1774).

He did not try to evade the trouble of rediscovering ideas which he had already expressed, or the unpleasantness of repeating himself. The reason for this manner of working was the small value which he attached to what he had composed, and his total unawareness of any literary repute. Overflowing with his salutary and fruitful principles, he applied them to every question with the greatest ease. Completely preoccupied with propagating some useful idea, he did not think of himself as a writer. Free from personal attachment to what he had written, he gave it over, without reservations, to all those who wished to instruct themselves, or to write, on these matters, and more often than not he did not even keep copies of what he had written. These fragments, jotted down in haste and forgotten by him, are nevertheless precious, even if regarded purely from the point of view of composition: his writings, like his conversation, was characterised by a natural eloquence, a lucid precision when expounding his principles, a remarkable art of presenting them from all types of viewpoints, of adapting them for all minds and of having them appreciated by examples which were always just right, and whose very rightness was often striking; a politeness which never failed, and a shrewd logic in the discussion of objections; finally, a patriotic and humane tone, which was unintentional and therefore all the more genuine.

M. de Gournay did not content himself with advocating his ideas through writing or speech: to command respect for the ideas he thought useful he applied the same activity, the same warmth and the same perseverance which an ambitious man puts into the pursuit of his own interests. Incapable of losing heart when the cause was a worthy one, he did not hesitate to push his efforts to the point of obtrusiveness. No proprietor of our isles has clamoured with as much zeal for the freedom of trade for neutral vessels in our colonies during the war.[24] His solicitations were all the more animated and pressing because he demanded nothing for himself, even to the extent that he died without receiving any favour from the court.

Meanwhile, as he occupied himself solely with public work, his own for-
p. 285 tune, as well as his health, had wasted away. He had sustained losses on the funds which he had left in Spain, and the state of his affairs forced him to leave his position as Intendant of Commerce in 1758. Some important people who knew how useful he was suggested that he ask the Court for some favours for himself which would compensate him for the losses he had sustained. He replied: "that he did not esteem himself sufficiently to believe that the State had to buy his services, that he had always looked upon similar favours as a dangerous practice, especially in the circumstances in which the State was situated, and that he did not desire to be reproached for being a party to exceptions to his own principles in his own interest". He added, "that

[24] I.e. the Seven Years' War (1756–1763) in which France supported Austria against Prussia and England.

he did not believe himself to be excused by his retirement from occupying himself with objectives useful for the wellbeing of trade". For this reason, he requested to keep his seat at the Board of Trade, with the title *honorary*, which was accorded to him.

Some time previously, he had similarly sold his Office of Councillor at the Grand Council, but had kept the title of *honorary councillor*.

Retirement did not deprive M. de Gournay of his importance. His zeal was not lessened because of it, his insight could still be as useful as ever. M. de Silhouette,[25] whose regard for M. de Gournay speaks in praise of both of them, resolved, as soon as he had become Contrôleur-général, to remove from retirement a man whose talents and zeal were so fitted to furthering his own designs. He began by inviting him to be present at the conference which the Intendants of Commerce held every week with the Contrôleur-général, and at which M. de Gournay had ceased to be present. He also intended him to take up one of the positions of Royal Commissioner to the General-Farm.[26] In this office, M. de Gournay would have been in a position to appraise the reciprocal complaints of commerce and finance, and to search for a means of reconciling these two interests of the State as far as possible, but he was not able to profit from this token of esteem of M. de Silhouette. When this proposition was put to him he had already been stricken by the illness of which he died.

His health had been deteriorating for a long time. After spending carnival time at his estate of Gournay, he returned with a pain in the hip he at first took for sciatica. For a time the pain gradually grew worse, and at the end of two months a tumour was discovered which appeared to be the source of the trouble, but several different attempted cures could not dissipate it. Weakness p. 286
and emaciation increased. The waters had been suggested, but he was not strong enough to undertake the journey; a slow fever was consuming him. A last effort was made with the use of a resolvent which was regarded as more potent, but no sooner was it applied, than M. de Gournay lapsed into a violent fever accompanied by delirium. This state of affairs lasted for three days; at the end of this time, he regained consciousness, of which he made use to make his will and to receive the last rites of the church. He died that same evening.

In the year ...[27] he married Clothilde Verduc, and he lived in great harmony with her. No children resulted from this marriage.

M. de Gournay would merit the gratitude of the nation even if it would

[25] M. Etienne de Silhouette (1709–1767), who was Contrôleur-Général from March to November 1759.

[26] I.e. the agency for collecting indirect taxation on behalf of the crown on a commission basis.

[27] This is left blank in the French text. The date of marriage between Gournay and Clothilde Verduc was apparently not known to Turgot. In fact, Gournay was married in 1748, on his retirement from trade.

have been obliged to him only for having contributed more than any other person to the directing of minds towards economic knowledge. This glory would be secured for him even if his principles were still liable to opposition; and truth would always have profited from the discussion of matters to which he had given occasion for debate. Posterity will decide between him and his adversaries. But until the nation delivers its judgement, the honour of being the first to diffuse the principles of Child and of Johan de Witt may be confidently claimed in his memory. And, if one day these principles are adopted for commerce by our administration, if they will ever be for France what they have been for Holland and England, that is, a source of abundance and prosperity, our descendants will know that gratitude for it is due to M. de Gournay.

The opposition which his principles encountered has led some people to portray M. de Gournay as a fanatic and a *man of systems*. This phrase, *a man of systems*, has become a type of weapon in use by all those who are biased or interested in maintaining some abuse, and directed against all those who propose changes in the *status quo*.

The philosophers of recent times have indeed, with as much strength as reason, striven against the spirit of *systems*. They understood by this term those arbitrary suppositions with the help of which it is attempted to explain all phenomena and which actually explain them all equally, because they do not explain any; that lack of observation, that overhasty reliance on obscure
p. 287 analogies by which a particular fact is rashly transformed into a general principle, and the whole is judged by a superficial glance at a part; that blind presumption which relates all it does not know to the little it knows; which, dazzled by an idea or a principle, sees it everywhere, like the eye, fatigued by an intense look at the sun, casts its image on all the objects to which it directs itself; which wants to know all, explain all, arrange all, and which, ignorant of the inexhaustible variety of nature, claims to subjugate it to its arbitrary and limited methods, and tries to circumscribe the infinite in order to embrace it.

But when men of the world in their turn condemn *systems*, it is not in the philosophic sense. These men, accustomed to receive all opinions, one after the other, like a mirror reflects all images without retaining them, accustomed to find everything probable without ever being convinced, to ignore the intimate connection of effects with their causes, to contradict themselves constantly without being aware of it or placing any importance on it, these men cannot help but be astonished when they meet with a man who is inwardly convinced of a truth, and deduces consequences from it with the rigour of exact logic. Today they will listen to him, tomorrow they will listen to entirely contrary propositions, and they will be surprised not to see in him the same flexibility. They do not hesitate to call him a fanatic and a *man of systems*. Thus, although in their language the word system applies to an opinion adopted after mature consideration, supported by proofs and consistent in its consequences, they none the less take it amiss because the little attention of which they are capable does not enable them to judge the reasons, and does not offer them any opinion to which they can refer constantly or which is clearly related to a particular principle.

Yet it is true that all thinkers have a *system*, that a man who has no system or logical connection between his ideas must either be an imbecile or a madman.[28] Never mind. The two senses of the word system are confused, and he who has a system in the sense of the men of the world, that is, a settled opinion resulting from a chain of observations, will incur the reproaches made by the philosophers to the spirit of systems taken in quite a different sense, that of an opinion not founded on sufficient observation.

Taking the word system in the popular sense, M. de Gournay, undoubtedly, was a man of systems, since he had a viewpoint to which he was strongly attached. His adversaries were all men *of systems*, as much as he was, since they held an opinion contrary to his. p. 288

But if the word *system* is taken in the philosophical sense, which I first developed, nobody was further removed from that than he. On the contrary, he would rather have had the right to lay this reproach at the door of the principles against which he fought, since his whole doctrine was founded on the complete impossibility of directing, by invariant rules and by continuous inspection a multitude of transactions which by their immensity alone could not be fully known, and which, moreover, are continually dependent on a multitude of ever changing circumstances which cannot be managed or even foreseen; and since he therefore wanted the administration not to attempt to lead everybody by the hand, and not to claim the ability to do so, but rather to let them go their way and rely more on the natural motive of self interest, than on the external and artificial restraints of regulations which were always arbitrary in spirit and often so in application. If arbitrariness and a mania for fitting facts to ideas rather than ideas to the facts are the distinguishing marks of the spirit of *systems*, then assuredly M. de Gournay was not a *man of systems*.

He was even less so as far as an obstinate attachment to his ideas was concerned. The humility with which he held them proved strongly that he was not conceited about them and that he upheld them only as a citizen. It can be said that few men have been as perfectly free as he was from that type of vanity which shuts the door on new ideas. He searched for new information as if he knew nothing, and was ready to examine every assertion as if he had never held any opinion to the contrary.

[28] This sentence was changed by Du Pont in his edition of Turgot's works. It should apparently read as follows:

"In this last sense, it is however true that everybody who thinks has a *system* and that a system cannot be a matter for reproach, seeing that a system can only be confounded by an opposite system." (Note by G. Schelle.)

It must also be said that this so-called system of M. de Gournay had this peculiarity that its general principles have been adopted by nearly the whole world; that at all times the desire of commerce among all the nations has been expressed by those two words: *freedom* and *protection*, but above all freedom. M. le Gendre's phrase to M. Golbert is well known: laissez-nous faire.[29] Often M. de Gournay differed from the men who treated him as a man
p. 289 of systems only in this: that he objected with the strictness of a just and righteous heart, to the exceptions which they allowed in favour of their own interests.

For example, the world is full of people who condemn exclusive privileges, but who believe that there are certain commodities for which they are necessary. This exception is generally based on their personal interest, or on that of individuals with whom these people are connected. Thus the majority of people is by nature well disposed towards the sweet principles of commercial freedom. But nearly all, either through interest, or through habit, or through subordination, insert some small modifications or exceptions.

M. de Gournay, in objecting to any exception in particular, had the majority with him, but by objecting to all exceptions at the same time, he ranged against him all the people who each wanted one exception, even though they were not united on the type of exception they desired. The result of this was a misleading unanimity of feeling against his principles, and an almost universal imputation of the title of *man of systems* against him personally.

This imputation was seized upon as a rallying cry by those who were turned into his adversaries because of envy or an excessive zeal for their own opinion, and gave them the excuse to oppose him as a solid body, instead of the empty shadow they really were, of which any man less zealous for the public welfare and less indifferent to his own interests, would have been terrified.

Opposition only served to stimulate his courage. He knew that by declaring the universality of his principles less candidly, and by failing to acknowledge all the remote consequences which derived therefrom, by being a party to some slight modifications, he would have evaded this dreaded title of a *man of systems* and would have escaped the bias which people endeavoured to propagate against him. But he believed in the usefulness of developing principles to their fullest extent, and he wanted the nation to instruct herself; and only the clearest exposition of the truth could instruct her. He thought that

[29] Possibly François Legendre, author of *L'Arithmétique et sa perfection selon l'usage des Financiers, Banquiers, et Marchands* which was published in several editions between 1657 and 1687, who is here credited by Turgot of having coined the phrase "Laissez-nous faire". According to Oncken, *Die Maxime Laissez-faire et Laissez-passer*, this remark was probably made to Colbert in about 1680. See Palgrave, *Dictionary of Political Economy*, II, p. 534; while for a detailed discussion of the origin of the phrase, "laissez-faire, laissez-passer", see G. Schelle, *Vincent de Gournay*, pp. 214–217.

such circumspection would be useful only to himself, and he held himself of no account.

It is not true that he believed, as several people alleged he did, that there was no need for any moderation in the reform of abuses; he knew how necessary it was to prepare all improvements, how dangerous too sudden
p. 290 shocks are; but he thought that the necessary moderation should be in the action and not in the thought. He did not desire to have the whole old edifice knocked down before the foundations of the new one had been moulded, but he wanted an extensive plan to be drawn up before this task was started, to avoid acting blindly either in destroying, or conserving, or in reconstructing.

Finally, to M. de Gournay's very personal glory, there was his virtue, which was so well known that in spite of all the opposition which he had to endure, not the least shadow of suspicion ever tarnished the brightness of his reputation even for a moment. This virtue did not falter all through his life. Based on a deep feeling of justice and philanthropy, it made him a kindly and modest man, forbearing in society, irreproachable and even austere in his conduct and principles, but austere only for himself; even tempered at home, busy in his family circle to make all those around him happy, always ready to sacrifice, obligingly, all that he did not regard as duty. In public life he showed himself free from all self interest, ambition, and almost entirely free from love of glory, and yet, none the less active for it, nor less indefatigable, nor less ingenious in the pursuit of the fulfilment of his designs, whose sole objective was the general welfare. He was a citizen completely occupied with the prosperity and glory of his country and the happiness of mankind. Humanity was one of the motives which tied him most to what was called his *system*. He most vigorously reproached his opponents for the principle of always favouring the rich and idle part of society at the expense of the poor and industrious part.

It is unfortunate in a way that men commendable for the most deserving virtues, and who are most truly useful to the world, are most unfavourably endowed in the distribution of fame. Posterity considers almost exclusively those actions which take place in public and which are dazzling, and it is perhaps more sensitive to their brilliance than to their usefulness. But, even if we assume its judgement to be always equitable in this respect, the motives and the spirit which produce these actions and which alone can lend them the mark of virtue, are ignored. The finer details are lost in the narrative of history, like the glow of a complexion and the delicacy of features vanish under the painter's colours. Only lifeless brush strokes remain, and actions
p. 291 whose character is misjudged. Sometimes spite and sometimes flattery interpret them at their pleasure, and only too often succeed in making posterity's verdict fluctuate between the purest virtue, and clever vice masked as virtue.

This misjudgement never occurs while these people are still living, and there is an interval of time when spite in vain attempts to tarnish a well known virtue and when flattery that would offer undeserved honours can be repelled.

This moment passes with the life of the person. Therefore the only means of ensuring, for that small number of men whose virtue is generally recognised, the contination of the general esteem which they deserve, and of catching the fragrance of virtue which surrounds them, is to call forth the testimony of the present generation, and to call recent events to bear witness. In rendering this deserved public homage to the virtue of M. de Gournay, we feel sure that no voice will be lifted against us.

CHAPTER V

1766

REFLECTIONS ON THE FORMATION AND DISTRIBUTION OF WEALTH

1. *The impossibility of Commerce upon the supposition of an equal division of lands, where every man would possess only what is necessary for his own support.*

If the land was divided among all the inhabitants of a country in such a way that each of them possessed precisely the quantity necessary for his support, and nothing more, it is evident that all being equal, no one would be willing to work for others. Neither would any of them possess the wherewithal to pay for the labour of others, for each person having only so much land as was necessary to produce a subsistance, would consume all he had gathered, and would have nothing which he could exchange for the labour of others.

2. *The above hypothesis has never existed and could not have continued. The diversity of soils and the multiplicity of wants lead to an exchange of the products of the land for other products.*

This hypothesis could never have existed, because the earth was cultivated before it was divided; cultivation itself having been the only reason for a division, and for that law which secures to every one his property. The first people who engaged in cultivation probably cultivated as much land as their resources permitted, and consequently, more than was necessary for their support.

Even if this state of affairs could have existed, it could not possibly have endured; each man obtaining from his field only his subsistence, and not having the means wherewith to pay others for their labour, could only provide for his other wants of shelter, clothing etc. by his own labour, and this would be virtually impossible, *every type of soil by no means producing everything.*

The man whose land was fit only for grain, and would produce neither cotton nor hemp, would lack cloth to clothe himself. Another would have a piece of land suitable for cotton, which would not produce grain. A third would be without wood to keep himself warm, while a fourth would lack grain to feed himself. Experience would soon teach every one the kinds of products for which his land was most suitable and he would confine himself to the cultivation of that particular crop in order to obtain those things he required by means of exchange with his neighbours; who, having in turn reached the same conclusion, would have cultivated the crop best suited to their land, and given up the cultivation of all others.

3. *The products of the earth require long and difficult preparations in order to make them suitable for the wants of man.*

The crops which the earth yield to satisfy the different wants of man, cannot usually serve that purpose in the state in which nature gives them; they must undergo various changes and be prepared by art. Wheat must be converted into flour, then into bread; hides must be tanned or dressed; wool and cotton must be spun; silk must be drawn from the cocoon;[1] hemp and flax must be soaked, peeled, spun, and next, different fabrics must be woven from them, and then they must be cut and sewn into garments, footwear, etc. If the same man who, on his own land, cultivates these different articles, and uses them to supply his own wants, was also forced to perform all the intermediate operations himself, it is certain that he would succeed very badly. The greater part of these preparations require care, attention and a long experience, such as are only to be acquired by working continuously and on a great quantity of materials. Take, for example, the preparation of hides:[2] what labourer could attend to all the details necessary in this operation, which continues for several months, sometimes for several years? If he could, would he be able to, for a single hide? What a loss of time, space, materials which might have served either at the same time or successively, to tan a large quantity of hides! And even if he did succeed in tanning a single hide, he only needs one pair of shoes; what will he do with the rest? Shall he kill an ox to make this pair of shoes? Shall he cut down a tree to make a pair of wooden shoes? The same thing may be said concerning all the other wants of man, who, if he were reduced to his own field and his own labour, would waste much time and trouble in order to be very badly equipped in every respect, and would also cultivate his land very badly.

4. *The necessity of these preparations brings about the exchange of products for labour.*

The same motive which has established the exchange of various crops between the Cultivators of different types of soil, must also have brought about the exchange of crops for labour, between the Cultivators and another

[1] The anonymous translator of 1793 translated this as "cod". For a discussion of the alleged importance of this point, see I.C. Lundberg, *Turgot's Unknown Translator*, pp. 94–96. The correct word is, undoubtedly, cocoon.

[2] Tanning of hides was a favourite example with Turgot, see below, section 60, pp. 69–70. This may have been due to the fact that there were several large tanneries in the Generality of Limoges. See Schelle, *Oeuvres de Turgot*, II, p. 42.

part of society which came to prefer the occupation of preparing and working up the produce of the land to that of growing it.[3] Every one profited by this arrangement, for each, by devoting himself to a single kind of labour, succeeded much better in it. The Husbandman obtained from his field the greatest possible quantity of produce and procured for himself by means of exchange all his other wants with much greater facility than he could have done by his own labour. The Shoemaker, by making shoes for the Husbandman, secured for himself a portion of the latter's harvest. Each Workman laboured to satisfy the wants of all other types of Workmen, who in turn all worked for him.

5. *Pre-eminence of the Husbandman who produces, over the Artisan who works up materials. The Husbandman is the prime mover in the circulation of labour; it is he who causes the soil to produce the wages of every Artisan.*

It must, however, be observed that the Husbandman, who furnishes everyone with the most important and the most considerable objects of their consumption (I mean their food, and moreover the materials of almost every manufacture) has the advantage of a greater degree of independence. His labour, among the various kinds of labour which are divided between the different members of society, retains the same primacy and pre-eminence, as the procuring of food did among the different works he was obliged, when in a solitary state, to employ himself in, in order to supply himself with his wants of all kinds. This is not a pre-eminence of honour or of dignity, but of *physical necessity*. The Husbandman, generally, speaking, can get on without the labour of other Workmen; but no Workman can labour, if the Husbandman does not provide his food. In this circulation, which, by a reciprocal exchange of wants, renders men necessary to one another, and constitutes the bond of society, it is therefore the labour of the Husbandman which is the prime mover. What his labour causes the land to produce beyond his personal wants, is the sole fund for the payment of wages which the other members of society receive in exchange for their labour. The latter, by availing themselves of the price of this exchange to purchase in their turn the commodities of the Husbandman, only return to him precisely what they have received. There is here a very basic difference between these two kinds of labour, which it is necessary to emphasise in order to be convinced of the evidence on which it rests, before dealing with the innumerable consequences which flow from it.

6. *The wages of the Workman are limited to his subsistence by the competition among the Workmen. He gets only his livelihood.*

The mere Workman who depends only on his arms and his industry, has

[3] Daire and Schelle, following Du Pont de Nemours, divide this paragraph into two separate paragraphs at this point.

nothing except in so far as he succeeds in selling his labour to others. He sells it at a lower or higher price; but his low or high price does not depend on himself alone; it results from the agreement he makes with the buyer of his labour. The latter pays him as little as he can; because he has the choice among a great number of Workmen, he prefers the one who works cheapest. The Workmen are therefore compelled to lower their price in competition with one another. In every kind of work it must, and, in effect, it does happen, that the wages of the Workman are limited to what is necessary to procure him a subsistence.[4]

7. *The Husbandman is the only one whose industry produces more than the wages of his labour. He, therefore is the unique source of all wealth.*

The position of the Husbandman is materially different. The soil, independent of any other man, or of any agreement, pays him directly the price of his toil. Nature does not bargain with him to compel him to content himself with what is absolutely necessary. What she grants is neither related to his wants, nor a contractual valuation of the price of his days of work. It is the physical result of the fertility of the soil, and of the wisdom, far more than the laboriousness, of the means which he has employed to render it fruitful. As soon as the labour of the Husbandman produces more than his wants, he can, with the surplus which nature accords him as a pure gift above the wages of his toil, purchase the labour of other members of society. The latter, in selling to him, only obtain a livelihood; but the Husbandman, besides his subsistence, collects an independent and disposable wealth, which he has not purchased and which he sells. He is, therefore, the unique source of the wealth which, by its circulation, animates all the industry of society, because he is the only one whose labour produces more than the wages of his labour.

8. *Primary division of society into two classes, the one* productive *or the Cultivators, the other* stipendiary, *or the Artisans.*

Here then is the whole society divided, by a necessity founded on the nature of things, into two classes, both industrious, one of which, by its labour, produces or rather, draws from the soil, wealth which is continually regenerated, and which supplies the whole society with subsistence and with materials for all its needs; while the other is employed in giving to the said materials such preparations and forms as render them suitable for the use of man, and sells its labour to the first class, and receives its subsistence in exchange. The first may be called the *productive*, the latter the *stipendiary* class.

[4] For further details of Turgot's theory of wages, which is only outlined here, see 'Observations on a Paper by Graslin', below pp. 126–127, and 'Letters on the Grain Trade', below pp. 167–169.

9. *In Ancient times, the Proprietor could not have been distinguished from the Cultivator.*

Hitherto no distinction has been made between the Husbandman and the Proprietor of the land, and in early times they were not in fact so distinguished. It is by the labour of those who were the first to cultivate the fields, and enclosed them to secure their harvest, that all the lands ceased to be common, and that landed proprieties were established. Until societies were consolidated and until public power, or the law, becoming predominant over individual power was able to guarantee to each man the tranquil possession of his property against all invasion from without, a man could retain the ownership of a field only in the way he had acquired it, and by continuing to cultivate it. It would not have been safe to get his field cultivated by another who, having taken all the trouble would not easily have understood that the whole harvest did not belong to him. Moreover, in this early time, as every industrious man would find as much land as he wished, he could not be tempted to till the soil for another. Every proprietor had to cultivate his fields himself or abandon them completely.[5]

10. *Progress of society; all lands have an owner.*

But the land filled up and was cultivated to a greater extent. With the passage of time, the best lands all came to be occupied; there remained for those who came last nothing but the barren land, rejected by the first. But finally all land found an owner, and those who could not have properties had at first no other resources than that of exchanging the labour of their arms, in the occupations of the *stipendiary* class, for the surplus produce of the cultivating Proprietor.

11. *It begins to be possible for the Proprietors to transfer the labour of cultivation to hired Cultivators.*

However, since the land returned to the owner who cultivated it not only his subsistence, not only that wherewith to procure himself, by way of exchange, the other things he needed, but also a considerable surplus, he could with this surplus pay other men to cultivate his land, and for men who live on wages it was as good to earn them in this occupation as in any other. Thus ownership could be separated from the labour of cultivation, and it soon was.

12. *Inequality in the division of land: causes which make this inevitable.*

The original Proprietors at first occupied, as has already been said, as much land as their resources permitted them to cultivate with their families. A man of greater strength, more industrious, more concerned about the future, occupied more than a man of contrary character. He whose family was more

[5] The analysis in this paragraph is probably indebted to Locke, *The Second Treatise of Civil*

numerous, as he had more needs and more hands at his disposal, extended his possessions further: here was already a first inequality.[6]// All pieces of ground are not equally fertile; two men with the same area of land and the same amount of labour, may reap a very different harvest: (this is a) second source of inequality.// Property, in descending from fathers to their children, divided into greater or smaller portions, according to whether the descendants were more or less numerous; as one generation succeeds another, the inheritances are sometimes still further subdivided; sometimes they are reunited again by the extinction of some of the branches: (this is a) third source of inequality.// The contrast between the intelligence, the activity, and above all, the thrift of some and the indolence, inaction, and dissipation of others, was a fourth principle of inequality, and the most powerful of all.// The negligent and improvident Proprietor, who cultivates badly, who in years of abundance consumes in frivolous things the whole of his surplus, finds himself reduced on the slightest accident to request assistance from his more provident neighbour, and to live by borrowing. If by a further accident, or by a continuation of his negligence, he finds himself not in a condition to repay his debt, if he is obliged to have recourse to new loans, he will at last have no other means at his disposal but to abandon part, or even the whole of his property to his creditor, who will take it as an equivalent, or assign it to another, in exchange for other assets with which he will discharge his obligation to his creditor.

13. *Consequence of this inequality: the Cultivator distinguished from the Proprietor.*

Thus is landed property made subject to purchase and sale. The portion of the dissipating or unfortunate Proprietor serves to increase that of the Proprietor who has been more fortunate or prudent, and in this infinitely varied inequality of possessions, it is inevitable that many Proprietors must possess more than they can cultivate. Besides, it is very natural for a rich man to wish for a tranquil enjoyment of his wealth, and instead of employing his whole time in toilsome labour, to prefer to give part of his surplus to people who work for him.

14. *Division of the produce between the Cultivator and the Proprietor.* Net product, *or revenue.*

By this new arrangement, the product of the land is divided into two parts: the one includes the subsistence and the profits of the Husbandman, which are the rewards for his labour, and the condition on which he agrees to cultivate the field of the Proprietor; the other, which remains, is that indepen-

[6] Daire and Schelle, following Du Pont de Nemours, divide this long paragraph into five separate ones at the points indicated.

dent and disposable part which the soil produces as a pure gift to him who cultivates it, over and above his advances and the wages of his trouble, and this is the portion of the Proprietor or the *revenue*, with which the latter can live without labour, and which he takes wherever he wishes.

15. *A new division of Society into three classes: the Cultivators, the Artisans and the Proprietors, or the* productive, stipendiary *and* disposable *classes.*

We now behold Society divided into three classes: the class of Husbandmen, for whom the name of *productive class* may be reserved; the class of Artisans and others *receiving stipends* from the produce of the land; and the class of *Proprietors*, the only one which, not being confined by the need of subsistence to a particular species of labour, may be employed for the general needs of the Society, such as war, and the administration of justice, either by a personal service, or by the payment of a part of their revenue, with which the State, or Society, may hire men to discharge these functions. The name which, for this reason, suits it best, is that of *disposable class*.

16. *Resemblance between the two working, or non-disposable classes.*

The two classes of Cultivators and Artisans resemble each other in many respects, and particularly in this, that those who compose them do not possess any revenue, and both equally live on the wages which are paid them out of the product of the soil. Both have also this in common, that they gain only the price of their labour and their advances, and that this price is nearly the same in the two classes. The Proprietor bargains with those who cultivate in his land to pay them as small a part as possible of its product, in the same manner as he bargains with the shoemaker to buy his shoes as cheaply as possible. In short, neither the Cultivator nor the Artisan receives more than a bare recompense for his labour.

17. *Essential differences between the two working classes.*

But there is this difference between the two kinds of labour, that the work of the Cultivator produces not only his own wages, but also that revenue which serves to pay the whole class of Artisans and other stipendiaries, whereas the Artisans receive simply their wages, that is, their share of the produce of the land in exchange for their labour, and do not produce any revenue. The Proprietor has nothing but by the labour of the Cultivator. He receives from him his subsistence, and the wherewithal to pay for the labour of the other stipendiaries. He has need of the Cultivator because of a necessity arising from the physical order of things by virtue of which the soil produces nothing without labour; but the Cultivator needs the Proprietor only by virtue of human conventions, and of those civil laws which guaranteed, to the first Cultivators and to their heirs, the ownership of the land they occupied, even when they ceased to cultivate it.[7] But these laws can secure the man who does not work only that part of the produce which the land gives over and above the return due to the Cultivators. The Proprietor is obliged to give up the latter on pain of losing the whole.[8]// The Cultivator, confined though he is to the recompense for his labour, thus preserves that natural and physical primacy which renders him the prime mover in the whole machinery of Society, and which causes his own subsistence, as well as the wealth of the Proprietor and the wages of all the other labours, to depend on his labour alone.// The Artisan, on the contrary, receives his wages either from the Proprietor or from the Cultivator, and gives them by the exchange of his labour, only the equivalent of these wages, and nothing more.

Thus, although neither the Cultivator nor the Artisan gains more than the recompense of his labour, the Cultivator causes, over and above that recompense, the generation of the revenue of the Proprietor; while the Artisan generates no revenue, either for himself or for others.

18. *This difference justifies their being distinguished as the* productive *class and* barren *class respectively.*

We may then distinguish the two non-disposable classes as the *productive class*, which is that of the Cultivators, and the *sterile class*, which includes all the other stipendiary members of society.

19. *How the Proprietors can draw the* revenue *from their lands.*

The Proprietors who do not till their lands themselves, may adopt different methods of having them cultivated, or make different arrangements with those who cultivate them.

20. *First method: cultivation by wage labourers.*

They may, in the first place, pay men, by the day or by the year, to till their fields, and reserve to themselves the whole of the produce, a method which assumes that the Proprietor advances both the seed and the wages of the workmen until after the harvest.[9]// But this method has the drawback of

[7] Du Pont's versions, and that in Daire, leave out "human" and "civil" as qualifying adjectives to "conventions" and "laws" respectively. He also inserted the following material at this point:

"..., and this for the price of the *landed advances* (avances forcières) with which they have prepared these lands for cultivation and which are, as it were, incorporated in the soil itself."

Turgot was most annoyed with these changes as is shown in his letters to Du Pont on the subject. See Turgot to Du Pont, 2/2/1770, 20/2/1770, in Schelle, *Oeuvres*, III, pp. 373–374, 378–379. For reasons which may explain why Du Pont made these changes, see Schelle, 'Pourquoi les "Réflexions" de Turgot ...', op. cit., pp. 8–9.

[8] This last sentence is not in the 1793 translation.

Schelle and Daire, following Du Pont, divide this paragraph into three separate paragraphs at the points indicated.

[9] Daire and Schelle, following Du Pont de Nemours, divide this paragraph into four separate paragraphs at the points indicated.

requiring much labour and diligence on the part of the Proprietor, who alone can direct the workmen in their labour, watch over the employment of their time and on their trustworthiness in not diverting any of the produce to their own use.// It is true that he may also hire a man of more intelligence, whom he knows to be trustworthy, to direct the workmen and keep an account of the produce, as overseer or manager; but he will always be subject to fraud.// Besides, this method is extremely expensive, unless a large population, and want of employment in other kinds of work, forces the workmen to be content with very low wages.

21. *Second method: Cultivation by Slaves.*
In times not very distant from the origin of Society, it was almost impossible to find men willing to cultivate the land which belonged to others, because, all the land not as yet having been occupied, those who were willing to labour preferred the clearing of new lands, and cultivating them on their own account; this is more or less the case in all new Colonies.

Violent men have therefore conceived the idea of obliging other men by force to labour for them. They owned slaves. These latter had no justice to look for from the hands of people who could not have reduced them to slavery without violating all the rights of humanity. Yet, the physical law of nature still assures them their part of the products which they raised, for the master must necessarily feed them in order to profit by their labour. But wages of this kind are limited to the barest necessities and to their subsistence.

This abominable custom of slavery has formerly been universal, and is still spread over the greater part of the earth. The principal object of the wars carried on by the People of antiquity was to carry off Slaves, whom the Conquerors either compelled to labour for themselves, or sold to others. This brigandage and this trade still continue in all their horror on the coast of Guinea, where the Europeans encourage it by going thither to purchase Negroes for the cultivation of the American Colonies.

The excessive labour to which avaricious masters force their slaves, causes many of them to perish; and it becomes necessary, in order always to maintain the number requisite for cultivation, that this trade should annually supply a very large number of them. And as war is always the principal source which supplies this commerce, it is evident that it can exist only as long as men are divided into very small Nations who are incessantly plundering each other, and as long as every district makes war upon its neighbours.[10]// Let England, France and Spain carry on the most cruel hostilities, only the frontiers of each State will be affected, and that in a few places only. All the rest of the country will be peaceful, and the small number of prisoners they could

[10] Schelle divides this last paragraph into two separate paragraphs at this point.

make on either side would be an inadequate resource for the agriculture of each of the three Nations.[11]

[11] This passage was almost completely rewritten by Du Pont de Nemours and was broken up into three sections. It is therefore at this point that the numbering of the sections in the *Reflections* as published in *Ephémérides*, the Du Pont edition of Turgot's *Works* and the Daire edition start to differ from that of the other editions. See Concordance, Appendix, p. 196. These changes are as follows.

"XXI. *Another method, which is very bad, which has unfortunately been very common in the ages of barbarism, and which, to the shame of mankind, still exists in many countries which are neither enlightened nor civilised.*

"*In the ages of ignorance and ferocity, there were many occasions for dispute between men who were ill-armed and apprehensive, and, as a result, more susceptible to mutual fear and hatred; for experience shows that people fight almost only out of weakness, and in fear, well or ill founded, of misfortunes which they regard as certain, and to which they prefer the chances of combat – At first, the conquered were slaughtered mercilessly, as is still done by some American savages.*

"*The introduction of cultivation mitigated the customs a little, without entirely correcting them, or rather, it corrected them in a manner which made the depravity less cruel in appearance, but in reality more dangerous, and more widespread in fact. The stronger thought that instead of killing the weaker, they would benefit more if they appropriated them, and made them work the soil as slaves.*

"*As soon as this abominable custom was established, wars became even more frequent. Before this time, they happened only by accident; since then, they are waged for the very purpose of* carrying off slaves, whom the conquerors either compelled to labour for themselves, or sold to others. *This was* the principal object of wars carried on by the people of antiquity, and this brigandage and this trade still continue, in all their horror, on the coast of Guinea, where the Europeans encourage it by going thither to purchase negroes for the cultivation of the American Colonies.

"XXII. *The Share which nature assures the cultivators, even slaves of the product of their labour.*

"*The slaves* had no justice to look for from the hands of people who could not have reduced them to slavery without violating *all the laws of (natural) order and morality, and* all the rights of humanity". (See Turgot to Du Pont, 20/2/1770, in Schelle, *Oeuvres*, III, p. 378.)

"Yet, the physical law of nature still assures them their part of the products which they raise, for the master must necessarily feed them in order to profit by their labour. But wages of this kind are limited to the barest necessities and to their subsistence.

"XXIII. *To what extent cultivation carried out by slaves is unprofitable and costly for the master and for humanity.*

"(*The*) *Slaves have no motive to carry out the work they are forced to do with the intelligence and care which could assure its success: as a result, these labours produce very little.*

"*Avaricous masters know of no other way of making up for this lack of produce which is a necessary result of cultivation by slaves, than to force the latter to work even more arduously, more continuously, and more forcefully.* These excessive labours cause many of them to perish; and it becomes necessary, in order always to maintain the number required for cultivation, that this trade should supply annually a very large number of them *whom the masters are obliged to buy again. Thus they do not give any wages to their slaves, but they pay a considerable capital to procure these bad workers*, and since war is always the principal source which supplies this commerce, it is evident that it can exist only *through an enormous destruction of men*, and as long as men are divided into very small nations, who are incessantly plundering each other, and as long as every district makes war upon its neighbours.

"Let England, France and Spain carry on the most cruel hostilities, the frontiers alone of each State will be affected, and that in a few places only. All the rest of the country will be

22. *Cultivation by Slaves cannot continue to exist in large Societies.*
Thus when men gather together into large Societies, slave recruits are no longer numerous enough to take the place of those used up by agriculture. And although the labour of men is supplemented by that of beasts, there comes a time when the lands can no longer be worked by slaves. The employment of them is then retained only for domestic service, and in the end dies out; because as Nations become more civilised, they enter into agreements for the exchange of prisoners of war. These conventions are the more readily made, as every individual is very much concerned to be free from the danger of falling into a state of slavery.

23. *Bondage to the soil succeeds slavery proper.*
The descendants of the first slaves, originally attached to the cultivation of the lands, experience a change in their condition. As internal peace within the several Nations no longer leaves commerce the wherewithal to satisfy the excessive consumption of slaves, the masters are obliged to handle them with

---

peaceful, and the small number of prisoners they could make on either side would be an inadequate resource for the agriculture of each of the three nations."

(The above is the text as found in the *Ephémérides*, November 1769; in the *Works* of Turgot, as edited by Du Pont, and reprinted by Daire, the following, different version appears:)

"XXI. *Second Method: cultivation by slaves.*
"In times not very distant from the origin of society, it was almost impossible to find men willing to cultivate the land which belonged to others, because, all the land not as yet having been occupied, those who were willing to labour preferred the clearing of new lands, and cultivating them on their own account. *Thus it is not in the early stage of society that proprietors can cease to be cultivators; it is, as we have shown above (See XI and foll.) only when the progress of society and agriculture produced, and distinguished, the stipendiary class.*

"*But, in the early times of ignorance and ferocity, there were many occasions for disputes between men who were ill-armed, apprehensive, in need, who did not have the assurance of their subsistence, and who were, as a result, very susceptible to reciprocal fear and hatred; for experience shows that men fight almost only out of weakness, worry, well or ill founded fear of privation or misfortunes which they regard as certain, and to which they prefer the chances of combat. For a long time the conquered were slaughtered mercilessly, as is still done by some American savages.*

"*The introduction of cultivation mitigated the customs a little, without correcting them entirely, or in a way which made the depravity less cruel, but more widespread, and thus in reality more dangerous for humanity generally. The stronger thought that instead of killing the weaker, it would be profitable to appropriate them, and to make them work the soil as slaves.*

"*As soon as this abominable custom was established, wars became even more frequent. Before this time, they happened only by accident; since then, they are undertaken with the view of obtaining* slaves, whom the conquerors compel to work for themselves, or they sell to others . . . ."

(The rest of this section, and sections XXII and XXIII conform to the text of the *Ephémérides.*)

In order to distinguish the material added by Du Pont, these additions have been italicised.

more consideration.[12]// Those who were born in the house, accustomed from infancy to their condition, are less revolted by it, and their masters have less need to employ severity in controlling them. By degrees the land they cultivate becomes their country; they have no language other than that of their masters;[13] they become part of the same Nation; good relations develop, followed by trust and humanity on the part of their masters.

24. *Vassalage succeeds bondage to the soil, and the Slave becomes Proprietor. Third method: alienation of an estate in return for a fixed due.*

The administration of an estate cultivated by slaves is an onerous task and a constraint on one's place of residence. The master secures for himself a freer, easier and safer enjoyment of his property by interesting his slaves in the cultivation of it, and by yielding to each of them a certain portion of the ground, on condition of their paying him a share of the produce. Some have made a temporary agreement, and have left their *serfs*, or slaves, only a precarious and revocable possession. Others have given up the estate in perpetuity, retaining an annual rent payable either in kind or in money, and exacting from the possessors certain duties. Those who received these lands, under the condition prescribed, became proprietors and freemen, under the name of *tenants* or *vassals*; and the former proprietors, under the title of *lords*, reserved only the right of exacting the payment of rent, and other stipulated dues. Thus things have come to pass in the greater part of Europe.

25. *Fourth Method: Share cropping.*

These estates, rendered free on the condition of payment of rent, may again change their Proprietors, be divided and reunited in consequence of successions and sales, and such a *Vassal* may in his turn have more land than he can cultivate himself. As a rule the rent to which those lands are subject is not so large but that, with good cultivation, there can still be procured, over and above the advances, the expenses and the subsistence of the Cultivator, a surplus of produce which forms a revenue. Henceforth the *Vassal* Proprietor is also likely to desire to enjoy this revenue without labour, and to have his estate cultivated by others. Moreover, most of the lords alienated only those parts of their possessions, which are the least within their reach, and retain those which they can have cultivated with least expense. Cultivation by slaves being no longer practicable, the first method which offered itself, and the simplest to induce free men to cultivate estates which did not belong to them, was to give up to them a part of the produce; a plan which would induce them

[12] Daire and Schelle, following Du Pont de Nemours, divide this paragraph into two at the point indicated.

[13] The phrase "they have no language other than that of their masters", was omitted from the 1793 translation.

to cultivate the land better than labourers on fixed wages would be likely to do. The most common division has been that into two equal parts, one of which belonged to the Cultivator and the other to the Proprietor. This has given rise to the name of *Métayer* (medietarius), or share cropping. In arrangements of this kind, which occur in the greater part of France, the Proprietor pays all the advances of the cultivation, that is to say, he provides at his own expense the working cattle, the ploughs and other instruments of husbandry, seed, and the support of the Cultivator and his family, from the time the latter enters into the *métairie* until the first harvest.

26. *Fifth method: renting, or the letting-out of land.*

Intelligent and rich Cultivators, who suspected to what extent an active and well directed cultivation, for which neither labour nor expense was spared, would raise the fertility of the soil, rightly judged that they would gain more, if the Proprietor should consent to give up to them, for a certain number of years, the whole of every harvest, on condition of paying him annually a fixed revenue, and making all the advances of cultivation. Thereby they would be assured that the increase in product obtained by their expenses and labour, would belong entirely to themselves. The Proprietor, on the other hand, gained thereby a more tranquil enjoyment of his revenue, being freed from the care of making the advances and keeping an account of the product; a more steady enjoyment, since he received every year the same price of his lease; and a more certain enjoyment, because he never ran the risk of losing his advances, and the cattle and other effects with which the tenants had stocked his farm became a security for his payment. Besides, the lease being only for a small number of years, if his tenant had given him too low a price for his land, he could raise it at the end of the lease.

27. *The last method is the most advantageous of all, but it assumes an already wealthy country.*

This method of putting out lands to lease is the most advantageous of all both to the Proprietors and to the Cultivators. It is established everywhere where there are wealthy Cultivators, capable of making the advances of cultivation; and as wealthy Cultivators are able to bestow much more labour and manure upon the land, there results from it a prodigious increase in the productions and the revenue from estates.

In Picardy, Normandy, the neighbourhood of Paris, and in most of the Provinces in the north of France, the lands are cultivated by Tenant Farmers; in the provinces of the South, by share-croppers. Likewise the Northern provinces are incomparably richer and better cultivated than the Southern provinces.

28. *Recapitulation of the several methods of making estates productive.* I have just enumerated five different methods by which the Proprietors have been able to remove themselves of the labour of cultivation, and make their land productive by the hands of others.

Firstly, by workmen paid fixed wages.

Secondly, by slaves.

Thirdly, by giving up the estate in return for the payment of a rent.

Fourthly, by granting to the Cultivator a fixed portion of the produce, usually half, the Proprietor undertaking to make the advances of cultivation.

Fifthly, by letting their lands to Farmers, who undertake to make all the advances of cultivation, and who engage to pay the Proprietor a fixed revenue during the number of years agreed upon.

Of these five methods, the first is too expensive, and very seldom practised; the second can take place only in countries still ignorant and barbarous; the third is not so much a method of getting what one can out of a property as a surrender of the property in consideration of a lien upon the estate, so that the former Proprietor is, properly speaking, no more than a creditor of the new Proprietor.

The last two methods of cultivation are the most common, to wit: the cultivation by Share-croppers in the poor countries, and cultivation by Farmers in the richer countries.[14]

29. *Of capitals in general, and of the revenue of money.* There is another way of being rich, without labouring and without possessing lands, of which I have not yet spoken. It is necessary to explain its origin and its connection with the rest of the system of the distribution of wealth in the society which I have just outlined. This way consists in living by what is called the revenue of one's money, or on the interest drawn from money placed on loan.[15]

30. *Of the use of gold and silver in commerce.* Silver and gold are two articles of commerce like any other, and less precious than many others, because they are of no use for the real needs of life. To explain how these metals have become the representative pledges of every

[14] This is the end of the first part of the *Reflections* as published in the *Ephémérides*. At the end of this section, Du Pont inserted the following: "This systematic treatise is large enough to have filled this volume completely, if we had included the whole of it. We have found a natural break at this point; and it is this that has decided us to postpone the conclusion to the next volume."

[15] This last sentence was changed by Du Pont in his edition of Turgot's *Works* (V, pp. 31–32), though not in the version in the *Ephémérides*. This text, and that of Daire, reads as follows in translation: "This way consists in living on one's capital, or rather, on the interest drawn from money placed on loan. This is something which the use of gold and silver helps greatly, by facilitating small savings."

kind of wealth, what influence they exercise in the progress of commerce, and how they enter into the composition of fortunes, it is necessary to go back a little and to retrace our steps.

31. *Rise of Commerce. Principle of valuation of exchangeable objects.* Reciprocal wants led to the introduction of exchange of what people owned for what they did not own. Commodities began to be exchanged for one another, and for labour. In exchanging, it is necessary that each party should agree to the quantity and quality of each of the things exchanged. In this agreement it is natural that each should desire to receive as much, and to give as little, as he can, both being equally masters of what they have to give in exchange, each has to balance the attachment he has for the commodity he gives, against the desire he has for the commodity he wishes to receive, and to fix accordingly the quantity of each of the things exchanged. If the two persons do not agree, they will have to approach one another by yielding a little on both sides, offering more and contenting themselves with less. I will assume that one needs corn and the other wine, and that they agree to exchange *one bushel of corn* for *six pints of wine.* It is evident that by both of them *one bushel of corn* and *six pints of wine* are looked upon as exactly equivalent, and that in this particular exchange, the price of *a bushel* of corn is *six pints* of wine, and the price of *six pints* of wine is *one bushel* of corn. But in another exchange between other men, this price will be different, according as one of them shall have a more or less urgent need for the commodity belonging to the other; and *a bushel* of corn may be exchanged against *eight pints* of wine, while *another bushel* shall be exchanged for *four pints* only. Now it is evident that not one of these three prices can be looked on as the true price of a bushel of corn, rather than the other; for, to each of the dealers, the wine he has received was equivalent to the corn he had given. In short, so long as we consider each exchange as isolated and standing by itself, the value of the thing exchanged has no other measure than the needs or desires of one party weighed with those of the other, and is fixed only by their agreement.[16]

32. *How current value is established in the exchange of commodities.* However, it happens that several Individuals have wine to offer to the man who has corn. If one is not willing to give more than *four pints* for *one bushel*, the Owner of the corn will not give him his corn, when he comes to learn that someone else will give *six* or *eight pints* for the same *bushel.* If the former wishes to have corn, he will be obliged to raise his price equal to what is offered by others. The Sellers of wine profit on their side by the competition among the Sellers of corn. No one resolves to part with his commodity until

[16] For a full evaluation of Turgot's theory of value, exchange and price determination, see my 'A Reappraisal of Turgot's Theory of Value, Exchange and Price Determination', op. cit.

he has compared the different offers that are made to him of the commodity he needs and he gives preference to the highest offer. The value of the corn and wine is no longer debated between two isolated individuals in relation to their respective wants and resources, but is fixed with those of all the Sellers of wine. For he who would willingly give *eight pints* of wine for *one bushel* of corn, will give but *four* when he learns that an Owner of corn is willing to give *two bushels* for *eight pints*. The price will become the current price to which all the Buyers and Sellers will conform in their exchanges; and it will be true to say that *six pints* of wine will be to everyone the equivalent of *one bushel* of corn, if that is the mean price, until a diminution of offer on the one side, or of demand, on the other, causes this valuation to change.

33. *Commerce gives to all commodities a current value with respect to every other commodity; from which it follows that every commodity is the equivalent of a certain quantity of every other commodity, and may be looked on as a pledge which represents it.*

Corn is not only exchanged for wine, but also for all other commodities which the owners of corn may need, such as wood, leather, wool, cotton, etc.; it is the same with wine and every other particular commodity. If *one bushel* of corn is equivalent to *six pints* of wine, and *one sheep* is equivalent to *three bushels* of corn, this same sheep will be equivalent to *eighteen pints* of wine. He, who, having corn, wants wine, may, without inconvenience, exchange his corn for a sheep, in order afterwards to exchange the sheep for the wine which he needs.

34. *Each commodity may serve as a scale or common measure, by which to compare the value of all others.*

It follows from this, that in a country where Commerce is brisk, where there is much production and much consumption, where there are many offers and demands for all sorts of commodities, each kind will have a current price relative to every other kind; that is a certain quantity of one will be of equal value with a certain quantity of each of the others. Thus the same quantity of corn which is worth eighteen pints of wine, will also be worth one sheep, a piece of dressed leather, or a certain quantity of iron, and all these things will have an equal value in commerce.[17]// To express or make known the value of any particular thing, it is evident that it is sufficient to state the quantity of any other known commodity which will be looked on as if equivalent. Thus, to make known what a piece of leather of a certain size is worth, we may say indifferently that it is worth *three bushels of corn*, or *eighteen pints of wine*. We may similarly express the value of a certain quantity of wine by the number of sheep, or bushels of corn which it is worth in commerce.

[17] Daire and Schelle, following Du Pont, have divided this paragraph into two at the point indicated.

From this it can be seen that all the kinds of commodities which are exchangeable objects, measure one another, so to speak, and that each may serve as a common measure, or scale of comparison to which to refer the value of all the others; and in like manner each commodity becomes in the hands of its owner, a means to obtain all the others, a sort of universal pledge.

35. *Every commodity does not present an equally convenient scale of values. The preference, therefore, has in practice necessarily been given to those which, not being susceptible to any great difference in quality, have a value principally related to the number and the quantity.*

But although all commodities have essentially this property of representing all others, being able to serve as a common measure to express their value, and as a universal pledge to procure all of them by way of an exchange, all cannot be used with the same degree of facility for these two purposes.[18]// The more susceptible any commodity is to changing its value on account of its quality, the more difficult it is to use it as a scale to which to relate the value of other commodities.// For example, if *eighteen pints* of wine of *Anjou* are the equivalent of *one sheep, eighteen pints* of *Cape* wine may be the equivalent of *eighteen sheep*. Thus the person who, to express the value of a sheep, would say that it is worth eighteen pints of wine, would be using ambiguous speech which would not communicate any precise idea, at least until he added a good many explanations, which would be very inconvenient.// Men, therefore, have been obliged to prefer for their scale of comparison such commodities, which being more commonly in use and consequently of a better known value, were more like each other, and of which, consequently, the value had more relation to the number of the quantity than to the quality.

36. *The want of an exact correspondence between the value and the number or quantity is supplied by average valuation, which becomes an ideal money.*

In a country where there is only one race of sheep, the value of a fleece or of a sheep may easily be taken for the common measure of values, and it may be said that a barrel of wine, or a piece of stuff, is worth a certain number of fleeces or sheep. There is in reality some inequality among sheep, but when it is a question of selling sheep, care is taken to estimate that inequality, and to reckon, for example, two lambs as one sheep. When it is a question of valuing any other commodity, the common value of a sheep of medium age and condition is taken as the unit.[19]// In this way, the expression of values in terms of

[18] Daire and Schelle, following Du Pont, divide this paragraph into four at the points indicated.

[19] Daire and Schelle, following Du Pont, divide this paragraph into two at the point indicated.

sheep becomes an agreed form of expression, and this word *one sheep*, in the language of commerce, simply signifies a certain value which, in the minds of those who hear it, carries not merely the idea of one sheep, but of a certain quantity of the more common types of commodities which are regarded as the equivalent of this value, and this expression will end by being so entirely applied to a fictitious and abstract value, rather than to a real sheep, and that to purchase one of them, it becomes necessary to give double the quantity of corn or wine that was formerly given, people will rather say that one *sheep* is worth *two sheep* than change the expression they have been accustomed to for all the other values.

37. *Examples of those mean valuations which become an ideal expression of value.*

In the commerce of all Nations, several examples are known of these fictitious valuations in terms of commodities which are, so to speak, only an agreed form of expression of their value. Thus the Cooks of Paris, and the Fishmongers who provide great houses, generally sell *by the piece*. A fat pullet is reckoned as one piece, a chicken as half a piece, more or less, according to the season, and so on. In the Slave trade to the American Colonies, a cargo of Negroes is sold at the rate of so much per Negro head, *a piece of India*. The women and children are valued in such a way that, for example, three children, or one woman and one child, are reckoned as one head of Negro. The valuation is increased or diminished on account of the strength or other qualities of the slaves, so that certain slaves are reckoned as *two head of Negro*.

The *Mandingo* Negros, who carry on the gold dust trade with the Arabian Merchants, relate all their commodities to a fictitious scale whose parts are called *macutes*, so that they tell the Merchants that they will give so many *macutes* in gold. They value likewise in *macutes* the commodities they receive, and bargain with the Merchants on this valuation.

In the same way in Holland people reckon by *Bank florins*, which are only fictitious money, and which in commerce, have sometimes a higher, sometimes a lower value than the coins called *florins*.

38. *Every commodity is a pledge representing all other commodities, but it is more or less convenient in practice according to the ease with which it can be transported and stored without deterioration.*

The variation in the quality of commodities, and in their prices in accordance with that quality, which renders them more or less suitable than others to serve as a common measure, is also more or less an impediment to their being a representative pledge of every other commodity of a like value.[20]// But with

[20] Daire and Schelle, following Du Pont, divide this paragraph into three at the points indicated.

respect to this last property there is also a very great difference between the different types of commodities.// For example, it is evident that a man who owns a piece of cloth, is far more certain of obtaining a certain quantity of corn for it, when he wants it, than if he had a barrel of wine of the same value, the wine being subject to an infinity of accidents which in an instant may cause it to lose its entire value.

39. *Every commodity has the two essential properties of money, of measuring and representing all value; and in this sense all merchandise is money.*

The two properties of serving as a common measure of all values, and of being a representative pledge of all other commodities of a like value, include everything that constitutes the essence and use of what is called money; and it follows from the details which I have just given, that all merchandise is, in some respect, *money*, and shares more or less, according to the nature of each, in these two essential properties. All are more or less suitable to serve as a common measure in proportion as they are in more general use, of more similar quality, and easier to divide into parts of equal value. All are more or less suitable to be a universal pledge of exchanges in proportion as they are less susceptible to deterioration or alteration in quantity or quality.

40. *Reciprocally, all money is essentially merchandise.*

We can take only what itself has a value as a common measure of value, that which is received in Commerce in exchange for other values; and there is no universal, representative pledge of value, except something of equal value. Purely conventional money is therefore an impossibility.

42. *Different substances have been able to serve, and have served, as ordinary money.*

Many Nations have adopted in their language and in their Trade, as a common measure of value, different substances, more or less precious; there are even at this day some Barbaric Peoples who make use of a species of little shells called *Cowries*.[21] I remember having seen, when at College, apricot stones exchanged and passed as a type of money among the Scholars, who used them to play certain games. I have already spoken of the reckoning by head of cattle; traces of this can be found in the Laws of the ancient Germanic Nations who broke up the Roman Empire. The early Romans, or at least the Latins, their ancestors, made use of it also. It is claimed that the first coins they struck in copper, represented the value of a sheep, and bore the im-

[21] Daire, following Du Pont in *Oeuvres de Turgot*, V, p. 45, adds after "cowries"; "which are used to make bracelets and necklaces for the adornment of their women". This addition does not occur in other editions.

age of that animal, and that the name of *pecunia*, has come from *pecus*. This conjecture has a great deal of probability.

42. *Metals, and particularly gold and silver, are the most suitable for this purpose: and why.*

We have now come to the introduction of the precious metals into Commerce. All the metals, as they have been discovered, have been admitted into exchange, on account of their real usefulness: their splendour has caused them to be sought after, to serve as ornaments; their malleability and their solidity have rendered them suitable for making utensils, more durable and lighter than those of clay. But these substances could not be brought into Commerce without almost immediately becoming a universal Money. A piece of any metal, of whatever sort, has the same qualities as another piece of the same metal, provided they are both equally pure. Now, the ease with which we can separate, by different Chemical operations, a metal from other metals with which it is incorporated, enables us always to bring it to the degree of purity, or, as it is called, the *standard*, which is desired, and the value of metal can only vary then according to its weight. In expressing, therefore, the value of all commodities by the weight of metal which may be had in exchange, we shall have the clearest, the most convenient, and the most precise expression of value; and hence it is impossible that it should not, in practice, be preferred to every other. Nor are the metals less suitable than other commodities for becoming the universal pledge of all the values that they can measure; as they are susceptible for all imaginable divisions, there is no commodity whose value, great or small, cannot be exactly paid for by a certain quantity of metal. To this advantage of lending themselves to every kind of division, they join that of being unalterable, and those which are scarce, like gold and silver, have a very great value in a very inconsiderable weight and bulk.

These two metals then, are, of all commodities, the most easy to verify as to their quality, to divide as to their quantity, to keep for a long time without deterioration,[22] and to convey to all places at the least expense. Every one who has a surplus commodity and who does not need, at the time, any other commodity for use, will hasten to exchange it for money, with which he is more certain than with anything else, to procure himself the commodity he wants at the moment he needs it.

43. *By the nature of things, gold and silver are constituted money and universal money, independently of any convention and of any law.*

Here then are gold and silver constituted money, and universal money, and

[22] This last phrase is omitted in the 1793 translation. Curiously, it contains one of the few differences between the 1788 edition and the *tirage à part* and all other editions. For the phrase in question, the 1788 edition has: "... à conserver longtemps sans alteration" (p. 51). All other editions have "éternellement" instead of "longtemps" so that the English in the Ashley translation, for example, becomes: "... to keep forever without alteration" (p. 38).

that without any arbitrary agreement among men, without the intervention of any law, but only by the nature of things. They are not, as people imagine, signs of value; they have a value themselves. If they are capable of being the measure and pledge of other values, they have this property in common with all other commodities which have a value in Commerce.[23]// They differ from them only because, being at the same time more divisible, more unchangeable, and of more easy conveyance than other commodities, it is more convenient to use them to measure and represent value.

44. *The employment of other metals for these purposes is only subsidiary.* All metals would be capable of being used as money.[24]// But those which are very common have too little value in too large a bulk to be used in the everyday exchanges in Trade. Copper, silver, and gold are the only ones which have been brought into constant use.// And even copper, except among some Peoples to whom neither mines nor Commerce have supplied a sufficient quantity of gold or silver, has never been used except in exchanges of the smallest values.

45. *The use of gold and silver as money has augmented their value as substances.*
It is impossible but that the eagerness with which every one has sought to exchange his superfluous commodities for gold and silver, rather than for any other commodity, must have greatly augmented the value of these two materials in Commerce. They are thereby rendered more suitable for their employment as pledge, or common measure.

46. *Variations in the value of gold and of silver, compared with the other commodities, and with one another.*
This value is susceptible to change, and in fact does continually change so that the same quantity of metal which answered to a certain quantity of such or such a commodity, ceases to correspond to it, and more or less money is required to represent the same commodity. When it requires more, the commodity is said to be dearer; when it requires less, it is said to be cheaper; but it might just as well be said that it is the money which is cheaper in the first case, and dearer in the latter.[25]// Silver and gold vary in price not only as compared with all other commodities, but they also vary in price among themselves, according as they are more or less abundant. It is well known that

[23] Daire and Schelle, following Du Pont, divide this paragraph into two at the point indicated.

[24] Daire and Schelle, following Du Pont, divide this paragraph into three at the points indicated.

[25] Daire and Schelle, following Du Pont, divide these two paragraphs into four at the points indicated.

in Europe at the present time from *fourteen to fifteen ounces of silver* are given for *one ounce of gold*, and that in former times only *ten to eleven ounces of silver* were given for *one ounce of gold.*[26]// In China, even at present only about *twelve ounces of silver* are given to get *one ounce of gold*, so that there is a very great advantage in carrying silver to China, to exchange for gold to bring back to Europe. It is evident that, in the long run, this Commerce will make gold more common in Europe and less common in China, and that the value of these two metals must finally come to the same proportion everywhere.//

A thousand different causes compete to determine at any moment the value of commodities when compared either with each other, or with silver, and cause them to change incessantly. The same causes determine the value (of money), and cause it to vary, when compared either with the value of each particular commodity, or with all the other values which are in Commerce at the time. It is not possible to disentangle these different causes, and to unfold their effects, without entering into very extensive and very difficult details, and I shall abstain from entering upon this discussion.

47. *The practice of making payment in money has given rise to the distinction between Seller and Buyer.*

In proportion as people have become accustomed to the practice of valuing everything in money, of exchanging all their superfluous commodities for money, and of not parting with that money but for the things which are useful or agreeable to them at the moment, they have become accustomed to consider the exchanges of Commerce from a new point of view.[27]// They have distinguished two persons, the Seller and the Buyer: the Seller was the one who gave commodities for money, and the Buyer was the one who gave money for commodities.

48. *The use of money has greatly facilitated the separation of the different labours among the different Members of Society.*

The more money came to stand for everything else, the more did it become possible for everyone, by devoting himself entirely to the kind of cultivation and industry he had chosen, to relieve himself completely of all care of supplying his other wants, and to think only of obtaining as much money as possible, by the sale of his fruits or his labour, very sure that by means of this money he could get all the rest: in this way the use of money has prodigiously hastened the progress of Society.

49. *Of the reserve of annual produce, accumulated to form capitals.*

As soon as men were found whose property in land assured them an annual

[26] The 1793 translation also divides this paragraph into two at the point indicated.

[27] Daire and Schelle, following Du Pont, divide this paragraph into two at the point indicated.

revenue more than sufficient to satisfy all their requirements, there were sure to be found men who, anxious about the future, or merely prudent, put aside part of what they gathered every year, either to meet contingencies, or to increase their comforts. When the produce they gathered was difficult to preserve, they must have sought to obtain, by exchange, articles of a more durable nature, whose value would not be destroyed by time, or which could be employed in such a manner, as to procure profits which would more than make up for their deterioration.

50. *Moveable wealth;*[28] *accumulation of money.*

Possessions of this kind, resulting from the accumulation of annual produce not consumed, are known by the name of *moveable wealth.* Furniture, houses, plate, commodities in warehouses, the tools of each trade, and cattle, belong to this kind of wealth. It is evident that men toiled hard to procure themselves as much as they could of this kind of wealth, before they became acquainted with money; but it is no less clear that, as soon as it was known, as soon as it was proved to be the most changeable of all commodities, and the easiest to keep without trouble, it could not fail to be sought after by whoever wished to accumulate. It was not only the Proprietors of landed estates who thus accumulated their surplus produce. Although the profits of industry are not, like the revenue of the soil, a gift of nature, and the working man draws from his labour only the price which is given him by the persons who pay him his wages; although the latter economises as much as possible in the payment of these wages, and competition obliges the working man to content himself with a price less than he would like, it is nevertheless certain that this competition has never been numerous or keen enough in any kind of labour, to prevent, at any time, a man who is more expert, more active, and above all, more thrifty than others in his personal consumption, from earning a little more than was necessary for the subsistence of himself and his family, and from setting aside this surplus to create therewith a little store.[29]

51. *Moveable wealth is an indispensable prerequisite for all lucrative work.*

It is also necessary that in every trade the Workmen or the Entrepreneur who set them to work have a certain fund of moveable wealth, accumulated

[28] The French, *richesses mobilières*, translated here as "moveable wealth", has a wider connotation in that it is also the antonym of real property. In this sense, Turgot's division of wealth into *bien-fonds* and *richesses mobilières* also implies the legal distinction between real and personal property. The 1793 translator, quite correctly, sometimes translates *richesses mobilières* as "circulating wealth", and sometimes as "personal property".

[29] Cf. with section 6, above pp. 45–46. The above modifies the view expressed there. See also 'Letters on the Grain Trade', below pp. 167–169, where a similar opinion is expressed.

In his edition of the *Works* (V, p. 55), Du Pont inserted a note at this point on the subject of the manner in which the introduction of gold and silver as money has facilitated the accumulation of capital. This, and other notes by Du Pont will not be reproduced here.

beforehand. Here we are again obliged to retrace our steps and to recall several matters which at first were only hinted at in passing, when the division of the several professions was discussed, and the different methods by which Proprietors could make their estates productive; because this could not be explained at that time without breaking the line of argument.

52. *Necessity of advances in agriculture.*
Every type of labour, in agriculture, in industry or in commerce, requires advances. Even if the soil were cultivated by hand, it would be necessary to sow before reaping; it would be necessary to live until after the harvest. The more agriculture is brought to perfection, and the more energetic it becomes, the more considerable these advances are. There is need of cattle, implements of husbandry, buildings to house the cattle and store the produce; it is necessary to pay a number of people proportioned to the extent of the enterprise, and to enable them to subsist until the harvest. It is only by means of considerable advances that a large return is obtained, and that the lands yield a large revenue. In any craft whatsoever, it is necessary that the Workman has tools in advance, that he has a sufficient quantity of materials on which to work; and he has to subsist while waiting for the sale of his finished goods.

53. *First advances furnished by the land while still uncultivated.*
It is the land which is always the first and unique source of all wealth; it is the land which by cultivation produces all the revenue; it is the land also which provided the first fund of advances, prior to cultivation. The first Cultivator took the seed which he sowed from the plants which the earth had of itself produced; while waiting for the harvest, he lived by hunting, by fishing, and upon wild fruits; his tools have been the branches of trees, torn down in the forest, and shaped with stones sharpened against other stones; the animals wandering in the woods he took himself in the chase, or caught in his traps; he brought them into subjection and tamed them; he used them at first for food, afterwards to help him in his labour. The first fund grew gradually; cattle were in early times the most sought after of all moveable wealth, and also the easiest to accumulate; they die, but they reproduce themselves, and the wealth of which they consist is in a way indestructible: this fund itself grows by the mere process of generation, and gives an annual product, either in dairy produce, or in wool, in hides or other materials, which, with the wood obtained in the forest, was the first fund for the works of industry.

54. *Cattle, moveable wealth even before the cultivation of the soil.*
In times when there was still a large quantity of uncultivated land which did not belong to anyone, cattle could be maintained without there being a Proprietor of land. It is even probable that mankind has almost everywhere begun to collect herds and to live on their produce before devoting themselves

to the more toilsome labour of cultivation.[30]// It seems that the Nations which cultivated the earth in the earliest times, were those which found in their Country types of animals more susceptible of being tamed, and which were led in this way from the wandering and restless life of Hunters and Fishermen to the more tranquil enjoyment of Pastoral Pursuits.// Pastoral life requires a longer residence in the same place, affords more leisure, more opportunities to study the difference between lands, to observe the way of nature in the production of plants which serve for the support of cattle. Perhaps it is for this reason, that the Asiatic Nations were the first to cultivate the earth, and that the peoples of America have remained so long in a Savage State.

55. *Another kind of moveable wealth, and of advances of agriculture: Slaves.*[31]

Slaves were another kind of moveable wealth, procured at first by violence, and afterwards by way of Commerce and exchange.[32]// Those who had many slaves employed them not only in the cultivation of the land, but also in different works of industry. The ease with which these two kinds of wealth could be accumulated almost without limit, and used independently from the land, made it possible to value the lands themselves, and to compare their value to that of moveable wealth.

56. *Moveable wealth has an exchangeable value relative to the land itself.*

A man who happened to have a good many pieces of land, but no cattle or slaves, would certainly make an advantageous bargain by surrendering a part of his land to a person who gave him in exchange cattle and slaves to cultivate

[30] Daire and Schelle, following Du Pont, divide this paragraph into three paragraphs at the points indicated.

[31] Du Pont joined this section to the next one in his editions by omitting the title as well as the first sentence. In Daire, and in Du Pont editions, sections 55 and 56 are combined into a single section numbered 57. Du Pont also made several other alterations, so that his section 57 (the present 55 and 56) reads:

"57. *Moveable wealth has a value exchangable against land itself.*

"Those who had a good deal of moveable wealth could employ it not only in the cultivation of the land, but also in different works of industry. The ease with which this wealth could be accumulated and used independently from the land, made it possible to value the lands themselves, and to compare their value to that of moveable wealth.

"A man who happened to have a good many pieces of land but no beasts or equipment, or insufficient beasts or equipment, would certainly make an advantageous bargain by surrendering part of his land to a person who gave him in exchange beasts and equipment to cultivate the rest ...."

(The remainder of this section is the same as the text in section 56 above.)

These changes were undoubtedly inspired by the difference in opinion on the subject of slavery between Turgot and Du Pont. See above, *Reflections*, pp. 52–53, n. 11; and also Turgot to Du Pont, 2/2/1770, 6/2/1770, 20/2/1770, in Schelle, *Oeuvres*, III, pp. 374–375, 378–379.

[32] Schelle starts a new paragraph at the point indicated.

the rest. It is principally in this way that landed estates themselves entered into Commerce, and had a value comparable with that of all other commodities. If *four bushels* of corn, the net product of an acre of land, were worth *six sheep*, the acre itself which produced them, could be transferred for a certain value, larger of course, but always easily determined in the same manner as the price of other commodities; i.e. first by the chaffering between the dealers, and afterwards by the current price established by the competition of those who wish to exchange land for cattle, and those who wish to give up cattle for land. It is in accordance with this current price that lands are valued when a Debtor is sued by his Creditor, and is compelled to surrender his estate to him.

57. *Valuation of lands in accordance with the proportion of the revenue to the amount of moveable wealth, or the value for which they are exchanged: this proportion is what is called the penny of the price of land.*[33]

It is evident that if a piece of land which produces a revenue equivalent to *six sheep*, can be sold for a certain value which may always be expressed by a number of *sheep* equivalent to that value, this number will bear a definite proportion with that of *six*, and will contain it a certain number of times. Thus the price of an estate will be simply so many times its revenue; *twenty times* if the price is *one hundred and twenty* sheep; *thirty* times, if it is *one hundred and eighty* sheep. And so the current price of land regulates itself in accordance with the relation between the value of the estate and the value of the revenue; and the number of times that the price of the estate contains the revenue is called so many years purchase of land. It is sold at the price of *twenty, thirty,* or *forty years purchase*, when twenty, thirty, or forty times the revenue is paid to obtain it. It is also no less evident that this price or this rate must vary according to the number of purchasers or sellers of land, in the same manner as the price of all other commodities varies in accordance with the varying proportion between the offer and the demand.

58. *Every money capital, or every sum of value, whatever it may be, is the equivalent of a piece of land producing a revenue equal to some definite fraction of this sum. First employment of capitals. Purchase of a landed estate.*

Let us now go back to the time after the introduction of money. The ease with which it can be accumulated made it the most sought after form of moveable wealth, and furnished the means of accumulation unceasingly by the simple

[33] This phrase, "the penny of the price of land" is synonymous with the English expression, "the number of years' purchase of the annual rent". The 'penny' was also another expression for a rate per cent, the twentieth penny, for example, being five per cent. See, for example, Voltaire, *Siècle de Louis XIV*, p. 564, for a similar usage.

means of thrift. Whoever, either from the revenue of his land, or from the wages of his labour or industry, receives each year more value than he needs to spend, may set aside this surplus and accumulate it: these accumulated values are what is called *a capital*. The timid Miser who accumulates money with the objective of preventing worries about lacking the necessaries of life in an uncertain future, keeps his money in a hoard. If the dangers which he foresaw should eventuate, and he in his poverty should be reduced to live each year upon his treasure, or if a prodigal Heir should spend it by degrees, this treasure would soon be exhausted, and the capital entirely lost to the Owner. The latter can draw a far greater advantage from it. Since a landed estate of a certain revenue is only the equivalent of a sum of value equal to this revenue multiplied a certain number of times, it follows that any sum whatsoever of value is equivalent to a landed estate producing a revenue equal to a definite fraction of this sum: it is perfectly the same whether this sum of value, or this capital consists of a mass of metal, or of any other matter, since money represents every kind of value, just as every kind of value represents money. In the first place, therefore, the Owner of *a capital* can use it to purchase lands, but he has other possibilities as well.

59. *Another employment of money in advances for enterprises of manufacture or industry.*

I have already observed that all labours, whether of cultivation or industry, require advances, and I have shown how the earth, by the fruits and herbs which it produces of itself for the nourishment of man and beast, and by the trees of which men have formed their first tools, had furnished the first advances of cultivation, and even of the first handmade articles that each man might fashion for his own use. For instance, it is the earth that provided the first stone, clay and wood of which the first houses were built; and, before the separation of occupations when the same man that cultivated the earth provided also for his other wants by his own labour, there was no need of other advances: but when a large part of Society had only their arms to maintain themselves, it was necessary that those who thus lived on wages, should have something in advance to begin with, either to procure the materials upon which they worked, or to maintain them while waiting for their wages.

60. *Further explanations of the use of the advance of capitals in enterprises of industry, on their return and on the profits which they ought to yield.*

In early times, he who set men to work, supplied the materials himself, and paid the wages of the Workmen from day to day. It was the Cultivator or the Proprietor himself that gave the Spinner the hemp he had gathered, and he maintained her during the time of her working; then he passed the yarn to a Weaver, to whom he gave, every day, the wage agreed upon; but those slight daily advances could be sufficient only for works of the simplest and roughest kind. A vast number of Crafts, and even of those Crafts engaged in by the poorest Members of Society, require that the same materials should pass through a multitude of different hands, and undergo, for a very long time, exceedingly difficult and varied operations. I have already mentioned the preparation of leather,[34] of which shoes are made: whoever has seen the workshop of a Tanner, cannot help feeling the absolute impossibility of one, or even several poor persons providing themselves with hides, lime, tan, utensils, etc. and causing the buildings necessary for establishing a Tannery to be erected, and of their living for several months until their leather was sold. In this Craft, and in many others, must not those that work at it have learnt the trade before they venture to touch the materials, lest they should spoil them in their first attempts? Here then is another indispensable advance. Who then will collect the materials for the work, the ingredients, the tools necessary for the process? Who is to construct canals, markets, and buildings of every kind? Who will enable that great number of workmen to live until their leather is sold, of whom none individually would be able to prepare a single hide, considering moreover that the profits of the sale of a single tanned hide could not furnish subsistence for any one of them? Who will defray the expenses for the instruction of Pupils and Apprentices? Who will maintain them until they are sufficiently instructed, guiding them gradually from an easy labour proportionate to their age, to works that demand the utmost strength and ability? It will be one of those Owners of *capitals*, or moveable accumulated values, who will employ them partly in advance for the construction of the establishment and the purchase of materials, partly for the daily wages of the Workmen who labour in the preparation of them. It is he who will wait for the sale of the leather to return him not only all his advances, but also a profit sufficient to compensate him for what his money would have been worth to him, had he turned it to the acquisition of an estate, and moreover, the wages due to his labour and care, to his risk, and even to his skill; for surely, if the profits were the same, he would have preferred living without any exertion on the revenue of the land which he could have purchased with the same capital. As fast as this capital returns to him by the sale of his products, he uses it for new purchases to furnish and maintain his Manufactory by this continual circulation; he lives on his profits, and lays aside what he can spare to increase his capital, and to direct it to his business, thereby increasing the amount of his advances, in order to increase his profits even more.

61. *Subdivision of the industrial stipendiary Class into capitalist Entrepreneurs and simple Workmen.*

Thus the whole Class employed in supplying the different wants of Society with an immense variety of industrial products is, so to speak, subdivided into

[34] See above, section 3, note 2, p. 44.

two orders: that of the Entrepreneurs, Manufacturers and Mastercraftsmen, all owners of large capitals, which they invest profitably as advances for setting men at work; the second order, composed of simple Artisans, who have no other property than their arms, who advance only their daily labour, and receive no profit but their wages.

62. *Another employment of capitals, in advances for Agricultural enterprises. Explanations as to the use, the return and indispensable profits of capitals in Agricultural enterprises.*

In speaking first of the employment of capitals in Manufacturing enterprises, I had in view to present a more striking example of the necessity and effect of large advances, and of the course of their circulation; but I have slightly reversed the natural order, which would have required that I should rather begin to speak of enterprises of agriculture, which also can neither be performed, nor extended, nor afford any profit, but by means of considerable advances. It is the Owners of large capitals who, in order to make them productive in agricultural enterprises, take leases of land, and pay the Proprietors large rents, taking on themselves the whole burden of advances. Their position is essentially the same as that of Entrepreneurs of Manufacturing Industry: Like them, they are obliged to make the first advances of the enterprise, to provide themselves with cattle, horses, tools of husbandry, to purchase the first seeds; like them they must maintain and nourish their Carters, Reapers, Threshers, Servants and Labourers of every kind, who have nothing but their arms, who advance only their labour, and earn only their wages; like them, they have to obtain from the harvest, apart from the return of their capital, i.e. their original and annual advances, firstly, a profit equal to the revenue they would be able to acquire with their capital without any labour; secondly, the wages and the price of their labour, of their risk and their industry; thirdly, the wherewithal to replace annually the wear and tear of their property, the cattle that die and the tools that wear out, etc.[35]// All this must be first deducted from the price of the produce of the earth; the surplus serves the Cultivator to pay the Proprietor for the permission he has given to use his field for establishing his enterprise. This is the price of the lease, the revenue of the Proprietor, the *net product*, for all that the earth produces up to the amount of the advances, and the profits of every kind due to him who made these advances, cannot be regarded as a *revenue*, but only as the *return of the expenses of cultivation*, considering that if the Cultivator did not get them back, he would be loath to risk his wealth and trouble in cultivating the field of another.

[35] Daire and Schelle, following Du Pont, divide this paragraph into two at this point.

63. *The competition between the capitalist Entrepreneurs establishes the current price of lands and farming on a large scale.*[36]

The competition between rich Entrepreneurs in agriculture fixes the current price of leases, in proportion to the fertility of the soil, and the price at which its produce is sold, always according to the calculations which the Farmers make both of their expenditures, and of the profits they ought to draw from their advances. They cannot give the Proprietors more than the surplus.[37]// But when the competition among them is very keen, they give him the whole of this surplus, the Proprietor only leasing his land to him who offers the highest rent.

64. *The lack of Capitalist Entrepreneurs in agriculture restricts cultivation to small scale farming.*[38]

When, on the contrary, there are no rich men who have large capitals to put into agricultural enterprises, when, through the low price of the products of the land, or for any other reason, the crops are not sufficient to assure the Entrepreneurs, besides the return of their funds, profits at least equal to those they would derive from their money by employing it in some other way, then Farmers cannot be found who are willing to lease lands.[39]// The Proprietors are forced to hire *Colons* or *Métayers*, who are unable to make any advances, or to cultivate properly.// The Proprietor himself makes some small advances, which produce him a very small revenue: if the land happens to belong to a Proprietor who is poor, in debt, or neglectful, to a widow, or a Minor, it stays out of cultivation.// Such is the true origin of the difference I have already noticed, between Provinces where the lands are cultivated by wealthy Farmers, as in Normandy and the Ile de France, and those where they are cultivated only by poor *Métayers*, as in Limousin, Angoumois, Bourbonnais and many others.

65. *Subdivision of the Class of Cultivators into Entrepreneurs or Farmers, and mere Wage Farmers, whether Servants or Daylabourers.*

Hence it follows, that the Class of Cultivators, like that of the Manufacturers, may be divided into two orders of men, that of the Entrepreneurs or Capitalists, who make all the advances, and that of the mere wage earning

[36] Farming on a large scale is what Quesnay first called "*la grande culture*". In the first part of the *Reflections* Turgot had distinguished *petite culture* from *grande culture* under different names. See sections 25–27 above pp. 54–55.

[37] Daire and Schelle, following Du Pont, divide this paragraph into two at this point.

[38] Previously Turgot had stated that *Métayage* was practised in the poor part of France, and large scale farming in the few wealthy provinces of the North. See section 27 above, p. 55.

[39] Daire and Schelle, following Du Pont, divide this paragraph into four at the points indicated.

workmen. It is also evident, that capitals alone can form and support great enterprises of Agriculture which give the estates an invariable rental value, so to speak, and which assure the Proprietor a revenue which is always constant and as large as possible.

66. *Fourth Employment of capitals, in advances for Commercial Enterprises. Necessity of the Interposition of Merchants, properly so called, between the Producers of the commodity and the Consumers.*

The Entrepreneurs either in Agriculture or in Manufacturing, draw their advances and their profits only from the sale of the fruits of the earth, or of the manufactured commodities.[40]// It is always the wants and the *means*[41] of the Consumer that sets the price of the sale; but the Consumer does not always need the good at the moment of harvest or at the completion of manufacture.// Yet the Entrepreneurs require that their funds should return to them immediately and regularly, in order that they may put them back into their enterprises. The harvest must be followed without interruption by the ploughings and the sowing of the seed. The Workmen of a Manufactory must be kept at work continuously, a fresh set of articles must be begun as soon as the first are finished, materials must be replaced as they are being consumed. It would not be safe to interrupt the workings of a going enterprise, and they could not be taken up again just when desired.// The Entrepreneur, therefore, has the greatest possible interest in having his funds returned promptly by the sale of his crops or commodities. On the other hand, it is in the Consumer's interest to find the things he needs when and where he wants them; it would be extremely inconvenient for him to be obliged to purchase, at the time of the harvest, his provisions for a whole year.// Among the articles that are commonly consumed there are many that require long and expensive labours, labours that cannot be undertaken with profit except on a large quantity of materials, so large that the consumption of a small number of men, or of a limited district, cannot suffice as a market for the products of a single Manufactory even.// Enterprises of this kind must then necessarily be few in number, at a considerable distance from each other, and consequently very far from the homes of the great majority of Consumers. There is no man above extreme poverty who is not in a position to consume several things, which are neither gathered nor fabricated, except in places considerably distant from his home, and no less distant from each other. A man who could only obtain the objects of his consumption by buying them directly from the

[40] Daire and Schelle, following Du Pont, divide the two paragraphs of this section into eight paragraphs at the points indicated.

[41] This phrase, "and the *means*" is probably an addition by Du Pont. See Turgot to Du Pont, 20/2/1770, in Schelle, *Oeuvres*, III, pp. 378–379, where he wrote: "As for your third correction, I had not even noticed it. It is surely very obvious that the ability to pay is a strong consideration in the demand, but I did not believe it necessary to say this in the passage concerned . . . ." (My translation.)

hand of the person who gathers or manufactures them, would either go without a good many things, or spend his life in travel.//

This double interest on the part of both the Producer and the Consumer, of the first to find an opportunity to sell, of the other, to find an opportunity to buy, and yet not to lose precious time in waiting for the purchaser, or in seeking the Seller, must have suggested to a third party to act as intermediaries between the two. This is the purpose of the profession of Merchants, who purchase goods from the hands of the Producer, to store them in warehouses, wither the Consumer goes to get what he needs.// In this way, the Entrepreneur, assured of the sale and the return of his funds, devotes himself undisturbedly and continuously to further production, and the Consumer finds within his reach, and at any moment the things which he needs.

67.[42] *Different orders of Merchants. They all have this in common, that they purchase to sell again; and that their business depends upon advances which must return with profit in order to be once more put into the enterprise.*

From the Huckster who displays her herbs on the market place, to the Shipowner of Nantes or Cadiz who carries on his sales and purchases even to India and America, the profession of a Merchant, or, more correctly, of commerce, is divided into an infinity of branches, and, as it were, levels. One trader confines himself to stocking up several types of commodities which he sells in his shop to all those who present themselves; another goes with certain commodities to a place where they are in demand, to bring from thence in exchange such things as are produced there, and are wanting in the place from whence he departed; one makes his exchanges in his own neighbourhood, and by himself, another by means of Correspondents, and with the services of Carriers whom he pays, and whom he sends and brings from one Province to another, from one Kingdom to another, from Europe to Asia, and from Asia to Europe. One sells his merchandise in small quantities to the several individuals who consume them; another sells only in large quantities at the time to other Merchants who retail them to the Consumers; but all have this in common that they *buy to sell again*, and that their first purchases are an advance which returns to them only in course of time. It must return to them, like those of the Cultivators and Manufacturers, not only within a certain period, to be employed again in new purchases, but also firstly, with a profit equal to the revenue they would be able to acquire with their capital without any labour; secondly, with the wages and the price of their labour, their risk, and their industry. Without the assurance of this return, and of these indispensable profits, no Merchant would engage in commerce, nor could anyone possibly continue therein: it is from this point of view that he

[42] The 1788 edition here repeats the numbering of the previous section, i.e. 66. The remaining sections are then numbered consecutively 67, 68, etc. to 100 instead of 101.

guides himself in his purchases, when he calculates the quantity and the price of the things which he can hope to sell in a certain period. The Retailer learns by experience, and by the outcome of limited trials made cautiously, what are the approximate wants of the Consumers whom he is in a position to supply. The trader learns from his Correspondents about the abundance or scarcity, and the price of merchandise in those different Countries to which his Commerce extends; he directs his speculations accordingly, he sends his goods from the country where they bear a low price to those where they are sold for a higher price, it being understood that the expenses of Carriage enter into the calculation of the advances that have to return to him.[43]

Since Commerce is necessary, and it is impossible to undertake any commerce without advances proportionate to its extent, we see here another method of employing moveable wealth, a new use to which the owner of a mass of values saved and accumulated, of a sum of money, *of a capital*, in short, can put it[44] to obtain his subsistence, and to increase, if he can, his wealth.[45]

68. *The true idea of the circulation of money.*

From what has just been said it can be seen that the cultivation of estates, manufactures of all kinds, and all the branches of trade, depend upon the mass of capitals, or of moveable, accumulated wealth, which, having been first advanced by the Entrepreneurs in each of these different classes of work, must return to them again every year with a steady profit; that is, the capital to be again invested and advanced in the continuation of the same enterprises, and the profits for the more or less comfortable living of the Entrepreneurs. It is this advance and this continual return which constitutes *what ought to be called the circulation of money*; this useful and fruitful circulation, which gives life to all the labour of society, which maintains all the movement and life of the body politic, and which is correctly compared to the circulation of the blood in the animal body. For if, by any disorder whatsoever in the sequence of expenditure of the different classes of society, the Entrepreneurs cease to get back their advances with such profit as they have a right to expect, it is evident that they will be obliged to reduce their enterprises; that the amount of labour, of the consumption of the fruits of the earth, of the production and of the revenue would be equally diminished; that poverty will

[43] In his edition of the *Works* (V, p. 78), Du Pont inserted at this point a long note on mercantile credit and bills of exchange, and on the relationship between credit, saving and investment. This note is not in the *Ephémérides* edition, and is also not reproduced in the Schelle edition.

[44] This point marks another divergence between the text of the 1788 edition and that of the *tirage à part*. The *tirage* and all the other editions read: "... en un mot, peut en faire pour en tirer avantage pour se procurer sa subsistence, & pour augmenter s'il se peut ses richesses". (*Tirage à part*, p. 103.) The 1788 edition (p. 84) leaves out "pour en tirer avantage", and this has been followed for the translation.

[45] This section is one long paragraph in the 1793 translation.

take the place of wealth, and that the common Workman, ceasing to find employment, will fall into the deepest misery.

69. *All enterprises, especially those of manufactures and of commerce, could not fail to have been very limited before the introduction of gold and silver in trade.*

It is hardly necessary to remark that enterprises of all kinds, but especially those of manufactures and still more those of commerce, must have been very limited before the introduction of gold and silver in trade; since it was almost impossible to accumulate large capitals, and even more difficult to multiply and divide payments as much as is necessary to facilitate and increase the exchanges to the extent which a spirited commerce and circulation require. The cultivation of the land alone may support itself to a certain degree, because cattle are the principal object of the advances required therein; moreover, it is probable that there was no other Entrepreneur in agriculture than the Proprietor. As to crafts of all kinds, they must necessarily have languished greatly before the introduction of money; they were limited to the rudest types of occupation, for which the Proprietors furnished the advances by feeding the Workmen and by providing them with materials, or which they caused to be carried on at home by their Domestics.

70. *Capitals being as necessary to all enterprises as labour and industry, the industrious man shares voluntarily the profit of his enterprise with the Capitalist who furnishes him with the funds he needs.*

Since capitals are the indispensable foundation of all lucrative enterprises; since with money we can furnish means for cultivation, establish manufactures, and set up trade, the profits of which accumulated and frugally saved, will become a new capital; since in short, money is the principal means of begetting money,[46] those who, with their industry and love of labour, have no capitals, or do not have sufficient for the enterprise they wish to embark on, have no difficulty in deciding to give up to the owners of such capital or money who are willing to trust it to them, a portion of the profits they expect to receive over and above the return of their advances.

[46] The first part of this section appeared in a shorter form in the *Ephémérides*, in Du Pont's edition of the *Works*, in Daire, and even in Schelle. It was, however, corrected in the *tirage à part*. This shorter version, in translation, reads as follows: "Since capitals are the indispensable foundation of all enterprises, since money is also a principal means of economising from small gains, amassing profits and growing rich, those who . . .". Ashley also gives this shorter version in his section 70. Cf. also Turgot to Caillard, 16/3/1770, where he writes: "If you have my manuscript of *Wealth*, I would like you to send it back to me . . . On page 96 of the December issue of the *Ephémérides* there is a sentence which I find ambiguous and unintelligible. I suspect two or three lines have been left out, and I cannot recollect them." (Schelle, *Oeuvres de Turgot*, III, pp. 407–408.)

Schelle (ibid., II, p. 576, n. a) claims that "Aucune correction n'y avait été faite par Turgot dans le *tirage à part*" but he fails to comment on the change in text between the *tirage* and 1788 editions on the one hand, and the other versions on the other in this context.

71. *Fifth employment of capitals, lending at interest. Nature of the loan.* The Owners of money balance the risk their capital may run, if the enterprise does not succeed, with the advantage of enjoying a definite profit without labour, and regulate themselves thereby to require more or less profit or interest for their money, or to consent to lend it for such interest as the borrower offers. Here another opportunity is open to the Owner of money; lending at interest, or the trade in money. Let no one mistake me here, lending at interest is nothing but a commercial transaction, in which the Lender is the man who sells the use of his money, and the Borrower is a man who buys; precisely as the Proprietor of an estate and a Farmer sell and buy, respectively the use of a piece of land which is let out.[47]// The Latin term for a loan of money at interest expresses it exactly, *usura pecuniae*, a word which, translated into French has become hateful by consequence of false ideas being formed as to the interest of money.[48]

72. *False ideas about the lending at interest.*
The price of the loan is by no means founded, as might be imagined, on the profit the Borrower hopes to make with the capital of which he purchases the use.[49] This price, like the price of every commodity, is determined by the chaffering of seller and buyer; by the balance between the offer and the demand.[50]// People borrow for all kinds of purposes, and with all sorts of motives. One borrows to undertake an enterprise which will make his fortune, another to buy an estate, another to pay a gaming debt, another to make up for the loss of his revenue, of which some accident has deprived him, another to keep himself alive, while waiting for what he can get by his labour; but all these motives which influence the borrower are quite immaterial to the lender. The latter is only concerned with two things; the interest he is to receive, and the safety of his capital. He does not trouble himself about the use the borrower will make of it, any more than the merchant concerns himself with the use the buyer makes of the commodity he sells him.

[47] Daire and Schelle, following Du Pont, divide this paragraph into two at the point indicated.

This sentence also includes a textual difference between the *tirage* and 1788 editions. The *tirage* (pp. 108–109) has: "précisement comme le Propriétaire d'une terre et son Fermier"; the 1788 reads: "précisement comme le Propriétaire d'une terre et un Fermier . . ." (p. 89).

[48] This concludes the second part of the *Reflections* as published in the *Ephémérides*, December 1769. Du Pont inserted the following passage to indicate that the piece was to be continued (see Ashley, p. 66): "The Author here adds some very wise reflections upon the loan at interest, and continues the explanation of his doctrine as to the formation and employment of Capitals. It is with much regret that we find ourselves obliged, by the abundance of the material, to postpone this continuation of his Work to our next Volume, in which we shall give the conclusion of it."

[49] Cf. with section 74, below, p. 80.

[50] Daire and Schelle, following Du Pont, divide this paragraph into two at the point indicated.

73. *Errors of the Schoolmen refuted.*[51]

It is for want of having examined the lending at interest in its true light, that moralists, more dogmatic than enlightened, have endeavoured to have it looked upon as a crime, The scholastic Theologians have concluded from the fact that money does not produce anything by itself that it was unjust to exact interest from money placed on loan. Full of their prejudices, they have believed their doctrine was sanctioned by this passage from the Gospel, *mutuum date nihil inde sperantes.*[52]// Those Theologians who have adopted more reasonable principles on the subject of interest, have endured the harshest reproaches from Writers of the opposite party.

Nevertheless, it needs but a little reflection to realise the lack of depth in the pretexts which have been used to condemn the taking of interest. A loan is a reciprocal contract, free between the two parties, which they make only because it is advantageous to them. It is evident that, if the lender finds it to his advantage to receive something as the hire for his money, the borrower is no less interested in finding the money he needs, since he decides to borrow and to pay the hire of this money. Now on what principle can a crime be discovered in a contract advantageous to two parties, with which both parties are satisfied, and which certainly does no injury to anyone else? To say that the lender takes advantage of the borrower's need of money to demand interest, is as absurd an argument as saying that a baker who demands money for the bread he sells, takes advantage of the buyer's need for bread. If in this latter case, the money is an equivalent for the bread the buyer receives, the money which the borrower receives today is equally an equivalent of the capital and interest he promises to return at the end of a certain time; for, in short, it is an advantage for the borrower to have, during the interval, the use of the money he needs, and it is a disadvantage to the lender to be deprived of it. This disadvantage is capable of being estimated, and is estimated: the *interest* is the price of it. This price ought to be higher if the lender runs the risk of losing his capital by the insolvency of the borrower. The bargain therefore is perfectly equal on both sides, and consequently just and honest. Money

[51] This paragraph does not appear in Du Pont, *Oeuvres* V, or Daire, since Turgot had asked Du Pont to remove the theological sections on interest, which were to be the subject of another paper. See Turgot to Du Pont, 12/1/1770, in Schelle, *Oeuvres*, III, p. 371. In his edition of the *Works*, Du Pont therefore deleted both sections 73 and 75, but not in the *tirage à part* made for Turgot.

When the matter of a German translation came up in 1774, Turgot asked Caillard to make sure that section 75 was omitted, since it "interrupts the line of the argument". See Turgot to Caillard, 5/5/1774, in Schelle, *Oeuvres*, III, pp. 675–676. For this reason, only section 75 has been omitted by Schelle.

Since this translation follows the 1788 edition, I have left both sections 73 and 75 in the text. This also maintains the 101 sections which Turgot had originally intended.

[52] I.e. Luke 6:35, which in the authorised standard version reads as follows: "and lend, hoping for nothing again."

Schelle divides this paragraph into two at this point.

considered as a physical substance, as a mass of metal, does not produce anything; but money employed in advances in enterprises of agriculture, manufactured, commerce, procures a definite profit; with money an estate can be purchased, and a revenue procured thereby: the person, therefore, who lends his money, does not only give up the barren possession of such money, but deprives himself of the profit or the revenue he would have been able to procure by it, and the interest which indemnifies him for this loss cannot be looked upon as unjust. The Schoolmen, compelled to acknowledge the justice of these considerations, have allowed that interest may be taken, provided the capital is alienated, that is, provided the lender renounced his right to demand the repayment of his money in a certain time, and leave the borrower free to keep it as long as he wished while paying only interest. The reason for this toleration was that then it is no longer a loan, for which an interest is taken, but a rent which is purchased with a sum of money, just as an estate is purchased. This was a petty subterfuge to which they had recourse in order to concede the absolute necessity of loans in the course of transactions of Society, without clearly acknowledging the falsity of the principles upon which they had condemned it. But this condition of the alienation of capital is not an advantage to the borrower, who remains no less burdened with the debt until he has repaid this capital, and whose property is always destined as security for this capital. It is even a disadvantage, as he finds it more difficult to borrow money when he needs it; for persons who would willingly consent to lend for a year or two a sum of money which they had destined for the purchase of an estate, would not lend it for an indefinite period. Moreover, if it is permissible to sell money for a perpetual rent, why would it not be permissible to let it for some years in return for a rent which only continues for that number of years? If a rent of *a thousand francs* per year is equivalent to the sum of twenty thousand francs in the case of a man who keeps this sum in perpetuity, a thousand francs will be the amount for the possession of that sum for one year.

74. *True foundation of the interest of money.*

A man then may let out his money as lawfully as he may sell it; and the owner of money may do either one or the other, not only because money is equivalent to a revenue, and a means of procuring a revenue, not only because the lender loses, during the time of the loan, the revenue he might have procured by it, not only because he risks his capital, not only because the borrower can employ it in advantageous acquisition, or in enterprises from which he may draw large profits; the Owner of money may lawfully draw the interest of it by a more general and decisive principle. Even if all the foregoing were not the case, he would none the less have the right to require an interest for his loan simply because the money is his property. Since it is his property he is free to keep it, nothing obliges him to lend; if then he does lend, he may attach conditions to the loan as he sees fit. In this he does no injury to the borrower, since the latter agrees to the conditions, and has no right of any kind over the sum lent. The profit that may be procured by the use of money is doubtedlessly one of the commonest motives influencing the borrower to borrow on interest; it is one of the means which facilitates his payment of the interest, but this is by no means what gives the lender the right to require it;[53] it is enough for him that his money is his own, and this right is inseparable from property. He who buys bread does it for his support, but the right the Baker has to ask a price is quite independent of the use of the bread; it is the same right he would have to sell him stones, a right founded on this principle alone, that the bread is his own, and no one has any right to force him to give it for nothing.[54]

75. *Reply to an objection.*[55]
This reflection makes us realise how false and how distant from the meaning of the Gospel, is the application which the dogmatists made of the passage *mutuum date nihil inde sperantes* (lend without expecting gain).[56] The passage is clear, as interpreted by moderate and reasonable Theologians, as a precept of charity. All mankind are bound to assist one another; a rich man who would see his fellow creature in distress, and who instead of providing for his wants, would sell him what he needed would be equally deficient in the duties of Christianity and those of humanity. In such circumstances, charity does not only require us to lend without interest, she orders us to lend, and even to give if necessary. To convert the precept of charity into a precept of rigorous justice, is equally repugnant to reason, and to the sense of the text. Those whom I attack here do not claim that it is a duty of (Christian) justice to lend their money; they must then agree that the first words of the passage, *mutuum date*, contain only a precept of charity; now I ask why they seek to extend the close of the passage into an obligation of (Christian) justice.[57] What, shall the lending itself not be a strict precept, and shall only its accessory, the condition of the loan, be made one! This is in effect what men would have been told: "You are free to lend or not to lend, but if you do lend, take care you do not require any interest for your money, and even when a Merchant shall require a loan of you for an enterprise from which he hopes to make large profits, it will be a crime for you to accept the interest he offers

[53] Cf. with section 72 above, p. 77.

[54] This bread example was given previously in section 73, above p. 78. It also occurs in the 'Paper on the Lending of Money', below, p. 155.

[55] This section is omitted by Du Pont, by Daire and by Schelle in their editions of Turgot's works for reasons given in note 51 above.

[56] Luke 6:35.

[57] Turgot here contrasts the loose interpretation of Christian charity of the first part of the Gospel quotation, with the strict prohibition of charging interest as an interpretation of the second part.

you; you must absolutely either lend him gratuitously, or not lend to him at all. You have indeed one method of making interest lawful, that is to lend your capital for an indefinite term, and to give up the right of demanding its repayment allowing your debtor to do so when he pleases or when he can. If you find any inconvenience on the score of security, or if you foresee you will need your money in a certain number of years, you have no other course to take but not to lend: it will be better to cause this Merchant to miss a precious opportunity, than to commit a sin in helping him to take advantage of it." This is what has been seen in these five words; *mutuum date nihil inde sperantes*, when they have been read with the prejudices created by a false metaphysics.[58]// Everyone who reads this text without prejudice, will soon find its real meaning; that is, "*as men, as Christians, you are all brothers, all friends: act towards each other as brethren and friends; help each other in your necessities; let your purses be open to one another, and do not sell the assistance which you owe each other by requiring interest on a loan which charity commands you to make.*" This is the true sense of the passage in question. The obligation to lend without interest, and that to lend, are evidently connected together; they are of the same order, and both inculcate a duty of charity, and not a precept of rigorous justice, applicable to all cases of lending.

76. *The rate of interest ought to be determined just like that of all commodities, by nothing but the course of trade.*

I have already said that the price of money is regulated like that of all other commodities, by the balance of offer and demand: thus, when there are many borrowers who need money, the interest of money becomes higher; when there are many owners who are ready to lend, it falls. It is therefore a further mistake to believe that the interest of money in trade ought to be fixed by the laws of Princes. It is a current price, determined like that of all other commodities. This price varies a little according to the greater or less security which the lender has of not losing his capital; but on equal security, it ought to rise and fall in proportion to the abundance and the need, and the law no more ought to fix the rate of interest than it ought to regulate the price of any other commodity which circulates in commerce.

77. *Money has two different valuations in commerce. One expresses the quantity of money we give to procure different sorts of commodities; the other expresses the relation a sum of money has, to the interest it will procure in accordance with the course of trade.*

It appears from this explanation of the manner in which money is either sold or let out for an annual interest, that there are two ways of valuing money in

[58] The 1793 English translation divides this paragraph into two at this point.

commerce.[59]// In buying and selling, a certain weight of silver represents a certain quantity of value, or of commodities of every kind; for example, one ounce of silver is the equivalent of a certain quantity of corn, or of a certain number of days' labour.// In lending, and in the trade in money, a capital is the equivalent of a rent equal to a fixed portion of that capital; and conversely, an annual rent represents a capital equal to the amount of that rent repeated a certain number of times, according as the interest is at a higher or lower rate.[60]

78. *These two valuations are independent of each other, and are governed by quite different principles.*

These two different evaluations have much less connection, and depend much less on each other than one would be tempted to believe at first sight.[61]// Money may be very common in ordinary commerce, may have a very low value, answer to a very small quantity of commodities, and the interest of money may at the same time be very high.//

Assume that there are *one million ounces of silver* in currency circulating in commerce, and that *an ounce of silver* is given in the market for a bushel of corn; suppose that there is brought into the State, in some manner or other, a *second million* ounces of silver, and that this increase is distributed to every purse in the same proportion as the first million, so that he who had two ounces before, now has four. The silver considered as a quantity of metal will certainly diminish in price, or, which is the same thing, commodities will be paid for more dearly, and it becomes necessary, in order to procure the same measure of corn which was obtained with one ounce of silver, to give a good deal more silver, and perhaps *two ounces* instead of *one*.// But it does not by any means follow from this that the interest of money falls, if all this money is carried to the market and employed in the current expenses of those who possess it, as by supposition the first million ounces were; for the interest of money falls only when there is more money to be lent, in proportion to the wants of the borrowers, than there was before.// Now the money which is carried to market is not for lending; it is the money which is placed in reserve, the accumulated capitals, that are lent, and so far from the increase of the money in the market, or the diminution of its price in relation to commodities in the ordinary course of trade infallibly, and as an immediate consequence bringing about a decrease in the interest of money, it may, on the contrary, happen that the very cause which increases the money in the market, and

[59] Daire and Schelle, following Du Pont, divide this paragraph into three at the points indicated.

[60] Turgot here seems to indicate the relationship between capital and income, capital value being income capitalised by the current rate of interest. See his remarks on the price of land, above sections 56–57, pp. 67–68; below section 91, pp. 88–89.

[61] Daire and Schelle, following Du Pont, divide these four paragraphs into seven at the points indicated.

which increases the price of other commodities by lowering the price of money, is precisely that which increases the hire of money, or the rate of interest.//

Indeed, suppose for a moment that all the wealthy people in a nation, instead of saving from their revenues or from their annual profits, spend the whole of it;[62] suppose that, not satisfied with spending their revenue, they spend their capital; suppose that a man who has a hundred thousand francs in money, instead of employing them in a profitable manner, or lending them, consumes them piecemeal in foolish expenses; it is evident that on the one hand there will be more money employed in current purchases, in satisfying the wants and humours of every individual, and that consequently its price will fall; on the other hand there will certainly be much less money to lend, and, as many people will ruin themselves, there will probably also be more borrowers. The interest of money will consequently increase, while money itself will become common in circulation, and fall in price, and precisely for the same reason.//

We shall cease to be surprised at this apparently peculiar result, if we consider that the money brought into the market for the purchase of corn, is that which is daily spent to satisfy one's needs, and that which is offered on loan, is precisely that which is saved from one's daily expenditure to be laid by and formed into capitals.

79. *In the valuation of money with regard to commodities, it is the money considered as metal that is the subject of the estimate. In the evaluation of the penny of money,[63] it is the use of the money for a definite time that is the subject of the estimate.*

In the market a measure of corn is equivalent to a certain weight of silver; it is a quantity of silver that is purchased with the commodity; it is this quantity which is valued and compared with other different values. In a loan on interest, the object of the valuation is the use of a certain quantity of value during a certain time. It is no longer the comparison of a quantity of silver with a quantity of corn; it is now a quantity of values which is compared with a definite portion of itself, which becomes the price of the use of this quantity for a certain time. Let *twenty thousand ounces* of silver be equivalent in the market to *twenty thousand measures of corn*, or only to *ten thousand*, the use

[62] At this point, Du Pont added a long note on the relationship between productive, unproductive spending and the formation of capitals, as well as more general considerations on saving, spending, investing and hoarding. This note was strongly attacked by Turgot in a letter to Du Pont, 23/3/1770, in Schelle, *Oeuvres*, III, pp. 383–384 in which he accused Du Pont of "confusing the use of Capital with the formation of Capital. Calling expenses receipts, and assuming that saving and hoarding are synonymous words . . ." (my translation).

Du Pont remained unconvinced and repeated this, and similar notes in his edition of Turgot's *Works*. See Du Pont, *Oeuvres*, V, p. 103, n. 4, p. 104, n. 5.

[63] See note 33, above p. 68.

of those twenty thousand ounces of silver for a year will none the less be worth in the money market the *twentieth* part of the principal sum, or *one thousand ounces* of silver, if interest is at the twentieth penny.[64]

80. *The price of interest depends directly on the relation between the demand of the borrowers and the offer of the lenders, and this relation depends chiefly on the quantity of moveable wealth accumulated by the saving of revenues and of annual products to form capitals, whether these capitals exist in money or in any other kind of effects having a value in commerce.*

The price of silver in the market is relative only to the quantity of this metal used in current exchanges; but the rate of interest is relative to the quantity of values accumulated and laid by to form capitals. It does not matter whether these values are in metal or other effects, provided these effects are easily convertible into money.[65]// It is far from being the case, that the mass of metal existing in a State is as large as the amount of the values lent on interest in the course of a year; but all the capitals, in furniture, merchandise, tools and cattle, take the place of silver and represent it. A paper signed by a man who is known to be worth a *hundred thousand francs*, and who promises to pay a *hundred thousand francs* at a certain date, is worth a hundred thousand francs until that date: all the capitals of the man who has signed this note are answerable for the payment of it, whatever the nature of the effects he has in his possession, provided they have a value of a *hundred thousand francs*.// It is not therefore the quantity of silver existing as metal which causes the rate of interest to rise or fall, or which brings more money into the market to be lent; it is simply the sum of capitals to be found in commerce, that is to say, the current sum of moveable values of every kind, accumulated, saved gradually out of the revenues and profits, to be employed by the owner to procure himself new profits and new revenues. It is these accumulated savings which are offered to the borrowers, and the more there are of them, the lower the interest of money will be, at least if the number of borrowers is not augmented in proportion.

81. *The spirit of thrift in a nation continually increases the amount of capitals, luxury continually tends to destroy them.*

The spirit of thrift in a nation continually tends to increase the amount of the capitals, to increase the number of lenders, and to diminish that of borrowers. The habit of luxury has precisely the opposite effect, and by what has already been remarked on the use of capitals in all enterprises, whether of agriculture,

[64] I.e. five per cent.

[65] Daire and Schelle, following Du Pont, divide this paragraph into three at the points indicated.

manufacture, or commerce, we may judge if luxury enriches a nation, or impoverishes it.

82. *The fall in the rate of interest proves that thrift generally has prevailed over luxury in Europe.*

Since the interest of money has been constantly diminishing in Europe for several centuries, we must conclude that the spirit of thrift has been more general than the spirit of luxury. It is only people already rich who give themselves up to luxury, and among the rich, those who are sensible confine their expenses to their revenues, and are very careful not to touch their capitals. Those who wish to become rich are far more numerous in a nation than those who are already so. Now, in the present state of things, as all land is occupied, there is but one way to become rich, it is either to possess, or to procure in some way, a revenue or an annual profit above what is absolutely necessary for subsistence, and to reserve this surplus every year so as to form a capital, by means of which a person may obtain an increase in revenue or annual profit, which may again be saved and converted into capital. There are consequently a great many people interested and occupied in accumulating capitals.

83. *Recapitulation of the five different methods of employing capitals.*

I have reckoned five different methods of employing capitals, or of profitably investing them.

The first is to buy a landed estate, which brings in a definite revenue.

The second is to invest money in agricultural enterprises by taking a lease of land, the produce of which ought to yield, over and above the price of the lease, the interest on the advances, and the price of the labour of the man who devotes both his wealth and his toil to its cultivation.

The third is to invest a capital in industrial and manufacturing enterprises.

The fourth is to invest it in commercial enterprises.

And the fifth method is to lend it to those who need it, in return for an annual interest.

84. *The influence which the different methods of employing capitals have on each other.*

It is evident that the annual product which can be drawn from capitals invested in these different employments, are influenced by each other, and are all related to the current rate of the interest of money.

85. *Money invested in land is bound to bring the least.*

The person who invests his money in the purchase of an estate, leased to a solvent Tenant, procures himself a revenue which entails very little trouble, and which he can spend in the most agreeable manner, by giving free play to all his tastes. There is the additional advantage in the purchase of this kind of property over that of any other, that the possession of it is more secure against all kinds of accidents.[66] We must therefore purchase an equal revenue in land at a higher price, or content ourselves with a less revenue for an equal capital.

86. *Money placed on loan ought to bring a little more than the revenue of landed estates acquired with an equal capital.*

The person who lends money on interest, enjoys it even more peaceably and freely than the possessor of land, but the insolvency of his debtor may cause him to lose his capital.[67]// He will not therefore content himself with an interest equal to the revenue of the land which he might buy with the same capital.// The investment of money lent must consequently be larger than the revenue of an estate purchased with the same capital; for if the lender found an estate for sale with a revenue equal to the interest, he would prefer this way of using it.[68]

87. *Money invested in agricultural, manufacturing or commercial enterprises, is bound to bring more than the interest of money on loan.*

For a like reason, money employed in agriculture, in industry or in commerce, ought to produce a more considerable profit than the revenue of the same capital employed in the purchase of estates, or the interest of money placed on loan; for since these employments require, in addition to the capital advanced, much care and labour, if they were not more lucrative, it would be more advantageous to secure an equal revenue which might be enjoyed without having to do anything. It is necessary then, that, besides the interest of the capital, the entrepreneur should draw every year a profit to recompense him for his care, his labour, his talents and his risks, and to furnish him in addition that with which he may replace the annual wear and tear of his advances, which he is obliged from the very first to convert into effects which are liable to deterioration and which are, moreover, exposed to all kinds of accidents.

[66] There is a slight textual alteration at this point. In the editions of Du Pont, Daire and Schelle, this sentence reads: "There is the additional advantage that land is, of all forms of property, that whereof the possession is most secured against any kind of accident." The next sentence does not appear in these editions.

[67] Daire and Schelle, following Du Pont, divide this paragraph into three at the points indicated.

[68] Du Pont added a note to this section at this point which stated that there was no legal obligation for the rate of interest to be greater than the rate of return to land. (See *Oeuvres*, V, p. 108, n. 6.)

88. *However, the products of these different employments are limited by each other, and notwithstanding their inequality, preserve a kind of equilibrium.*

The different uses of the capitals produce, therefore, very unequal products; but this inequality does not prevent them from having a reciprocal influence on each other, nor from establishing a kind of equilibrium amongst themselves, like that between two liquids of unequal gravity, which come into contact with each other at the base of an inverted siphon, of which they fill the two branches; they will not be on a level, but the height of the one cannot increase without the other also rising in the opposite branch.

Suppose that suddenly, a very great number of proprietors of estates wish to sell them: it is obvious that the price of estates will fall, and that with a less sum a larger revenue may be acquired; this cannot happen without the interest of money rising, for the owners of money would choose rather to buy estates, than to lend at an interest which was no higher than the revenues of the lands they could purchase. If, then, the borrowers want to have money, they will be forced to pay a greater rate. If the interest of money becomes higher, people will prefer lending it to using it in a more toilsome and hazardous fashion in enterprises of agriculture, industry and commerce, and they will only enter those enterprises which will produce, besides the wages of their labour, a profit much greater than the rate of interest on money placed on loan. In short, as soon as the profits resulting from an employment of money, whatever it may be, increase or diminish, capitals turn in that direction or withdraw from other employments, or withdraw and turn towards other employments; and this necessarily alters in each of these employments, the relation between the capital and the annual product. Generally, money invested in landed property does not bring in as much as money placed on loan; and money placed on loan brings less than money employed in enterprises involving labour; but whatever be the way in which money is employed, its product cannot increase or decrease without all the other employments experiencing a proportionate increase or decrease.

89. *The current interest of money is the thermometer by which the abundance or scarcity of capitals may be judged; it is the measure of the extent to which Nation can expand its enterprises of agriculture, manufacture and commerce.*

Thus the current interest of money placed on loan may be considered as a kind of thermometer of the abundance or scarcity of capitals in a Nation, and of the extent of the enterprises of every kind on which she may embark: it is evident that the lower the interest of money is, the higher is the value of landed estates. A man that has fifty thousand livres in rent, has a property worth only one million, if estates are sold at the twentieth penny; he has two million, if land is sold at the fortieth penny.[69]// If the interest is at five per cent all uncleared land whose produce would not yield five per cent over and above the replacement of the advances, and the recompense of the care of the Cultivator, would remain uncultivated. No manufacture, no commerce will exist if they will not bring in five per cent over and above the wages of the Entrepreneur's exertions and risks.// If there is a neighbouring Nation in which the interest stands only at two per cent, it will not only carry on all the branches of commerce, from which the nation where interest is at five per cent finds itself excluded, but moreover, as its manufacturers and merchants can content themselves with a lower profit, they will place their goods on all markets at a much lower price, and will draw to themselves the almost exclusive trade in all those commodities of which the trade is not retained (by exceptional circumstances or by the excessive cost of carriage), for the commerce of the nation where money is worth five per cent.

90. *Influence of the rate of interest of money on all lucrative enterprises.* The price of interest may be looked upon as a kind of level, beneath which all labour, agriculture, industry and commerce come to an end. It is like a sea spread over a vast area; the summits of the mounts rise above the waters, and form fertile and cultivated islands. If this sea happens to flow back, in proportion as it descends, first the slopes, then the plains and valleys appear, and are covered with productions of every kind. It is enough that the water rises or falls a foot to inundate immense tracts, or throw them open to cultivation. It is the abundance of capitals which animates all enterprises, and the low interest of money is at the same time the effect and the index of the abundance of capitals.

91. *The total Wealth of a nation consists: firstly, in the net revenue of all landed estates, multiplied by the rate at which land is sold; secondly, in the sum of all moveable wealth existing in the nation.*

Landed estates are equivalent to a capital equal to their revenue multiplied by the current penny at which lands are sold. Thus if we add the revenue of all lands, that is, the net revenue they render to the proprietors, and to all those that share in the property, such as the Lord that levies a rent, the Curate that levies the tithe, the Sovereign that levies the tax; if, I say, we should add all these sums, and multiply them by the rate at which lands are sold, we would have the sum of all the wealth of a Nation in landed estates.[70]// To obtain the whole of a Nation's wealth, the moveable wealth ought to be added, which consist in the sum of capitals employed in enterprises of agriculture, industry

[69] Daire and Schelle, following Du Pont, divide this paragraph into three at the points indicated.

[70] Daire and Schelle, following Du Pont, start a new paragraph at this point.

and commerce,[71] which never come out of them (because) all advances, in any kind of enterprise, must continually return to the entrepreneurs, to be reinvested in the enterprises, which could not continue without them.[72]// It would be a very gross error to confound the immense mass of moveable wealth with the mass of money that exists in a State; the latter is but a very small thing in comparison. To be convinced of this, we need only remember the immense quantity of cattle, utensils and seed which constitute the advances of Agriculture; of raw materials, tools, furniture and merchandise of every kind which fill the workhouses, shops, and warehouses of all Manufacturers, Merchants and Traders,[73] and it will be plain that in the totality of wealth, both landed or moveable, of a Nation, the specie makes but a very small part. But as all wealth and money are continually exchangeable, they all represent money, and money represents them all.

92. *The sum of capitals on loan cannot be included in this without double counting.*

The amount of capitals which are placed on loan must not be included in the calculation of the wealth of the Nation; for these capitals can only have been lent either to Proprietors of estates, or to entrepreneurs who invest them in their enterprises, since only these two kinds of people can answer for that capital, and pay the interest; a sum of money lent to people who have neither estate nor industry, would be a dead capital, and not an active one. If the proprietor of an estate of four hundred thousand francs borrows a hundred thousand,[74] his land is charged with a rent that diminishes his revenue in a like proportion, and if he should sell his property, out of the four hundred thousand francs he would receive, a hundred thousand would belong to the creditor. The capital of the lender would, therefore, in the calculation of existing wealth, be a repetition of an equal part of the value of the land. The land is always worth four hundred thousand francs: when the proprietor borrows a hundred thousand francs, this does not make it five hundred thousand francs; it only brings about that out of the four hundred thousand francs, a hundred thousand belong to the lender and that there remains no more than three hundred thousand francs for the borrower.

[71] In the *Ephémérides*, January 1770, p. 153, Du Pont inserted a note at this point on another type of division of national wealth, that is, into *richesses stables et durables* or fixed capital including landed property, and *richesses renaissantes* or the annually reproduced expenses of production. This note was presumably intended to connect Turgot's terminology with that of the *Tableau économique*.

[72] Schelle starts a new paragraph at this point.

[73] In the editions of Du Pont, Daire and Schelle, there is a slight textual variation in the last clause. Their text, in translation, reads: "... of materials, tools, furniture of all sorts which constitute the stocks of the manufacturers, and which fill the warehouses of all merchants and all those engaged in trade".

[74] The French, "en emprunte cent" is extended to "en emprunte cent mille" in Schelle only. Ashley mistranslates the first phrase as "borrows a hundred" instead of "borrows a hundred thousand" since the "mille" is clearly understood in the French text.

The same double counting would take place if the total sum of capitals were to include the money lent to an entrepreneur to be employed in the advances of his enterprise; for this loan does not increase the total sum of advances necessary for that enterprise. It only brings about that that sum, and the part of the profits which represent its interest, belong to the lender. Whether a merchant employs ten thousand francs of his own property in his trade and takes the whole profit, or whether he has borrowed these ten thousand francs from another to whom he pays interest, contenting himself with the surplus of the profit, and the wages of his industry, there are never more than ten thousand francs.

But if we cannot include in the calculation of the wealth of a nation the capital which corresponds to the interest of money placed on loan without counting it twice over, we ought to include the other kinds of moveable property, which, though they were originally an object of expenditure, and do not bear any profit, become, however, by their durability, a true capital which is continually accumulated, and which, when required, may be exchanged for money, making, as it were, a reserve fund which may return into commerce and, when desired, make up for the loss of other capitals. This includes the furniture of every kind, jewels, plate, paintings, statues, ready money shut up in the chests of misers: all these things have a value, and the sum of all these values may reach a considerable amount in rich nations. Yet be it considerable or not, it is still true that it must be added to the sum of the prices of landed estates, and to that of the advances circulating in enterprises of every kind in order to make up the sum total of the wealth of a nation. Besides it is superfluous to say that, though it is easy to define, as has just been done, of what consists the sum of the wealth of a nation, it is probably impossible to discover to how much it amounts, unless some rule be found to determine the proportion of the total commerce of a nation, to the revenue of its land: a thing perhaps feasible, but which has not yet been executed in such a manner as to dispel all doubts.

93. *In which of the three classes of Society the Capitalists who are lenders of money are to be included.*

Let us now see how what we have just discussed about the different ways of employing capitals, agrees with what we have established before about the division of all the members of Society into three classes, the productive class or that of cultivators, the industrial or commercial class, and the disposable class, or that of proprietors.

94. *The capitalist lender of money belongs to the disposable class as far as his person is concerned.*

We have seen that every rich man is necessarily owner either of a capital in moveable wealth, or of an estate in land equivalent to a capital. Every landed estate is the equivalent of a capital; consequently every proprietor is a capitalist, but not every capitalist is a proprietor of a landed estate; and the owner of a moveable capital may choose whether to use it in acquiring a landed estate, or to invest it in the enterprises of the agricultural class, or the industrial class. The capitalist who has become an entrepreneur in agriculture or industry, is no more of the disposable class either as regards himself or his profits, than the mere workmen in those two classes; they are both set aside for the carrying on of their enterprises. The capitalist who confines himself to lending money, lends it either to a proprietor, or to an entrepreneur. If he lends it to a proprietor, he seems to belong to the class of proprietors, and he becomes part-owner of the property; the revenue of the land is assigned to the payment of the interest of his loan, the value of the estate is pledged to provide security for his capital to its full amount.[75]// If the lender of money has lent to an entrepreneur, it is certain that his person belongs to the disposable class; but his capital is sunk in the advances of the enterprise, and cannot be withdrawn without injuring the enterprise, unless it is replaced by a capital of equal value.

95. *The interest drawn by the lender of money is disposable so far as the use he can make of it is concerned.*

Indeed, the interest he draws from that capital seems to be disposable, since the entrepreneur and the enterprise can do without it; and it seems also that we may conclude from this, that in the profits of the two working classes, there is a disposable portion, namely, that which corresponds to the interest of the advances, calculated at the current rate of interest of money placed on loan. It appears also that this conclusion is in conflict with what we have said before, that only the class of proprietors had a revenue properly so called, a disposable revenue, and every member of the two other classes had only wages and profits. This deserves some explanation.[76]// If we consider the thousand *écus* received annually by a man who has lent sixty thousand francs to a merchant, in relation to the use he may make of them, it cannot be doubted that they are absolutly disposable, since the enterprise can do without them.

96. *The interest of the money is not disposable in this sense, that the State can, without harm, appropriate part of it for its wants.*

But it does not follow that they are disposable in the sense that the State can, with impunity, appropriate part of them for the public wants. Those thousand *écus* are not a return which agriculture or commerce bestows gratuitiously on the person who has made the advances, it is the price and the condition of

[75] The 1793 translation divides this paragraph into two at this point.

[76] Daire and Schelle, following Du Pont, divide this paragraph into two at the point indicated.

these advances, without which the enterprise could not be carried on. If this return is diminished, the capitalist will withdraw his money, and the enterprise will come to an end. This return ought then to be inviolable, and enjoy an entire immunity, because it is the price of an advance made for an enterprise, without which the enterprise could not go on. To encroach upon it, would cause an augmentation in the price of advances in all enterprises, and consequently, diminish the enterprises themselves, that is, agriculture, industry and commerce.

This answer should lead us to conclude, that if we said that the capitalist who had lent money to a proprietor, *appeared* to belong to the class of proprietors, this *appearance* had something equivocal about it which needed to be unravelled.[77]// In fact, the strict truth is that the interest of his money is no more disposable, that is, is no more capable of being encroached upon, than the money lent to the entrepreneurs in agriculture, and commerce. This interest is equally the price of a free agreement, and cannot be encroached upon without altering or changing the price of the loan;[78]// now, it matters little to whom the loan has been made; if the price changes or increases for the proprietor of lands, it will also change or increase for the cultivator, the manufacturer, and the merchant. In short, the capitalist lender of money ought to be considered as a dealer in a commodity absolutely necessary for the production of wealth, which cannot be at too low a price. It is as unreasonable to burden this commerce with a tax as it would be to lay a tax on a dunghill which serves to manure the land. Let us conclude from this, that the person who lends money belongs properly to the disposable class as to his person, because he has nothing to do; but not as to the nature of his wealth, whether the interest of his money is paid by the proprietor of land, out of a portion of his revenue, or whether it is paid by an entrepreneur, out of the part of his profits designed to pay the interest of his advances.

97. *Objection.*

It will undoubtedly be replied, that the capitalist may indifferently either lend his money, or employ it in the purchase of an estate; that in either case he draws only an equal price for his money, and that, whichever way he has employed it, he ought none the less to contribute to the public charges.

[77] Daire and Schelle, following Du Pont, divide this paragraph into two at the point indicated.

There is, at the beginning of this sentence, also a minor textual difference between the *tirage à part* and the 1788 edition on the one hand, and all the other editions.

In the *tirage* (p. 155) and the 1788 edition (p. 128) the first part of this sentence reads: "Cette réponse nous doit faire conclure que, si nous avons dit que le capitaliste . . .". In the *Ephémérides*, and all other editions, this becomes: "Ceci doit faire comprendre ce que nous avons dit que le capitaliste . . .".

The motivation for this minor change appears to be style rather than anything else.

[78] Only the 1793 translation breaks this paragraph into two at this point.

98. *Answer to the objection.*

In the first place, I answer that in fact, when the capitalist has purchased an estate, the revenue is the equivalent to him of what he would have drawn from his money by lending it; but there is this essential difference with respect to the State, that the price which he gives for his land does not contribute in any respect to the revenue it produces. It would not have yielded a smaller revenue, if he had not purchased it. The revenue, as we have already explained, consists in what the land produces, beyond the wages of the cultivators, their profits, and the interest of their advances. It is not the same with the interest of a loan; it is the very condition of the loan, the price of the advance, without which neither the revenue nor the profits which serve to pay it, would exist.

I answer, in the second place, that if the lands alone were burdened with the contribution to the public charges, as soon as that contribution would be regulated, the capitalist who purchased these lands would not reckon in the interest of his money that part of the revenue which is set aside for this contribution; just as a man who now buys an estate, does not buy the tithe which the Curate receives, but only the revenue which remains after the tithe is deducted.[79]

99. *There exists no truly disposable revenue in a state except the net product of land.*

We see by what has been said, that the interest of money lent is taken from the revenue of lands, or from the profits of agricultural, industrial and commercial enterprises.[80]// But we have already shown that these profits themselves were only a part of the produce of lands; that the produce of land is divided into two portions; that the one was designed for the wages of the cultivator, for his profits, for the return and interest of his advances; and that the other was the share of the proprietor, or the revenue which the proprietor expended at his pleasure, and from which he contributed to the general expenses of the State.[81]// We have demonstrated, that what the other classes of Society received, was merely the wages and profits paid either by the proprietor from his revenue, or by the agents of the productive class from the

[79] A slight textual change between editions should be noted here. In Du Pont (*Oeuvres* V p. 125) and in Daire, the last part of this sentence reads in translation: "... does not buy the tithe which the Curate receives, or even the tax, as far as it is known, but only the revenue which remains after the tithe and tax are deducted".

In his edition of the works, but not in the *Ephémérides*, Du Pont inserted a note at the end of this section in which he commented on the truth of the physiocratic doctrine of taxation.

[80] Daire and Schelle, following Du Pont, divide this paragraph into three at the points indicated.

[81] Along with Daire, Schelle and Du Pont, the 1793 translation also starts a new paragraph at this point.

part destined for their needs, and which they are obliged to purchase from the industrial class. Whether these profits be distributed in wages to the workmen, in profits to entrepreneurs, or in interest on advances, they do not change in their nature, and do not increase the sum of the revenue produced by the productive class over and above the price of its labour, in which the industrial class shares only to the extent of the price of its labour.

It therefore remains true that there is no revenue save the net produce of land, and that all other annual profit is paid, either by that revenue, or forms part of the expenditure that serves to produce the revenue.

100. *The land has also furnished the whole amount of moveable wealth, or capitals in existence, which are formed only by part of its produce being saved every year.*

Not only is it true that there does not exist, nor can exist, any other revenue than the net product of land, but it is also the earth that has furnished all capitals that form the total of all the advances of agriculture and commerce. It has produced, without cultivation, the first rude advances indispensable to the earliest labours; all the rest are the accumulated fruits of the thrift of successive ages since men began to cultivate the earth. This thrift undoubtedly takes place not only out of the revenues of proprietors, but also out of the profits of all the members of the working classes. It is even generally true, that, although the proprietors have a greater surplus, they save less; for, as they have more leisure, they have more wants, and more passions; they regard themselves as more assured of their fortune; and think more about enjoying it contentedly, than about increasing it: luxury is their lot. The wage-receivers, and especially the entrepreneurs of the other classes, receiving profits proportionate to their advances, talents and activity, have, though they do not possess a revenue properly so called, a surplus beyond their subsistence; and almost all of them, devoted as they are to their enterprises, and occupied with increasing their fortune, removed by their labour from amusements and expensive passions, save all their surplus, to invest it again in their enterprise, and to increase it. Most of the entrepreneurs in agriculture borrow little, and they almost all invest only their own funds. The entrepreneurs of other employments, who want to consolidate their fortunes, strive to attain the same position, and, unless they have great ability.[82] those who carry on their enterprises on borrowed funds, run great risk of failing. But, although capitals are formed in part by saving from the profits of the working classes, yet, as those profits always come from the earth, since they are all paid, either from the revenue, or from the expenses that are used to produce the revenue, it is evident that the capitals are derived from the earth just like the revenue, or rather, that they are but an accumulation of a part of the values produced by the earth, which the proprietors of the revenue, or those

[82] The phrase "unless they have great ability" does not occur in the 1793 translation.

who share it, are able to accumulate every year, without using it for the satisfaction of their wants.

101. *Although money is the immediate object of saving, and is, so to speak, the first material of capitals when they are being formed, yet specie forms an almost inappreciable part of the sum total of capitals.*

We have seen that money forms scarcely any part of the sum total of existing capitals, but plays a great part in the creation of capitals. In fact, almost all savings are made only in money; it is in money that the revenues return to the proprietors, that the advances and profits return to the entrepreneurs of every kind; it is therefore from money that they save, and the annual increase in capitals takes place in money; but all the entrepreneurs make no other use of it than to convert it immediately[83] into the different kinds of effects on which their enterprises depend; thus, this money returns to the circulation, and the greater part of capitals exist only in effects of different kinds, as we have already explained above.

November 1766

[83] Daire, Schelle, and Ashley in his translation, following Du Pont in his editions, italicise the "immediately" (sur-le-champ). For the importance of this emphasis, see my 'Turgot and Adam Smith', op. cit., pp. 278–279.

CHAPTER VI

1763

PLAN FOR A PAPER ON TAXATION IN GENERAL, ON LAND TAXES IN PARTICULAR, AND ON THE PROJECT OF A LAND REGISTER

D.D. I 392–408

The subject on which M. le Contrôleur-Général[1] has consulted the Intendants
p. 393 is one of the most interesting which can be examined. It contains the foundations of the whole political administration of a nation.

The question is no less than the determination of the most advantageous manner, for the sovereign and for the people, of securing the revenues of the State, and of distributing the contribution which the society as a whole owes itself for the supply of all public expenditures.

M. le Contrôleur-Général has contented himself with asking some questions; but I think that since each of these questions is closely related to the first principles of the matter, they cannot be resolved in a satisfactory and practical manner unless this matter is treated fully and its principles are developed in their natural order. It seems to me that this is the only way of realising what is the best thing to do; for it is always *the best* with which theory should be concerned. Neglecting this procedure, on the pretext that what is *best* is not practical in actual circumstances, is like wishing to resolve two questions at the same time. It is like surrendering the advantage of putting questions in the simplicity which alone can render them susceptible to proof. It is like rushing into an inextricable labyrinth without any clues and like wishing to unravel all
p. 394 the paths at the same time, or rather, like voluntarily closing your eyes to the light by making it impossible for you to find it.

I will therefore treat the subject with all the rigour of theory by a separate study and discussion of the following two very different questions: What should be done. And what can be done?

I will not conform to the order in which the succinct questions have been put forward. The answer to each of these questions will be discovered as a

[1] The Contrôleur-Général to whom this paper was directed was presumably Bertin (1719–1792), who held this post from 1759 to 1763. He was keenly interested in agricultural reform, and took charge of a new secretariat d'Etat which included agriculture, in 1763.

matter of course through the development of the principles, and I will take care to recall them and to recapitulate them separately.

To the questions on the land register, M. le Contrôleur-Général has added some questions on the establishment of corporations. This subject is so important in itself that I believe I must treat it in a separate paper in which I also intend to approach it from the two points of view of the best possible, and the most feasible.

PLAN OF THE VARIOUS CHAPTERS

Of the necessity of taxation, or of the contribution to public expenditure.

Examination of Rousseau's idea[2] that the *corvées* are preferable; show how much more costly this is, how much less equitably distributed, and impractical in a large society.[3]

General principles of the distribution of taxation.

Of distributive justice.

Of the necessity of never injuring the sources of wealth.

False ideas of some people on distributive justice.

Who is liable to taxation? Proof that only the proprietor of the soil is liable |to taxation|, (because he alone earns a net revenue which is ascertainable), for the maintenance of all other types of property of which the conservation and free use necessarily turn to his profit.

Refutation of the arguments used in attempts to prove that people with *purely personal property* have the same interest.

Different types of taxation.

There are only three possible types.

Direct taxation of landed property.

Direct personal taxation, which becomes a tax on the use of labour.

Indirect taxation, or that on consumption.

Indirect taxation is divided into general taxation on consumption, like sales p. 395
tax (*aides*) and excise duties; and into local taxation.[4]

The latter is subdivided into duties or impositions on consumption by virtue of their admission into the place where they are to be consumed;

[2] See J.J. Rousseau, *The Social Contract*, Bk. III, ch. 15: "In a country that is truly free, the citizens do everything with their own arms and nothing by means of money; . . . I hold enforced labour to be less opposed to liberty than taxes."

[3] Turgot himself, as Intendant of Limoges, abolished the *corvées* in his generality in the early 1760s; see D. Dakin, *Turgot and the Ancien Régime in France*, pp. 63–78. As Contrôleur-Général, Turgot later introduced similar reform for the whole of France; see ibid., pp. 239–251.

[4] The *aide* and *accise* were taxes on consumption goods. For a different classification of direct and indirect taxation, see Turgot 'Programme d'un Concours sur l'impôt indirect', in Schelle, *Oeuvres*, II, p. 431, where he wrote: "L'impôt que le propriétaire paye immédiatement sur son revenu est appelé *impôt direct*. L'impôt que n'est point assis directement sur le revenu du propriétaire, mais qui porte, ou sur les frais productifs du revenue, ou sur les dépenses de ce revenu, est appelé impôt *indirect*."

Taxes on trade or on commodities passing through certain places, like tolls;

Taxes on certain transactions in the society, sales, etc., which are direct in some respects, and indirect in others;

And monopolies, like those of salt or tobacco.

All these different types of taxation ultimately fall entirely on the proprietors of the soil.

In order to demonstrate this, it is necessary:

To develop accurately the concept of the revenue, and to prove that only the proprietor has a revenue;[5]

Proof that industry has no revenue at all; distinction between profit and revenue.

Enumeration of different taxes. Their incidence.

Only the tax on consumption admits of difficulty. Now, it is obvious that the proprietor pays it by buying services more dearly, and selling his products at a lower price, or by the decrease either of the price or of the quantity of consumption: the decline in quantity leads also to the decline in price.

Examination of the question whether the proprietor pays the indirect tax twice.

The loss may be greater or smaller, but whatever the proportion and the manner in which the question is decided, there is no doubt that preference must be given to direct taxation.

Firstly, because, as I have said already, only the proprietor is liable [to taxation];

Secondly, because direct taxation is less expensive to levy, and thus the proprietor gains the whole amount of the costs and the gain of the chief collectors, tax farmers or agents;

p. 396 Thirdly, because the indirect taxation imposes a multitude of constraints on commerce; because it entails lawsuits, frauds, penalties, the loss of a large number of people, a war between the government and its subjects, a lack of proportion between crime and punishment, and a continual and almost irresistible temptation to fraud, which is yet subject to cruel punishment;[6]

Fourthly, because indirect taxation attacks liberty in a thousand ways;[7]

Fifthly, because it is greatly prejudicial to consumption, and by this destroys itself;

[5] I have heard a man calculating the revenue of a province by saying: There are so many men; each man, in order to live, spends so many *sous* per day, therefore the province has so much revenue. Tax a similar revenue proportionately, and these people must die of hunger, or at least from misery. I believe that it all comes back to the great question of the soup of the Franciscans; it is in them when they have eaten it. It is the same with the so-called revenue from industry. When a man has eaten the reward proportioned to his talent or to the usefulness of his service, he has nothing left, and taxation cannot be levied on nothing. (Note by Turgot.)

[6] Cf. 'In Praise of Gournay', above pp. 30–31.

[7] Cf. ibid., pp. 30–31.

Sixthly, because the expenses of the State are increased by it, since the State pays it on its own expenditure and on that of all its agents;

Seventhly, because it gives a competitive advantage in trade to foreign merchants;

Eighthly and finally, because its results cannot be calculated precisely, while a proprietor is always able to determine what proportion of his revenue he pays.

In the case of direct taxation, the State knows what it is inflicting; it also clearly knows what it is able to inflict. Everything desirable in administration is present in it, that is, simplicity, surety, and rapidity.

DIRECT TAXATION

On persons or on the land.

That on persons, by its very nature offends reason; only laziness, and undue haste can have suggested it.

It cannot possibly be uniform.

Firstly, because there are people who own nothing;

Secondly, because, if the whole idea is to tax the individual, who is but a mass of wants, it would at any rate be necessary to tax at the rate appropriate to the lowest class of society; and at such a low rate, taxation would not yield a great deal.

It is therefore necessary to come back to classifying people more or less according to their means. Then this is no more than taxation of wealth, imposed arbitrarily and without rules.

If all so-called means are included in this, such as industry, commerce, their wages, the profits necessary for the exercise (of their business), etc., this poll-tax is in this respect an indirect tax.

The part proportioned to the means originating from landed property is p. 397
direct taxation; but it has all the disadvantages of arbitrariness.

It is still possible to distinguish between personal and real taxation, even in the case where the personal taxation would be proportioned to landed property only, for the taxation resting on landed property may be payable by the person, as in the *taille personelle*, or by the capital, as in the *taille réelle*. This is the difference from real taxation with regard to the assessment and with regard to the collection.

If all direct taxation were left in existence in amended form, a great deal of the taxation would still remain and fall directly on the soil, and it would still have to be imposed in the most equitable way possible, and even then the indirect taxes would still hit landed property on the rebound.

It is therefore of some use to discuss the question in general terms, and to run through the particular disadvantages of the various types of indirect taxation.

INDIRECT TAXATION

Impositions on general consumption; their disadvantages. They cause the payment of the same tax on products of the same type, some of which are costly, and others not. Poor consumers are taxed excessively. And similarly, the same tax is paid on output of which a part, originating from fertile soil, has cost little, while the rest, from barren ground, has cost a great deal which it barely repays. These taxes therefore bear no relation to the revenue, and cause the abandonment of cultivation of mediocre soil, the output of which would only cover costs.

The import duties of towns. They have the same disadvantages and, moreover, this difficulty, that their rates could not be made to follow the relative value of commodities; because, for commodities with a high value, smuggling would increase in line with the duties.

The less necessary commodities are, the more duties will diminish their consumption.[8]

A sure yield can therefore be counted on only to the extent that the taxes are imposed on commodities which the people use, which they cannot do
p. 398 without, and which are at the same time sufficiently bulky to prohibit fraud; but then the poor pay, or, at least advance, the whole of the tax, which causes them great hardship. The wealthy, who repay this advance, at first pay almost nothing, and even in the end pay only tardily.

It is a common belief that through these duties the towns are made to pay; but in reality, it is a charge on the country side which produces the taxed commodities. For the inhabitants of towns have limited revenues, and can pay the tax only by offering a lower price to the producers and the initial sellers of the commodity, or by curtailing their consumption. And we have already seen that these two transactions which naturally occur together, have the same results.

The ridiculous tariffs which the inhabitants of the towns have been allowed to establish, have almost completely the objective of placing the whole burden of the tax on what they call *foreigners*.

Foreign merchandise must therefore be sold at a higher price than local goods. This gives the local merchants a monopoly which is prejudicial to the ordinary inhabitants of the towns.

In the case of most of these duties, it is felt that everything must be taxed.

[8] Cf. Hume's essay 'Of Taxes', in David Hume, *Writings in Economics*, ed. E. Rotwein, 1953, p. 85.

Because of this, an inextricable labyrinth of valuations, disputes, etc. has been created.

Moreover, taxation of commerce tends to reduce its volume.

The natural result of all these urban taxes would be to change the location of towns, or to extend them beyond the genuine convenience of the inhabitants by building in the suburbs in order to evade the duties. The only reason which prevents this effect is another evil, which is even worse: It is the sad condition of the inhabitants of the countryside and the manifold vexations which pursue them, while the city dwellers, by reason of their wealth and their proximity to the government, their better education and greater prestige, and because, through closeness, they form a much more imposing body than those living in the country, even though the latter are twice as numerous, have been able to avoid much of the wrongs and the bad treatment which the cultivators have had, and still have, to endure.

If the countryside were subjected to territorial taxation only, the majority of the town dwellers would soon settle there, and this would not be a bad thing, for then consumption would come closer to the place of production; there would be fewer wasteful expenses of transportation and the cultivator, p. 399
enjoying the whole of the consumer's expenditure, would be able to extend his activities profitably to less fertile lands of which the additional produce would enable citizens to live whose existence is at present impossible, because if they were born, they would have no sustenance.

Taxation by way of monopoly is much worse still. By the extreme disproportion in price, it becomes a cruel lure to smuggling. The king is made to play the same role as those people who scatter corn for the birds in order to trap them.

With all indirect taxation, the maladministration of the customs officers is impossible to avoid. In order to ascertain frauds, it is necessary to give customs officers the privilege of being believed on the basis of their reports, and this may become a source of vexations which cannot be curbed.

The intricacy of the tariffs and the laws which regulate their collection and which seek to prevent their violation, make it a physical impossibility for the people to hold out against these vexations, for in the midst of so many obscurities, what individual would dare to hazard the expenses of a lawsuit against the agents of the authorities?

The taxation on transfers of property and Commercial deeds, is a type of taxation no less odious.

It seems that Public Finance, like a greedy monster, has been lying in wait for the entire wealth of the people, and all this through a gross misunderstan- p. 400
ding. For why so many tricks when all real wealth is *out in the open*, as the saying goes?

The hundredth penny (centième) takes a portion from property itself. However, when people agreed to pay taxes to preserve the society of which they are members, they did this only to preserve their property, and not to lose it.

There are undoubtedly cases in which people would consent to sacrifice part of their property in order to save the remainder, but this would not be the normal case. They want an assured and constant tenure of property, and they also want their sacrifice to be constant. Taxation must therefore be levied on the revenue and not on the capitals.

Moreover, the State has the greatest possible interest in preserving the stock of capitals. It is this stock which provides the advances of all agricultural and commercial enterprises, as well as the acquisition of real property. These capitals are formed by the slow process of thrift. To cause payment, as revenue of the State, of part of these capitals, which are accumulated for the advances necessary for work, is to destroy in part the source of these same revenues.

Having decided that direct taxation of landed property is the only form of taxation conforming to our principles, it is necessary to establish: firstly, on what part of the product of landed property it should be levied, and then how it can be distributed and collected.

I have already said that only the owner of real property is liable to contribute to taxation; a first ground for this is that he alone has a stake in the preservation of an abiding social order. What does it matter to a working man what becomes of the government? He would always own the same resources in the form of his arms; he is perfectly indifferent as to whether it is Jack or Peter who furnishes the work. A second ground, and the more peremptory, is that only the owner of landed property has a true revenue.

p. 401

DISCUSSION OF THE REVENUE

M. Quesnay was the first to establish the correct notion of the revenue, when he learnt to distinguish the *gross product* from the *net product*, and not to include the profits of the cultivator in the *net product*.[9] These products are the bait, the sufficient and necessary motive for cultivation; why would the cultivator work if he could not count on his legitimate profit? And will he not work with all the more eagerness and success as he is assured that he will not labour in vain?

An estate may produce commodities in quite large quantities and not yield any net product; for this result it is sufficient to assume that it costs more to till than the sale of its fruits can yield.

[9] See e.g. Quesnay, 'Impôts, in *François Quesnay et la Physiocratie*, II, p. 582. Although this paper was not published till 1908, Turgot was familiar with it, since he owned a manuscript copy, on which he made several comments. This copy is at present in the Archives of Limoges. See ibid., I, p. 255.

It is well known that soil, manured and ploughed to the point where it is as light as that of an ants nest, yields a prodigious harvest; but if in order to work the soil in this manner, spades and many days' labour are required, this output may become expensive. If the quantity of output is such that it is not matched by consumption, and has no exchange value, the revenue will be zero in spite of the abundance of the harvest. When the philosopher's stone is discovered, its inventor would not be any richer from it if he could only make gold to the value of a hundred *louis* by spending the value of a hundred *louis* on charcoal, and if it were to cost him a hundred and one *louis* he would certainly leave the trade.

This truth is well known; but what has not been so well realised is that it is just as necessary to subtract similarly from the gross product the recovery of the expenses of the cultivator in order to ascertain the *net product*.

M. Quesnay has developed the mechanism of agriculture[10] which is based entirely on very large original advances and requires in addition annual advances which are equally necessary. It is therefore necessary to deduct from the sale of the produce: firstly, all the expenses or *annual advances*; secondly, the interest on the *original advances*; thirdly, their maintenance and the replacement of their inevitable decay, at least equal to the interest; fourthly, the subsistence and reasonable profit of the entrepreneur farmer and his agents, the wages of their labour and of their industry.

The cultivator has made these calculations when he leases a piece of land. It is the surplus which he gives to the proprietor that makes up the revenue, p. 402
and it is only on this revenue that taxes can be levied. When the proprietor cultivates the land himself, he has no greater disposable revenue, but he combines in one person his revenue as a proprietor and his profits as a cultivator, a profit which is not disposable at all.

M. Quesnay has, moreover, demonstrated[11] that, if the exchange value is diminished, the revenue would diminish gradually to the point where finally the soil would produce nothing beyond the reproduction of advances and the profit of the cultivator; that from then on, there would be no more letting out of land; that the proprietor, it is true, would still be able to farm it for his own subsistence, by making the advances himself, but that this slender revenue would no longer be disposable. And it would be possible that, in a nation where the estates would be reduced to this sort of cultivation, there would be absolutely no revenue, no means of sustaining the State, other than by gradually consuming the capitals; this situation would be self-destructive and of necessity transitory.

[10] See Quesnay, 'Fermiers', op. cit., esp. pp. 454–455; 'Grains', op. cit., esp. pp. 471 ff.; 'Analyse de la Formule Arithmétique du Tableau économique', op. cit., pp. 798–799; 'Explication du Tableau économique', op. cit., pp. 675–682.

[11] See Quesnay, 'Impôts', op. cit., p. 591; 'Philosophie Rurale', op. cit., pp. 691–692; 'Maximes Générales du Gouvernement économique d'un Royaume Agricole', op. cit., p. 954, where the following maxim is given: "Telle est la valeur vénale, tel est le revenu".

To appreciate this, it is sufficient to consider that the proprietors must have their livelihood. Let a family need a hundred *écus* in order to subsist, and let the land be so distributed that each proprietor, by farming it himself, earns only one hundred *écus*, and he will not be able to pay the tax without taking from his subsistence.

This so-called revenue would only be the wages of his labour. The true revenue is the portion of the proprietor over and above that of the cultivator, that which the cultivator gives to the proprietor in order to acquire the right to work his field. All other notions of the revenue are illusions. When landed property is purchased, it is this revenue alone which is purchased.

p. 403 Now it is obvious that it is this revenue alone in which the tax can share, since it could not encroach upon the share of the cultivator without removing his interest in cultivation, without forcing him to consume his advances and consequently to reduce his activities and his productive expenditure. As the output of successive years becomes less, the encroachment of the tax would become more and more destructive, and the output and the sources of the State's revenues would be exhausted together with the revenue of the proprietors.

There is no further need to return to indirect taxation, which would destroy
p. 404 the capitals even more quickly, for the very reason that its blows would at first be less perceptible and would give less warning of the danger.

In this context the question is solely one of territorial taxation; and since it has already been shown that taxation should respect the portion of the cultivator, it follows directly that it must be paid by the proprietor. For if it were demanded from the farmer, the latter would be intelligent enough to withhold it from the proprietor in the price of his lease. Thus, the taxing of the cultivator as such would never have been considered, but for the impediments placed in the way of true principles by the privileges of the Nobility and the Church which the lawmaker desires to dodge. The disadvantages of this method will be discussed below. For the time being, we will deal with the question considered by itself, and, in a nation where no obstacle is placed in the way of pursuing correct principles, there is no doubt but the proprietors would be approached directly.

However, this proposition is contrary to the opinion held by those who originally conceived of the device of the royal tithe (*dîme royale*),[12] or those who have praised it.This method may in fact dazzle one by its simplicity, by

[12] The system of the *dîme royale*, or royal tithe, had been suggested by Sebastien le Prestre de Vauban in the book *Dîme Royale*, which appeared in 1707. The *dîme royale* consisted of a tax levied proportionately on everything bearing a revenue, and was to be modelled on the *dîme ecclésiastique* which was then in existence in France; see Vauban, *Dîme Royale*, Paris 1887, p. 9. Vauban's scheme was severely criticised at the time by Boisguilbert, in a mémoire to Chamillart, then Contrôleur-Général; see Hazel van Dyke Roberts, *Boisguilbert*, New York, 1935, pp. 34–35, 81–83. Cf. also Quesnay, 'Impôts', op. cit., II, p. 590, note 11; this note was written by Turgot.

the ease with which it is collected, by the appearance of distributive justice, and at least, because each knows what he must pay. The ecclesiastical tithe is a fascinating example among the poor and non-trading people. This form of taxation may be established more easily than any other. It is certain that the taxpayer always has the wherewithal to pay; he pays immediately and without expense. This mode of taxation is established in China. Yet, it has a number of disadvantages.

First disadvantage of the tithe: its lack of proportion. No regard whatsoever to the expenses of cultivation. It is possible that the gross tithe is greater than the net product. If by expending the value of nine *setiers* of corn, one managed to produce ten *setiers* per *arpent*, the net product would be only one *setier*. This would yet be a very sufficient revenue for engaging in agriculture: well, the tithe would take it all; it would therefore destroy the whole revenue; and if the cultivation had been more expensive, the tithe would destroy itself; it would destroy the motive for cultivation, and put an end to it.

Second and more direct reason, but which is partly contained in the first. The tithe, being a portion of the crop, may encroach upon the share of the cultivator, and may therefore take more than it should. The whole crop belongs at first to the cultivator; it is up to him to make his calculations in p. 405
order to know what he ought to give up to the proprietor, and it is only on this portion, surrendered to the proprietor, that taxation may and should be levied.

Proposing to set up a cadaster for the tithe in order to remedy these shortcomings, and to ask less from land that produces less relative to the expenses, would mean rushing into a difficulty greater than that of evaluating the revenues in terms of money, because, for the latter operation, the leases and contracts of sale can be used at least, while there is nothing like this for evaluating the expenses of cultivation, which can only be ascertained through an analysis of cultivation. This is impossible for anyone but the cultivator, who knows how to calculate them accurately. The farmers calculate them approximately, and come closer by trial and error.

The tithe would be an excessive tax in some provinces; but it would be far from adequate for the public needs, unless it was extremely outrageous, which would make it more unequal, and even more destructive of cultivation, and consequently of itself, on land of inferior quality.

If it is assumed that the clergy have no other revenue than the tithe (setting off its other wealth against the enfeoffed tithes, and other tithes it does not own), the whole of the tithe, levied, it is true, at a multitude of different rates, would not go much beyond sixty million, and I do not believe the clergy to be a great deal more wealthy.

Let us thus turn back to approaching the proprietor directly, and asking p. 406
from him in coin that part of his revenue which the State needs.

What would be asked of him? How would it be asked from him?

Two different systems.

Ask from each a part of the revenue, a constant proportion. This is the method of the *dixième,* of the *vingtième,* this is what has been put forward in the *Théorie de l'impôt,* in the *Philosophie Rurale,* it is the method used in the English land tax.[13]

On the other hand, a fixed sum may be exacted from the nation, from each province, from each municipality; this sum being distributed among all the proprietors in proportion to their prosperity.

This second system, embodied in the arbitrary *taille,* has also been adopted in the provinces with land surveys or with *taille réelle* (property tax). In fact, it is only to this system that the land survey is truly appropriate. For what purpose would an unchangeable land survey serve in the case where a proportional part of a variable revenue is demanded? However, when a tax distribution is made, a fixed table is required. In all, there are only four possible methods of distributing the land tax.

Firstly, that of a portion proportional to the crop. This is the method of the tithe, of which I have already spoken and whose advantages and disadvantages I have sufficiently discussed.

Secondly, that of a portion proportional to the revenue. This is the method of the *vingtième.*

Thirdly, that of a fixed sum distributed each year among the taxpayers according to their mutual knowledge of the produce. This is more or less the method of the arbitrary *taille,* confined to landed property.

Fourthly, that of a fixed sum, distributed according to an invariable valuation of the property. This is the method of the land survey or the *taille réelle.*

The method based on the tax proportional to the revenue would have considerable advantages.

An unchangeable law could forever put an end to all the disputes between the government and the people, especially if it fixed one proportion for war and one for peace. People would compound at this rate in purchases and
p. 407 sales, and the part of the net product belonging to taxation would not be bought any more than that belonging to the priest is bought. After some time, in truth, no one would be paying taxes. But the king would be proprietor of a proportional part of the revenue of all the estates.

This revenue would increase with the wealth of the nation, and if the increase in wealth should augment the needs, it would be equally sufficient in that case. The wealth of the king would be the measure of the wealth of the people, and the administration, always affected by the repercussions of its

[13] Mirabeau (with the collaboration of Quesnay), *Philosophie Rurale ou Economie générale et politique de l'agriculture,* Amsterdam, 1763, II, p. 345–346 (Maxime VII), and, on taxation in general, II, pp. 265–298; Mirabeau, *Théorie de l'Impôt,* n.p., 1760, chapter VII, esp. p. 132, and, on the English land tax, *The History of our National Debts and Taxes,* second edition, London, 1753, p. 10. Turgot had a copy of this book in his library. See *Catalogue des livres . . .,* p. 135, item 2797.

mistakes, would learn once and for all, that is, by the simple calculation of the yield of the tax.

These advantages are considerable, especially in a monarchy; for in a republic or a limited monarchy like England, the people might not be so pleased if the prince would never have to reckon with them. With a law like this, the English Parliament would lose its greatest influence, and the king would soon be as absolute a monarch as in France, since it would no longer be to any one's advantage to oppose him.[14]

If, therefore, it were possible to succeed in establishing a tax like this, proportional to the revenue, there could be no hesitation in preferring this manner of levying the public revenue to any other.

But I confess that this seems completely impossible to me: under this system, the king or the government stands alone against all, and every one is interested in hiding the value of his wealth. In the provinces where the *grande culture* exists, the value of the leases serves as a valuation; but firstly, not all land is leased; and secondly, I think it impossible to guard against the disadvantage of defeasances.[15] I know it is said that an administration which inspires confidence, as that of the States could be, would persuade people to declare accurately; but I believe this to be a lack of understanding of human nature. Fraud would be very common, and straightaway would no longer be deemed dishonourable. Even in the case of the distribution method, where all frauds are regarded as odious in that they affect all the taxpayers, people scarcely scruple to commit fraud. The principles of honesty and patriotism have far from taken root in the provinces; only in the course of time and by the slow means of education could they be established.

It is proposed to make defeasances null and void, but this would encourage false testimony. The proper remedy for fraud is to take away all advantage in it.

Moreover, there still remains the objection relating to the provinces where leaseholding is not practised, that is, more than two thirds of the kingdom. p. 408
Would declarations be demanded from the proprietors? What has been their use for the *vingtième*? But, it is said in the *Théorie de l'impôt*,[156] the old forms of taxation can be left in existence in the provinces where there is no leaseholding, until cultivation has made sufficient progress there for this to be

[14] The interrelationship between the decreasing power of the sovereign and the increasing dependence of the crown on the parliament for its revenue was frequently illustrated by David Hume in his *History of England*, and can be said to be an important thesis of this work. Turgot had a copy of it in his library. See *Catalogue des livres*, p. 136, item 2810.

[15] Defeasance: a collateral deed, made at the same time with a feoffment or other conveyance, containing certain conditions, upon the performance of which the estate then created may be defeated or totally undone. So, a defeasance on a bond or recognizance, or judgement recovered, is a condition which, when performed, defeats or undoes it. *Mozley and Whitely's Law Dictionary*, sixth ed., P.A. Jones and J.C. Fisher (eds.), Butterworth and Co., London, 1950, p. 100.

[16] Mirabeau, *Théorie de l'Impôt*, pp. 237–238.

introduced. This is all right in the case of an entire province, but in connection with parishes for the distribution among the proprietors of each estate, it would entail returning to estimates.

And then, it would be rather a long wait until leaseholding is established everywhere. I will show below, when I will be concerned with developing the progress of *la grande culture*, that this will not be as speedy as M. de Mirabeau images it will be.[17]

The restoration of agriculture must start with the proprietors. The stock of capitals required for the establishment of rural enterprises will take a long time to eventuate.

It is therefore necessary to rest content with the distribution of a fixed sum, except that its increase could be regulated according to a certain proportion with the revenues of the nation; I will show below that this is possible, and how it may be done.

This distribution cannot be made arbitrarily without incorporating many of the disadvantages with which the *taille* has been reproached. I say a part, not all, for it must be understood that part of the disadvantages of the current taxation arises from the fact that it is not levied directly on the proprietor but on the cultivators, and on the unfortunate inhabitants of the countryside. Yet many of the disadvantages would remain.

One can be sure that in this annual distribution the poor proprietors would always be overburdened, and that the large proprietors, whose voice would always be preponderant. . . .[18]

[17] This was not done in this paper. Turgot dealt with it in a special paper dealing with taxation in his province. See 'Mémoire sur la surcharge des impositions qu'éprouvoit la Généralité de Limoges, dans lequel l'Auteur traite incédemment de la grande et de la petite Culture' in Schelle, *Oeuvres*, II, pp. 445–468. The material on 'la grande et la petite culture' appeared separately in the *Ephémérides*, 1767, No. 6, pp. 77–97.

The reference to Mirabeau is to his *Théorie de l'Impôt*, p. 237.

[18] This paper was not finished, and the manuscript has not been found. Schelle, in *Oeuvres*, II, pp. 308–312, prints some other manuscript fragments on the subject of taxation as well as Turgot's notes to Quesnay's article 'Impôt'. (Ibid., II, pp. 313–319, and see footnote 9 above.)

CHAPTER VII

1767

OBSERVATIONS ON A PAPER BY SAINT-PÉRAVY ON THE SUBJECT OF INDIRECT TAXATION[1]

D.D. 418–433

The author assumes firstly, that the proprietors spend half their income on purchases from the productive class and the other half on purchases from the industrial class; secondly, that the productive class spends only a quarter[2] of its income on manufactured goods.[3]

These two propositions are to be regarded as hypotheses only, which contain some degree of realism, and which may be used in mathematical formulae, but from which completely precise conclusions can never be drawn. The proportion between the various expenditures of each class is too variable to permit of accurate calculation. Assumptions of this type may only be p. 419
usefully employed to give a clearer idea of the circulation.

The author argues and calculates later[4] on the basis of an assumption which he has already put forward as a principle, that the proportion between the annual advances in agricultural production, and its total product is as two is to five.[5] The dubiousness of this assumption does not weaken what has

[1] There are two versions of this paper: a manuscript copy in Lantheuil among the Turgot papers, which is reprinted by Schelle in *Oeuvres*, II, pp. 641–658, and the Du Pont version, also reprinted in Daire, in his *Oeuvres*, IV, pp. 312–343. The differences between these two versions have been indicated in footnotes.

[2] Turgot's "quarter" should be "a third"; see Saint-Péravy, *Mémoire sur les effets de l'impôt indirect*, London, 1768, p. 45, and cf. Quesnay, 'Analyse de la formule arithmétique du Tableau économique', in *François Quesnay et la Physiocratie*, II, pp. 793–799, 801.

[3] This note is presumably based on Saint-Péravy's remarks in the following two paragraphs of his *Mémoire*, pp. 45–46, beginning: "A considérer l'ordre raisonnable de la dépense du revenu dans l'état de prospérité, il parait natural que . . .".

[4] The "later" in Turgot's text refers presumably to Part II of Saint-Péravy's *Mémoire* where these calculations are made.

[5] This assumption is stated quite clearly by Saint-Péravy, and derives from Quesnay's work. See Saint-Péravy, op. cit., p. 34, and e.g. Quesnay, 'Analyse de la formule arithmétique du Tableau économique', op. cit., II, p. 795 and the diagram on p. 801. In Part II of his *Mémoire*, Saint-Péravy occasionally changes this assumption by varying the ratio of the *avances primitives* to the *avances annuelles*; see ibid., pp. 151–152.

It should also be noted that the above three paragraphs are a translation from the text in Daire, which follows that of Du Pont. Schelle, as shown in note 1 above, has a quite different previously been said to demonstrate that the indirect tax falls entirely on the proprietors, because this truth results purely from the impossibility of encroaching upon the advances and the wages of the agricultural and the industrial classes without ruining them. These classes can only pay at the expense of the proprietors, who are the only ones to receive the disposable portion of the crop, that gratuitous portion which the soil yields over and

---

text for this earlier section based on the manuscript version of these observations at Lantheuil. This reads as follows in translation:

"On what is said of the difference between small commercial States and large agricultural States (a), see the observations on the paper (by Graslin). The details there (b) may be used to separate what is correct from what is wrong in this manner of considering these different constitutions of States.

"The deadly contrivance of borrowing (c) derives from the mania of spending more than one owns, and sometimes has been the system of taxation adopted by European kings of the last century; the ambition of Louis XIV and other princes has no less been a cause of it [the borrowing] through their stubborn wars pushed to the point of exhaustion. With the mania of war, which still excites kings and even the people, the fighting continues as long as there are troops left. When the revenue is exhausted, one borrows, and borrows while lenders can still be found. Now, lenders will be found so long as there are resources to pledge. A proprietor of an estate and a king ruin themselves in exactly the same way by each year spending more than their revenue. The nature of this revenue is here an absolutely immaterial consideration.

"The only difference between the individual and the king is the means which the latter has of going bankrupt in the preservation of his stock and revenue. I assume that instead of making the first loans for sustaining the war, the amount to be borrowed has been raised in taxes, the yield of these taxes was spent first of all, and soon recourse would have been had to borrowing. All the abuses about which here are complained are an inevitable consequence of the limited means to increase expenditure.

"Some views and reasoning on manufactures, of which he probably never thought, are her ascribed to Colbert. (d)

"These two propositions (e): 1 that the proprietors class spends half of what it receives in buying commodities from the productive class and the other half in purchases of manufactured goods from the industrious class (classe industrieuse); 2 that the class of cultivators can expend only a quarter of its returns on manufactured goods, can only be regarded as arbitrary assumptions which may be used in mathematical formulae but from which completely precise conclusions can never be drawn. The proportion between the different objects of expenditure of each class is too variable to be always calculatable with precision. The assumptions, however, can always be usefully employed to give a clear notion of the circular flow (la marche de la circulation). Here, a start is made by reasoning and calculating according to an assumption which has already been put forward as a principle."

(a) See Saint-Péravy, *Mémoire*, p. 20, n.: "C'est pour n'avoir jamais étudié la différence de constitution et d'intérêts des petits Etats republicains composés de comptoirs, de revendeurs que la sagesse de leur conduite a produit l'égarement des grandes puissances agricoles." (Note by Schelle.)

(b) See below, 'Observations on a Paper by Graslin', pp. 129–132.

(c) Saint-Péravy, *Mémoire*, p. 24. (Note by Schelle.)

(d) Ibid., p. 30 n. (Note by Schelle.)

(e) Ibid., pp. 33 ff. (Note by Schelle.)

These changes by Du Pont de Nemours were probably inspired by two different motivations. The first part, dealing with public borrowings and the "mania" of war, was probably not suitable for publication at the height of the first Empire of Napoleon, when the *Works* as edited by Du Pont were published. The second part, dealing with Saint-Péravy's assumptions derived from Quesnay's work, were probably removed for doctrinal reasons. The passage in this note was translated from Schelle, *Oeuvres*, II, pp. 641–642.

above the cost of working it. But since, in the subsequent estimation of the excess burden of the indirect tax by the effect which the decrease of the advances must cause, the starting point of the calculations is this assumed proportion between the annual advances and the total product of two to five, it is necessary to examine this assumption.

I would grant that this proportion has been established on the basis of exact calculations of the advances and the products of some farms *en grande culture* in a fertile region, which the author, or those who furnished him with the facts, visited in order to reassure themselves. But this procedure does not confer the right to draw from this particular calculation any general results; it takes little thought to realise that there can be no constant proportion between the advances and the product. Advances, which are only a form of expenditure, are not in themselves productive; they do not even have the productivity which the current rate of interest gives to loan money. If 20,000 livres put to interest return 1000 francs, it can be concluded that 40,000 will return 2000 francs. But from the fact that 2000 livres of annual advances applied to a farm will return 5000 francs worth of product, it cannot be concluded that another 2000 livres employed on another plot of ground would also yield 5000 francs, nor that 4000 employed on the same land would yield 10,000. The expenses of agriculture consist in giving the soil such preparation as is most likely to make it fruitful. Now, the outcome of these preparations, which determines the product, is by no means proportioned to the expenditure: the knowledge of the cultivator renders the same amount of expen- p. 420
diture more or less productive, depending on the extent to which his method of applying it is appropriate to the nature of the soil and all the seasonal factors. If as much ploughing is bestowed on a light soil as on a heavy soil, the cost may be higher while the return may be lower. If Tull's system contains some truth,[6] production may be increased while economising on the seed. Then the annual advances will diminish and the total product will increase. Production implies advances, but equal advances on soils of different fertility would yield very different total products, and this in itself would be sufficient to prove that product is not entirely proportional to advances. Even if applied to the same field it is not proportional, and it can never be assumed that double the advances will yield double the product. The earth certainly has a limited fertility, and assuming it to have been ploughed, manured, marled, ditched, watered, weeded, as far as it can be, it is obvious that all further expenditure would be useless, and that such increases could even become detrimental. In this case, the advances would be increased without increasing the product. There is therefore a *maximum* point of production which it is im-

[6] Presumably a reference to Tull's *The New Horse-Houghing Husbandry, or, an Essay on the Principles of Tillage and Vegetation,* Dublin, 1731, especially preface p. viii. Tull presents some estimates of costs and produce relating to his invention of the seed drill.

possible to pass, and when this point has been reached, advances will not only cease producing 250 for 100, but will produce absolutely nothing.

While it may be granted to the author that, in the case of ordinary good cultivation, the annual advances return 250 for 100, it is more than likely that as the advances are increased gradually past this point up to the point where they return nothing, each increase would be less and less productive. The fruitfulness of the soil may be compared in this case with a spring which is compressed by loading it successively with equal weights. If the weights are light and the spring is rather stiff, the effect of the first few weights may be almost negligible. When the total weight is heavy enough to overcome the initial resistance, the spring will yield visibly and will compress; but when it has been compressed to a certain point, it will offer more resistance to the force which compresses it, and such weights as would have compressed it an inch, can compress it no more than a fraction of an inch. The effect will thus diminish increasingly. This comparison is not entirely accurate, but it is
p. 421 sufficient to show how, as the soil approaches the point where it yields as much as it can produce, a very large outlay can only increase the product slightly.

If, instead of increasing the advances by equal degrees beyond the point at which they yield most, the farmer diminishes them, the same change in the proportion would be found. It is not just conceivable, but it is certain that very small advances yield a smaller profit than very large ones, and that the ratio between the profits is higher than that between the advances. If 2000 livres yield 5000, 1000 may not even yield 1500, and 500 will not yield 600.

Seed thrown on a soil which is naturally fertile, but has not been prepared at all, would be virtually a waste of expenditure. If the soil were tilled once, the produce would be greater; tilling it a second or a third time would not just double or triple, but quadruple or decuple the produce, which will thus increase in a much larger proportion than the expenditure, and this would be the case up to a certain point, at which the produce would be as large as possible relative to the advances.

Past this point, if the advances are still further increased, the product will still increase, but less so, and continuously less and less until an addition to the advances would add nothing further to the produce, because the fertility of the soil is exhausted and art cannot increase the product any further.

I will mention that it would be mistaken to imagine that the point at which the advances yield the most is the most advantageous one which the cultivator can attain, for, although further increments in advances do not yield as much as the preceding increments, if they yield enough to increase the *net product* of the soil, there is an advantage in making them, and it will still be a good investment. If it is assumed, for example, as it is by the author, that the annual advances in good cultivation yield 250 per cent, an increment which yields 225 per cent would still be exceedingly profitable. For, since the interest on fixed capital and the return of the first dose of annual advances has already been deducted from the 250 per cent, and since this deduction still leaves a very adequate *net product*, if from the product of the next dose of annual advances 100 is deducted for its replacement and 10 for the interest on the first dose, which becomes an addition to the fixed capital, of which the advances of the first year are always a part; if then, 110 per cent is deducted from the 225 produced by the new advances, a net product of 115 per cent would be obtained from the new advances, which would be added to the 250 per cent from the first advances, etc. p. 422

I have dwelt extensively on this point, because it is important not to surrender too easily to the hope of estimating with complete accuracy the decrease in total product caused by a decrease in annual advances when indirect taxation has broken into the latter. Here the author's calculations seem to be based on a fallacy, since he assumes that production is always in a proportion of five to two to the annual advances, and calculates the diminutions in the total product at this rate. It is evident from the above that the harmful effect of the diminution of the annual advances would be less when cultivation is already beyond the point at which the advances yield as much as possible. If, on the contrary, this diminution begins only when the annual advances yield the greatest product, the decrease must be greater; but below this, there must also be a point where the decrease in annual advances diminishes production in a still smaller proportion. In short, the decrease of advances must diminish the production in the same proportion as the gradual increase of advances had augmented it.

The fundamental principle of the paper, that the renewal of the cultivator's capital may not be impaired, and that he cannot decrease his advances without decreasing production, is beyond doubt; but the exact extent of this decrease does not appear to be susceptible to precise determination.

* * *

The rentier is a merchant of money.[7] Interest is the price of capital. Since the capital yields nothing by itself, but only by virtue of the agreement of the contracting parties, a tax on interest is exactly like any other tax on commodities. If part of the price of any commodity whatsoever is taken away, obviously this price is prevented from falling to the buyer's advantage by the whole of what is demanded from the seller. It is thus the buyer, who in the final analysis in this case is the proprietor of the property, who pays the tax on interest. This reasoning appears at first glance to be contradicted at times when applied to the facts, through the influence which the authority of the law regulating interest exerts in this matter. But it must be noted that the effect of p. 423

[7] This note refers to Saint-Péravy's remarks on rentiers or holders of the national debt, op. cit., pp. 65–68.

the law on interest is always to maintain it at a higher rate than would be the case in the absence of a law. This law, just like all other legal fixation of commodities, always raises the price, or interrupts commerce.

When the sovereign taxes interest, the whole impact of the law falls on the existing arrangements, and as the lender cannot demand reimbursement, he has no means at all of recouping his loss. As for new contracts, made after the passing of the Edict, if the lenders submit to the law of the tax, it is proof that the legal rate of interest was above the natural rate, for if the legal rate was too low, the lenders would evade the law by private arrangements, or else they would cease to lend.

If natural order, complete liberty and the competition which results from these existed in the trade in money, the reasoning put forward by the author would be as true in practice as it is in theory.

* * *

It is certain that houses do not produce any revenue which may be regarded as additional revenue for the State. Their rent is obviously a pure expense which, like all others, is paid from the produce of the soil. I believe, however, that houses should be taxed, not because of the value of the building, but because of the value of the land which they occupy and which is only used for building because in this way it yields more than in any other way.[8]

* * *

It is physically impossible for the taxes on consumption to be graded on the basis of the disproportion between luxuries and necessities.[9] The tax on consumption goods has a *maximum* which cannot be exceeded, and this maximum is determined by the relative ease of smuggling. The risks of smuggling are estimated like those of the sea, and it is a known fact that con-

[8] This is presumably a comment on Saint-Péravy's remarks on the rent of houses, op. cit., pp. 68–71. This was a standard Physiocratic argument, which Turgot here attacks. See for example, Mercier de la Rivière, *L'Ordre Naturel et essentiel des sociétés politiques*, London (i.e. Paris) 1767, p. 262. The same argument is presented by Quesnay, 'Impôts', op. cit., II, p. 580, and Turgot's note to this part, ibid., note 2, where he argues: "It seems to me that the rents of houses in towns should be regarded as a real revenue. In truth, the persons who pay it do not derive any profit from it and pay it from their own revenues, but it is none the less true that for the proprietor it is a free, net product, but one which is not based on the fruits of a productive and creative exploitation. Examining whether the tax on houses represents a form of double taxation on the annual revenue from estates; this seems to be true, but the double taxation does not occur if houses are charged only to the relief of the estates. Then it would not be so much a repetition as an indirect tax: but this indirect tax does not have the same disadvantages as those falling on industry and commerce, and there is some advantage as regards the uniformity and simplicity of taxation."

[9] This passage presumably is a comment on Saint-Péravy's remarks on indirect taxation or taxation of consumption, op. cit., pp. 71–77.

traband can be insured. If the tax on a commodity is fifteen per cent, and if the risk of smuggling is only ten per cent, obviously nearly all supplies would p. 424 be smuggled in, and the tax would produce so much the less for the government. Now the more precious the commodities are, the more value they have for their bulk, the easier it is to smuggle them. It is easier to hide 20,000 livres worth of lace work than twenty francs worth of corn; the duty must thus be diminished in proportion to the value of the commodities, and the expenditures of the rich are exactly those that are charged least. All excessive duties can be levied only by way of state monopoly; but the evils of this type of tax are innumerable, and the effects it produces, by disturbing trade and reversing all moral values in the minds of the people, are even more fatal than those it produces in its quality as an indirect tax, and which it has in common with all other taxes on consumption.[10]

* * *

It is certainly an evil that a very great part of private expenditure is made in the capital, but this disadvantage is not peculiar to the profit from the General-Farm. That of the Receiver-General, which arises out of direct taxation, that of the creditors, and pensioners of the government, the revenue of all great proprietors, are all spent in the capital. It is a great evil, but it derives from the general system of government rather than from the nature of the indirect tax.[11]

It seems that the author here envisages as an evil that part of the profits of the Farmers-General are set apart to create capitals, and that the money which they have gathered is not immediately returned to the circulation.[12] We may leave the Farmers-General, for the advantage, and what the author believes to be the disadvantage, of saving from profits, holds as much for any other profits as for theirs. Consider the question in general.

The author, and the majority of economic writers, seem to assume that the

[10] A paragraph has been omitted at this point by Du Pont. See Schelle, *Oeuvres*, II, p. 648. This paragraph reads in translation:

"I am not sure if it is absolutely impossible for a government to ascertain the product of a farm exactly. In a vast, and consequently complicated administration, where so many interested parties are entitled to have an account of the profits in which they share rendered to them, it is impossible that the farmers do not have their account books very much in order so that the government can always have them produced."

There seems to be no apparent reason why this paragraph was omitted by Du Pont de Nemours.

[11] This paragraph is presumably a comment on Saint-Péravy's remarks on the undesirability of large expenditures in the capital city. See his *Mémoire*, pp. 103 ff. The General-Farm is selected for special criticism on this ground. See ibid., pp. 113 ff.

[12] This presumably refers to Saint-Péravy's remarks in the paragraph, op. cit., p. 106, beginning: "Qu'on imagine un droit sur les consommations, prélevant la dixième partie du prix naturel des denrées"; cf. also his discussion on pp. 106–111, especially p. 107, note 8, where the matter is discussed in more detail.

whole of the revenue must necessarily be returned directly to the circulation, without any part of it being set aside for the formation of a monetary capital, and that, if it were otherwise, the reproduction would suffer by it. This
p. 425 assumption is far from true; it is sufficient, in order to see its falsity, to reflect on the importance of capitals in all the profitable enterprises of agriculture, of industry and of trade, and on the utter necessity of advances for all these enterprises.

What are these advances, and where lies their origin, if not in the savings from the revenue? The only true wealth is the produce of the soil; the advances can thus grow only by the setting aside of part of what the soil produces, and part of what is not absolutely necessary for the reproduction. It makes no difference whether this part is put aside by the entrepreneurs of the industrious classes, or by the proprietors. In the first case, the entrepreneurs retain part of their profits and accumulate capitals which they use to expand their enterprises; but for this it is necessary that their profits are a little higher than what is strictly required for the reproduction on the following year. This may occur in two ways; firstly, because besides the current return and replacement of their advances, besides the salary for their work and subsistence, they have a right to an interest on their advances equal to what the same capital would yield them in any other way without effort on their part, be it in the acquisition of landed property, or in lending at interest. Thus they need only a certain amount of capital to start with for the interest on this capital, accumulating with it, to swell it at quite a rapid rate, because their right to a subsistence in return for their work is independent of their right to profits from their capital. Secondly, because the absence of competition for some enterprises puts the entrepreneurs in the position of making profits which are higher than what is required for the continuation of those enterprises, and from which they can save a great deal each year. These profits are a portion of the net product which the entrepreneur appropriates over and above the returns which are necessarily due to him, and at the expense of the proprietors. The immediate result of this thrift is the accumulation of movable capitals, and these capitals are only accumulated for the purpose of obtaining a revenue or annual profit, which can only be done by employing this capital. The effect of this accumulation is to lower the interest of loan money; to increase the exchange value of landed property; to diminish the necessary returns of the entrepreneurs in all industry and the costs of all enterprises; to
p. 426 make profitable, and consequently possible, enterprises which were not so previously; to increase proportionately the total number of enterprises and the total output.

Of all the employments of money, that which requires the least effort on the part of the capitalists, is lending at interest; the second in order of ease is the acquisition of land; but the latter is first in order of security. Only the expectation of making a greater profit could urge the owner of a money capital to

employ it in uncertain and laborious enterprises. The rate of interest of money is thus the first established standard, the parameter (if I may call it this) on the basis of which the exchange value of landed property and the profits of the advances in agricultural, industrial and commercial enterprises are established. It is useless to declaim against the public stocks and their useless owners; as long as this use of money, that is to say, as long as this need for borrowing money, will exist, it will be preferred, because it is in the nature of things that it should be. Only what is left over can be used to call into existence, by way of advances, enterprises which take trouble. It is like the bed of the Nile, which must necessarily be filled before the flood is diffused over the fields to fertilise *them*. There should be no complaining over the water flowing into this bed, for the law of gravity inevitably directs it there. There is even less call for complaint about the fact that the water accumulates, for without this accumulation the fields would not be irrigated. The true evil is that the bed is hollowed out so much that it absorbs the greater part of the water; the evil is that the government, through its numerous borrowings, continually presents money with a use which the owner finds advantageous and which is sterile as far as the State is concerned; the evil is that by this ruinous transaction it competes with the luxuries of private citizens to maintain the rate of interest at a level which is high in itself, and higher than that in foreign nations. But once this evil exists, it is no less beneficial that the owners, of, or those who share in, the revenue of the State do not spend it in its entirety, and put part of it aside each year to convert it into capitals, since a low interest of money, and all its advantageous consequences result from the quantity of capitals offered by the lenders relative to the quantity demanded by the borrowers. If the whole of the net product had been spent each year without any accumulation, the stock of advances, of, I won't say *la grande culture*, but of the poorest cultivation, could never have been formed, and never could these advances grow. The whole thing is quite p. 427
obvious.[13]

But it is said, since the money does not return to the circulation, it diminishes the exchange values, and consequently the returns of the farmers who, when they sell more cheaply than they expected, pay the price of their p. 428
lease by encroaching upon the renewal of their advances.

Four things may be said in reply to this.

Firstly, this argument would prove too much, for it would prove that the whole of the money collected by the proprietors as revenue must always return immediately into the hands of the cultivators, and that is completely

[13] In a lengthy note to this passage, Du Pont (*Oeuvres*, IV, p. 329, n. 1), contrasts Quesnay's analysis of capital formation with that of Turgot. The statement that thrift leads directly to capital formation is questioned on the ground that hoarding may delay this. See also, *Reflections*, above, section 101, p. 95; and Quesnay, 'Hommes', op. cit., II, pp. 528–529. (Du Pont's note is reproduced in Daire, *Oeuvres*, I, p. 427, n. 1, and in Schelle, *Oeuvres*, II, p. 651, n. (a).)

untrue. The followers of the *Philosophie Rurale*[14] themselves agree to this when they maintain so strongly the utter unimportance of what is called the balance of trade settled in money. For certainly, if, by the settlement of the balance of trade, part of of the specie circulating as money in the State flows abroad, the whole of this specie will not come back to match the commodities produced by the cultivator in the circulation; and, according to the thinking of the author, goods will fall in price. Yet, the author is persuaded that nothing is of less importance than the manner in which this monetary settlement takes place.

Secondly, each year the mass of gold and silver circulating in the world increases by the continual working of the mines. The silver which the mines yield is spread first through the State where the mines are situated. It must either remain there in circulation, or be accumulated by the entrepreneurs, or leave the country to be exchanged for commodities. In fact the silver which is accumulated does not take long to return to circulation, and it is in the nature of things that the silver from the mines should leave the countries of origin in order to be exchanged for foreign commodities; for if it remained in the home countries, commodities would increase in price so stupendously, and silver would depreciate so strongly, that, on the one hand, part of the mines would cease to yield a profit to their entrepreneurs sufficient to meet the costs of exploitation, and the national production, being worthless, would cease; while, on the other hand, the difference in price between foreign goods and domestic goods would soon be so large that, in spite of all prohibitions by the government, the interest of all citizen-consumers would combine with that of the foreign sellers to break all the barriers with which the prejudiced administration would oppose the exportation of silver.

The silver which the States with mines draw from the bowels of the earth enters, through the monetary settlement of the balance of trade, into the
p. 429 States which sell their commodities to the owners of the mines. This silver, carried into the trading nation through commerce, has similar effects as that drawn directly from the mines in the State in which they are situated. Silver, having become plentiful, raises the price of commodities; soon they can no longer be given at the same price to the nation which settles (its balance) in silver, and nations in which silver is scarcer obtain the preference. The nation which had acquired the surplus of silver is itself compelled to draw part of its consumption goods from nations by virtue of their greater or smaller proximity to the country with mines, and by virtue of the stage in history during which they began to enter the system, or, if you wish, the great society of civilised and commercial nations; finally, by virtue of the extent to which their constitution and their domestic laws are favourable to the growth of produc-

[14] I.e. Quesnay and the other leading Physiocrats. See Mirabeau, *Philosophie Rurale*, III, chapter XI, e.g. pp. 236–238; Quesnay himself put this argument strongly in his 'Dialogue du commerce' in *Quesnay et la Physiocratie*, II, pp. 848 ff.

tion and to commercial activity. From Peru and Brazil, gold and silver pass into Spain and Portugal, from there to France, England and Holland, then to Germany and the Scandinavian countries. It is well known that gold and silver are still sufficiently scarce in Sweden for copper to be used as money there, as in the early days of the Roman Republic, when the word *aes* signified what the word silver money signifies today in the common usage of commerce and civil life.

As the mines do not cease to furnish a new increase of the stock of precious metals each year, the result is that, from the countries where these mines are exploited down to the last regions which share at the final stage and to the least extent in their annual distribution through trade, there is not one which, in the natural order of things, and disregarding the disturbances which may be occasioned by excessive expenditures abroad, war, and defaulting governments, does not experience every year an increase in the stock of its circulating medium.

In the type of scale which ranks these States by their relative wealth of silver, those which are the most fortunate and which approach most nearly a state of complete prosperity, are those where the abundance and the value of money are at the intermediate level to which perfect equilibrium would bring them if it were possible, over time, for the silver to be distributed over the earth in proportion to the total annual output of each district. The natural cir-
culation of money in trade approaches this universal level; but it can never be p. 430
reached as long as the mines are not exhausted, that is to say, as long as they yield in sufficient abundance to cover the expenses of production with a sufficient profit to encourage the entrepreneurs to make advances; for this determines the limit of their exploitation, and not their physical exhaustion.

This state of affairs would reduce the trade between all nations to the exchange of commodities,[15] and there would be no real balance. The nations which are at present in this intermediate stage which have neither an abundance nor a deficiency of gold or silver, are almost in the same position, and they have no settlement in bullion of the balance of trade because they deliver as much of it to nations which have less bullion as they receive from those nations that have more.

Let us return to the question of the need to restore to the cultivator all the money he has paid out: I say that, if the quantity of money withdrawn from immediate circulation by saving is less, or even, if it is no more than the quantity of money introduced each year into the circulation by way of trade, the commodities will maintain their exchange value, the cultivators will use as much money for the reproduction as in the preceding year, and there will be no decline in wealth; the saving, therefore, will not be prejudicial to either the

[15] This sentence reads slightly different in the version as published by Schelle. In his edition (II, p. 654), it reads as follows in translation: "In this state of affairs, the trade between all nations would be reduced to the exchange of commodities . . .".

reproduction, or the revenue. Not only will it not be prejudicial, but in fact it will increase them, since in the final analysis its effect is always to increase the stock of capitals and the total advances, and to lower the rate of interest. If it really withdrew from the circulation the money put aside, it would prevent the increase in the price of commodities which results from the increase in money, it would maintain the nation's ability to sell her superfluous commodities to foreign owners of silver, it would reduce the need to buy from less wealthy foreigners things necessary for her consumption, which her own artisans could no longer furnish at such a low price. Even when the effect of saving is not to withdraw money from the circulation, it would make up, through the low price of labour caused by the increase in the exchange value of commodities. It removes all disadvantages from the superfluity of money and leaves only the advantages. Is there any one who does not know that in p. 4
Holland wages are so high that they could destroy commerce if the low interest of money, and the resultant activity, did not compensate for this factor?

Thirdly, I assume for the moment that the immediate effect of saving is to withdraw money from circulation, and to lower the exchange value, to the detriment of the cultivator. I say that if the consequence of this saving is an increase in the advances, it will also cause a greater production, or, if you like, a decrease in the costs; so that the decrease in the exchange value resulting from the small amount of money withdrawn from circulation, is more than compensated by the number of articles sold, or by a smaller fundamental value[16] of each article sold; thus there is a real advantage in putting money aside. Now, it is most likely that the increase in the advances does more good than the harm done by the small decrease in the exchange value caused by saving. For this decrease will always be extremely small if unrestricted exportation continues to let our output share in the prices of the general market. Perhaps the increase in output caused by the introduction of new advances would bring about even more efficiently the decrease in exchange values. But the remedy for this disadvantage lies in this same communication with the general market; in the variety of output which the soil can produce, from amongst which the cultivator can choose those whose sale yields the highest

[16] Two types of value may be distinguished: fundamental value and exchange value. The fundamental value is what the thing costs to him who sells it, that is, the raw material cost, the interest of the advances, the wages of labour and industry. The exchange value is the price which the buyer agrees upon with the seller. The fundamental value is fairly stable and changes less frequently than the exchange value. The latter is ruled by supply and demand, it varies with needs, and often a single event suffices to produce very considerable and very sudden fluctuations. It is not in any essential proportion to the fundamental value, but it has a tendency to approach it continually, and can never move far away from it permanently. It is obvious that it cannot remain below it for a long time; for, as soon as a commodity can be sold only at a loss, its production is discontinued until the resulting scarcity has again raised it to a price above its fundamental value. The price can similarly not be much above the fundamental value for any length of time, for this high price, implying high profits, would call forth the commodity and generate lively competition among the sellers. Now the natural effect of this competition would be to lower the price until it again approaches the fundamental value. (Note by Turgot.)

profits, and prefer thistles to wheat if he finds this to his advantage; finally, in the increase of the population which follows naturally from the abundance of p. 432
output.

Fourthly, it is assumed without any grounds that savings decrease the exchange values by withdrawing the sums put aside from the circulation. They almost all return to it immediately, and to be convinced of this, it is but necessary to reflect on the use which is made of the money saved; either it is used in the purchase of land, or it is lent at interest, or used as advances in agricultural, industrial, or commercial enterprises. It is obvious that this third type of use returns the capitals immediately to the circulation and exchanges them for equipment, beasts of burden, raw materials, wages of labour, and the purchase of goods which are the object of commerce. The same is true of the other two uses. The money of the acquirer of landed property goes to the seller; the latter usually sells in order to obtain a more useful acquisition, or to pay debts, and it is always to this last object that the price of the sale goes; for if the first seller buys other land, it will be the seller of this land, or if you wish, a third, who sells only to redeem his debts; and if the debts are pressing, the money is spent again immediately and put back into circulation. If the debts bear interest, the reimbursed creditor has nothing more urgent to do than to lend his money once again. Let us therefore see what happens to the money lent, what the borrower does with it.

Dissipating young gentlemen, and governments, borrow in order to spend, and what they spend returns immediately to the circulation. When they are wiser, they borrow to put their affairs in order, to pay outstanding debts and redeem debts which carry an excessive rate of interest. Some people borrow in order to make up the purchase price of land which they wish to acquire; and to this type of borrowing applies what I said above about the acquisition of land, to wit, that the money, at second or third hand, returns to the circulation, redistributing itself through trade. As for the loans of entrepreneurs, manufacturers, and merchants, it is well known that they are immediately poured into their enterprises and spent on advances of all sorts.

It follows of course from this analysis that money which is saved, accumulated, put aside for the formation of capitals, is not lost to the circulation, and that the sum of monetary values which are counterbalanced in the p. 433
transactions of commerce with the other values to settle their price, neither decreases nor increases by it.

In a nation where agriculture, industry and commerce flourish, and where the interest of money is low, the stock of capitals is immense, and yet it is well known that the quantity of money placed in hoards is quite negligible; almost all the existing capitals are represented by paper which is equivalent to money because the assets which are responsible for their soundness are equivalent to money. But there really is no money in the tills other than what is required to meet the daily payments necessary for the flow of trade. Sometimes transfers involving several millions take place without a single *sou* in silver changing hands. The quantity of this money, which so to speak circulates in large stocks, is thus very limited, always proportioned to the intensity of commercial activity, and to the fluctuations which it gives to money, which are always about the same.

I believe to have shown two things: the one, that if saving withdrew money from circulation, it would not for this alone be a bad thing; the other, that in fact saving does not really withdraw from circulation the money it puts aside.

The outcome of this long note is that the reserves and the stock of money accumulated by the farmers of the indirect tax, are not a bad thing in themselves, and should not be counted among the drawbacks of this type of taxation. The excessive profits are undoubtedly an evil, because they are grasped from the people and because, as they never enter the coffers of the prince, they force the latter to raise the tax. It is an evil that these profits are spent in Paris, just as it is an evil that the large landowners spend their revenue in Paris. But it is a good thing that the Farmers-General spend only gradually part of them.

CHAPTER VIII

1767

OBSERVATIONS ON THE PAPER BY GRASLIN IN FAVOUR OF THE INDIRECT TAX, TO WHICH THE ROYAL AGRICULTURAL SOCIETY OF LIMOGES HAS GIVEN AN HONOURABLE MENTION[1]

D.D. I 434–444

The author inappropriately charges the writers whom he attacks with considering the net product of the soil only, that is, the revenue as wealth.[2] All that the earth produces is wealth. But these writers maintain correctly that the total of the *renascent wealth* of a State is confined to the total *annual output* of the soil. This output is divided into two parts, one of which is destined for the subsistence and the satisfaction of the wants of the cultivator, for the interest on and the replacement of the advances, in short, for all that is necessary, directly and indirectly, for the reproduction of the following year. But once this part is deducted, the surplus, which the cultivator gives to the proprietor of the soil forms the latter's revenue, which not being in any way necessary for the reproduction of the following year, is completely free, disposable, and susceptible to division among the titular owner, the recipient of the tithe, the *seigneur censier*,[3] the State, etc.

* * *

The author does not understand either the real distinction between the two working classes, one of which, applied directly to the work of the soil,

[1] Graslin's paper entitled, *Essai analytique sur la Richesse et sur l'Impôt*, was written for a competition organised by the Royal Agricultural Society of Limoges on the subject of indirect taxation. See 'Introduction', above pp. XXII–XXIII. Graslin's work was published in 1767, *à Londres*; subsequent page references refer to this edition.

[2] This presumably refers to the following passage: "The writers whom I am attacking are far from denying this analytical consequence. In fact, the concept of the elementary wealth seen uniquely and exclusively in the productive soil, and limited even to the *net product* of the soil, i.e. net of all expenses, is the basis of the new system of Political Economy." Graslin, op. cit., p. 5.

Graslin adds a note in which he explains what he regards as being the new system of political economy, tracing its origin to (Mirabeau's) *l'Ami des Hommes*, and its development in the same author's *Théorie de l'Impôt* and *Philosophie Rurale*. He also refers to the journals *Journal d'Agriculture, de Commerce et de Finance*, 1765–1766, and *Ephémérides du Citoyen*, 1766–1767.

[3] I.e. the feudal lord to whom the commoners owed their *sens* or dues.

produces, or, to remove all ambiguity, gathers directly all the wealth which the earth yields; the other, receiving nothing directly except by way of those who have gathered the fruits of the earth, earns its subsistence and receives it in exchange for its work, but does not add any new wealth to the total wealth produced by the earth alone.[4]

* * *

p. 435 It is not, as the author believes,[5] all real wealth which can pay the tax; it must also be disposable, i.e. it must not be essential for the reproduction of the following year, be it immediately or a little later. Any wealth can be seized by a superior power, but no wealth which is essential for the work of reproduction can be diverted from it without harming this production, the national wealth, and by consequence, the source of power of the government. This comprises the whole of the theory of taxation.

The three primary consequences of this doctrine of the economic writers are summarised in unlimited freedom of trade. The usefulness of this liberty as declaimed by the principles which the author attacks, is based, moreover, on so many other incontestible propositions that its certainty does not depend by any means on the system adopted as regards the nature of wealth and of the revenue. It should not be believed either than in permitting the selling and buying of what and to whom one pleases, the whole of industry is abandoned for this, as the author and the other partisans of protection imagine or argue:[6] the argument of those who, to create fear of freedom, assume that the foreigners will buy all our raw materials, will get hold of all of our industry, and will carry on the whole of our commerce, this argument is of the same type as that of the people who fear that the freedom of selling our grain abroad will cause us to die of hunger, although this freedom, of necessity, will increase our production and our stores, which will never seek an outlet in foreign parts when they find a profitable one at home.

* * *

I define as goods (*bona*) all objects of enjoyment, of property, of desire and of need. I define as value (*merae*) all things susceptible to exchange and evaluation. I define as wealth (*opes*) all goods which may be traded, all objects of enjoyment which have a value. The *revenue* is the wealth which the earth yields over and above the expenses and the returns to those who cultivate it.

[4] This note presumably refers to Graslin, op. cit., p. 5, the paragraph beginning: "Dela cette distinction des hommes en *classe productive* et en *classe stérile* . . .".

[5] This is presumably a comment on Graslin's statement in the paragraph beginning: "La richesse réelle pouvant seule payer l'Impôt . . .", op. cit., p. 9.

[6] Graslin claims these consequences of the freedom of trade in a footnote, op. cit., p. 9.

Water is a good which has no value at all. Work has a value, and is not in itself a good. Corn and cloth are wealth. What the farmer renders to the proprietor of an estate is a revenue.[7]

It follows from these definitions that the output of the land, when it is only equal to the expenses, is wealth, but *non disposable* wealth; WEALTH and not REVENUE. In the example cited[8] of a field planted with flax, which costs the cultivator *one hundred francs* and returns him only *one hundred francs*, this flax is *wealth* and has undoubtedly, like all other forms of wealth, its *usefulness*; but it is obvious that it does not yield any revenue either to the proprietor or to the State. The cultivator would not give a *sou* to the proprietor of such a field for permission to cultivate it; for what he gives could only be taken from his bodily needs. By the same argument, the State can draw nothing from this field, nor ask anything from the cultivator, without depriving him of his subsistence and consequently making it impossible for him to work. If all the fields of a kingdom were cultivated in this manner, it is obvious that the State could not levy any taxes, not because there would be no *wealth*, but because there would be no *revenue*, no disposable wealth; because, the whole annual output being set aside for the bodily needs of those who produce it, anything that might be taken from it would destroy the cultivation and the reproduction of the following year. p. 436

* * *

It is quite true, considering things vaguely, that as the subsistence of the cultivator makes up part of the expenses, the less the cultivator consumes for himself, the more remains for the net product.[9] It is certain that if a farmer wore clothes of velvet, and his wife wore lace, this expense would have to be recovered from the product of the earth by diminishing the portion of the proprietor. But it does by no means follow that the misery of the cultivator increases the net product. On the contrary, it has been shown that the wealth of agricultural entrepreneurs is no less necessary than work itself to obtain a plentiful output from the soil.[10] Since the fertility of the soil is limited, there is undoubtedly a point at which the augmentation of the advances would not increase the output in proportion to the increase of expenses; but at present this

[7] Turgot is very fond of etymological discussions, as is also revealed in 'Fairs and Markets', above p. 14, and 'Value and Money', below pp. 136–137. He contributed the article 'Etymologie' to the *Encyclopédie*; see vol. VI, pp. 98–111.

This discussion presumably refers to Graslin's definitions of such terms as *richesse, valeur,* etc. in the second chapter of his work.

[8] This example is given by Graslin, op. cit., pp. 11–12 in the paragraph beginning: "Pour prouver ma première proposition, je supposerai un paysan qui a employé toute sa vie à cultiver du lin . . .".

[9] This presumably refers to the paragraph beginning: "Si la richesse de l'Etat . . .", Graslin, op. cit., p. 12.

[10] Cf. Quesnay's articles 'Fermiers' and 'Grain', op. cit., II, pp. 454, 504–506.

limit is far from being attained, and experience proves that in those places where the advances are largest, that is, where the cultivators are most wealthy, there is not only the greatest output, but also the greatest *net product.*[11]

Assuming the output to remain the same, the smaller the share of the p. 437 cultivator, the larger that of the proprietor or the other partakers of the net product. But, if the cultivator would not receive a fair amount in proportion to his advances, if he were not sufficiently wealthy to have a right to a large profit from large advances, the output would no longer be the same at all, and it would become even more scanty as the cultivator grows even poorer, up to the point when, at a certain level of poverty, there would no longer be any net product. Thus it is very far from true that the principles attacked by the author contradict the resolution which humanity dictated to Henry IV.[12]

Moreover, the author does not appear to have distinguished here between the agricultural entrepreneur and the rural wage labourer, the ploughman, the day labourer, who works the soil with his arms. Yet these are two very different types of men who cooperate in quite different ways in the great work of the annual reproduction of wealth. The agricultural entrepreneur contributes to the reproduction through his advances; the man of toil contributes through his labour, for which the agricultural entrepreneur pays him his wages. It must, moreover, be admitted that the more the entrepreneur pays in wages to his carters, the more dearly he pays for the time of the reapers and other day labourers whom he employs, the more he lays out in costs, and that this outlay is always a deduction from the net product. What can be concluded from this? Is this not true in all systems? Is there any type of work in which profits are not diminished by the dearness of the labour? And is there any inhumanity in admitting a truth which only has to be expressed in words to become obvious? Moreover, there exists a natural proportion between the wealth produced, the revenue, and the wages, a proportion which establishes itself, and which causes that neither the entrepreneurs nor the proprietors have an interest in lowering the wages below this proportion. Apart from the fact that, in any kind of work, an ill paid man, who does not earn a plentiful livelihood by his work, works less well, the exchange value of the rural output is less. Now, if, when the cultivator pays his labourers less, he sells his grain for less, it is obvious that he is none the wealthier from this. The exchange value of the output of the soil is, normally, the measure of the wealth gathered each year by the cultivator, who shares it with the proprietor. A high

[11] Cf. Turgot, 'Observations on a Paper by Saint-Péravy', above pp. 111–113, for a more detailed discussion of the laws of returns.

[12] Henri IV, King of France (1553–1610). His Finance Minister, the Duc de Sully, was a great favourite with the Physiocrats. His *Economies Royales* were reprinted in the second edition of the *Tableau Economique*. Turgot may be referring to the following of these maxims: 8, 9 and especially 14; see 'Extrait des Economies Royales de M. de Sully', in *Quesnay et la Physiocratie*, II, 670–671.

exchange value of the produce of the soil and a large revenue enable the cultivator and the proprietor to pay high wages to men who live by their manual labour. High wages, on the one hand enable wage earners to consume more, and to increase their well-being: on the other hand, this well-being and these high wages offered, encourage population; the fruitfulness of the earth attracts foreigners, multiplies the people; and the increase in people in turn lowers wages through competition, while the number maintains the consumption and its exchange value. The exchange value of the produce, the revenue, the wage rate, the population, are things related to each other by a mutual dependence, which spontaneously reach their equilibrium according to a natural proportion; and this proportion is always maintained when commerce and competition are completely free.[13] p. 438

The single practical conclusion that can be drawn from this, is that wage labourers must be *completely free* to work for whom they desire, in order that the employers, by contending for them when they need them, may place a just price on their labour; and that, on the other hand, the employers must be *completely free* to use such men as they deem proper, in order that the local workers may not, by taking advantage of their small number, force them to increase wages above the natural proportion which depends on the stock of wealth, the value of subsistence goods, the amount of work available and the number of workers, but which can never be settled by anything other than competition and freedom.

* * *

Although the expenses of agriculture are spent in the State, it does not follow that, as the author believes,[14] the State will be just as wealthy when the costs increase at the expense of the *net product*. The State has not, and cannot have, any strength except for the *net product*, because all that is necessary for the reproduction is assigned to the needs of the individuals who work to create it, in such a way that nothing of it can be seized for the public expenditure. Now, if there can be no public expenditure, if there is no communal power to be used in the common interest, there is no State properly speaking; there is only a country peopled by inhabitants who are born, who live, and who die near each other. The expenses of agriculture remain in the State in the sense that they are expended between the Rhine, the Alps, the Pyrenees and the sea; but they neither are, nor can be, the property of the State con- p. 439
sidered as the body politic formed by the union of communal forces directed

[13] Cf. 'Letters on the Grain Trade', below, pp. 177–179, for a similar discussion.

[14] This presumably refers to Graslin's argument, op. cit., p. 13: "La dépense du cultivateur, ainsi que tous les frais de culture, ne diminuent rien de la richesse de la production du sol . . .".
The phrase, "as the author believes", appears to have been added by Du Pont (*Oeuvres*, IV, p. 352). It does not occur in Schelle (*Oeuvres*, II, p. 635).

towards a common interest. The comparison with the silver mine which costs one hundred marcs to exploit and which produces one hundred marcs, is fallacious.[15] This silver mine obviously returns nothing to its proprietor, nor to the entrepreneur who would exploit it at his pleasure, but it is true that it leaves a value of one hundred marcs which, not being consumed, increases the sum of value existing in the State until this money flows abroad by means of the exchanges. In this respect, the renascent wealth of the soil which is consumed and reproduced annually, is very different from the non-consumable values which circulate continually without ever being destroyed. Certainly, the sum of values spent each year on the expenses of agriculture is consumed and destroyed entirely as subsistence for the agents of the reproduction. As for the values which circulate without being destroyed, such as the products of mines, the expenditure of the costs of extraction does not completely annihilate them, and only causes them to change hands. It may therefore be said that the State has gained one hundred marcs, in the sense that one hundred marcs exist in the country. But what increase in the wealth of the State, considered as the body politic, results from this? None, except in so far as the existence of this new circulating value can increase the sum of the revenue or the net product of the earth, be it in augmenting the advances allocated to the reproduction or to commerce, if the money is set aside to form a capital which is directed to a profitable use; or be it in increasing the exchange value of the output, if this money, carried immediately to the circulation, is presented in the market in current purchases and causes their price to rise. This proposition is capable of proof, but in order to demonstrate it fully it would be necessary to develop the true use of money in trade and the result of its introduction into a State in greater or lesser quantity, by considering this State as if it were isolated, and then as if it were surrounded by other States with which it has different commercial and political relations. These questions, which have never been fully developed, are too lengthy to be treated here. I shall say only that the author is very much mistaken by regarding money purely as a *conventional token of wealth.*[16] It is not at all by vir-
p. 440 tue of a *convention* that money is exchanged for all the other values: it is because it is itself an object of commerce, a form of wealth, because it has a value, and because any value exchanges in trade for an equal value.

* * *

The author puts forward an objection to the principles of his adversaries

[15] Graslin gives this example in the rest of the passage referred to in note 14 above, but adds the following footnote: "I give this only for comparison; for the advantage of the legal increase in the Kingdom's specie is not as great as that of the increase in produce or the products of industry. In fact this advantage is real only because specie is the conventional token of wealth, in foreign nations as well as in ours. . . ."

[16] Cf. note 15 above.

which may be reduced to these questions: "If industry and trade do not produce any wealth, how do purely industrial and commercial nations live? How do they enrich themselves? If taxation can only be levied on the net product of the estates, how can these nations pay taxes? Would industry be a source of wealth in a commercial State but not in an agricultural State?"[17]

There are no nations which are industrial and commercial as opposed to agricultural; and neither are there any nations which are agricultural to the exclusion of all industry and trade. The word *nation* has not as yet been defined very exactly, because nations have often been confused with bodies politic or States.

A *nation* is a collection of people who speak the same language. Thus all Greeks belonged to the same nation, even though they were divided into a host of States. Nowadays the Italians form a nation, and the Germans another, even though Italy and Germany are divided into several independent sovereign States. In former times the French nation was not united into a single monarchy; several provinces obeyed various sovereigns, and all those who speak French are not even united into the Kingdom of France.

A *State* is a collection of men united under a single government. In this connection, this distinction is neither as strictly grammatical nor as irrelevant as it appears.

The term nation can only be applied to a large populace distributed over a vast stretch of country which yields the inhabitants enough to satisfy their needs. The soil, through the work of agriculture, gives them food and raw materials for their clothes, industry fashions these raw materials and makes them suitable for various uses. Commerce brings consumers and producers together, saving them the trouble of searching for each other, and assuring them that they will find the commodity in the place and at the time they need p. 441
it. Commerce, as the author of this paper says so well,[18] is responsible for transportation, warehouses, stocks, and for waiting. The mutual needs of buyers and sellers encourage them to come together and they must naturally gather in those places in every province which are the most conveniently located, most densely populated, at which the course which each follows for his own affairs cross in the greatest number.[19] Those points naturally become the commercial meeting places, the dwellings of the middle-men are gathered there, they develop into boroughs and towns where the gathering of buyers and sellers increases all the more as they are more certain of finding the opportunity to buy and sell there. Therefore, everywhere different centres of commerce spring up, more or less closely together and corresponding to dis-

[17] This presumably refers to the questions asked by Graslin in the paragraph beginning: "S'il n'y avait que le sol qui put produire la richesse renaissante . . .", op. cit., p. 14.

[18] See Graslin, op. cit., p. 98.

[19] The argument presented in this lengthy paragraph is also to be found, in a slightly different context, in Turgot's article 'Fairs and Markets', above pp. 14–17.

tricts of different sizes by reason of the abundance of the country's production, the size of the population, and the relative ease of transporting the commodities. The markets established in the principal places of each province for the retail trade and for the objects of daily consumption constitute as it were the first order of these centres of commerce, each of them corresponding to a very limited district only. There are also commodities with a less general and less frequent use, which are not consumed in sufficient quantity to allow the profitable establishment of their cultivation of manufacture in every individual place. The value of these commodities is normally high enough for a small volume to be able to bear the costs of long transport. The commerce in these goods is carried on in larger lots which are afterwards distributed to the retailers. The same principle which established markets for the trade in the most common commodities in the places with the most frequented gatherings, establishes markets of a higher order for the wholesale trade. These correspond to a more extensive district, and merchandise gathers there from further afield to be distributed to more remote places. These large markets (*emporia*) are exactly what are called *ports* of commerce, entrepots. They were towns of the kind which, in the centuries of feudal barbarism, having joined together for the general defence, formed the Hanseatic league. These ports of commerce are always large towns, and in any case they would become so by the gathering of citizens drawn to them by the commercial activity. It is the ad-
p. 442 vantageous situation of towns at the crossroads, if I may be so bold to speak like this, of large commercial routes, or at the mouth of navigable rivers, the good quality of the harbours, and sometimes the industry of the inhabitants and the flourishing state of certain manufactures which causes the great entrepots of commerce to be established there. Thus Nantes is the outlet of the Loire, Rouen that of the Seine, Bordeaux of the provinces through which the Garonne and Dordogne flow, the towns of Holland and Zealand of the Rhine, the Maas and the Scheldt, Hamburg of the Elbe, Venice of the Po. Tyre, Carthage, Messina, Genoa, and Cadiz have had an advantageous maritime location as their only advantage. Lyon, Geneva, Strasbourg, Orleans, Limoges, are entrepots of a slightly lower order. In all these towns, commerce and trade are the principal occupations of the inhabitants, and each town corresponds to a more or less extensive area of several districts or provinces of which it is the entrepot, from which it gathers the products, and to which it distributes their needs. The territory and commerce of these entrepot towns are two correlated things necessary to each other, and the distinction between the commerce in the produce of the soil and the entrepots or retail trade does not exist with respect to nations or regions. The fact is that certain towns and maritime coasts which served as entrepots to an extensive commerce, have been able, through chance of circumstances, to form little political States separated from the territory of which they are the entrepot; but this chance has changed nothing in the nature of things. Holland, whatever be its govern-

ment, will still be the outlet of the Rhine, the Maas and the Scheldt, and of the canals of prolific Belgium; she will still be a favourable place of commerce and entrepot for all the harbours of England, France and the Baltic States, and consequently also for most of the other countries which wish to keep up relations and exchange with these different States, for which Holland is particularly necessary.

Therefore to have advantage of location is to have a type of exclusive privilege in comparison with less happily situated places. Because of this privilege, which is a natural one and therefore not unjust, wages may be received which exceed the needs of those who earn them, even with economy for those who pay them, above all if the former are wise enough to live thriftily, as the Dutch do.

Consequently, from the excess of their wages over their needs, which they p. 443 are well able to curtail, people in this situation easily accumulate capitals which lower the interest of money among them. This assures them a further claim to preference, a further increase in wages. It is from the excess of these wages over their needs that the Dutch are able to discharge their public expenditure and continue to enrich themselves.

They have not produced these wages, nor the wealth which pays them; they have earned them legitimately by their work which their location has made both lucrative for them and useful to those who employ them; they have earned their wages like the commission agents of our cities earn theirs.

In wealthy, civilised countries, illustrious scholars, great doctors, artists, poets, and even great comedians, may also earn respectable salaries, live in ease, afford considerable expenditure, practise charity, accumulate capitals. No one thinks that they have produced any of this wealth which they acquire, which they can dispose of, and which is transmitted to them, by whom? by the proprietors of the estates; who obtain it – from whom? from the cultivators, from the advances and from the work of agriculture: advances, work of which the process can neither be constrained nor interrupted without ruin; and it is of this last maxim that the theory of taxation consists, as I have already said.

The author, and those who share his opinions, persist by saying: "Since there are people who earn high salaries, they are therefore able to pay the tax: you agree that the Dutch pay taxes which sustain their republic. In order that the tax may not be arbitrary and be proportioned approximately to resources, is it not proper to levy it on consumer goods?[20]

To this I reply:

Firstly, that the Dutch add the need to pay tax to their other needs, which

[20] This would seem to be a reference to Graslin's argument that when rich people have an income which exceeds their expenses, they can pay tax on that excess; op. cit., p. 21. The "proportionality" of taxes on consumption is discussed by Graslin in the second part of his paper, ch. IV, esp. pp. 310 ff.

must be provided for by their wages which other nations pay them; so that, apart from the portion which burdens the Dutch territory directly, the other nations pay the tax of that republic.

Secondly, that it is impossible to make consumers who are not proprietors pay tax on their consumption, because as soon as it is imposed, they are com-
p. 444 pelled either to curtail their consumption, or to lower the price which they are able to offer for the products which they consume, and because the one or the other measure throws this tax back on the producers and the sellers of these products.

Thirdly, that the price of high wages, like that of moderate ones, is regulated by competition and therefore cannot be impaired without the wage-earner recouping himself for it, for otherwise he would withdraw his labour and take it elsewhere.

To this must be added, fourthly, that if it is desired to place the tax on the more expensive consumption of the wealthier wage-earners,[21] it will yield almost nothing, because the number of these rich wage-earners is always very small. And that, if, in order to increase the receipts, common consumption goods are made to bear the burden, it becomes very disproportionate to wages, almost nothing on those of the wage earners who earn a lot, and crushing, at least temporarily and until they have been able to reimburse themselves, on those of the poor wage-earners who carry out the most laborious and most useful work, to whom belong naturally all the specifically agricultural wage earners, who make up the greatest part of the population. This inevitably raises the costs of cultivation, and this is the most onerous manner of shifting the tax back onto the proprietors; the most ruinous for the capitals set aside for the cultivation in countries where estates are leased; the manner which causes the speediest abandonment of mediocre land, which, therefore, most inevitably decreases the subsistence of the population and most rapidly leads a nation to misery.

[21] Graslin suggested that "luxuries" be taxed more than goods of prime necessity; cf. op. cit., pp. 314 ff.

CHAPTER IX

1769

VALUE AND MONEY[1]

D.D. I 75–93

Money has this in common with measures in general, that it is a type of language, differing among different peoples in everything that is arbitrary and conventional, but of which the forms are brought closer and made identical, in some respects, by their relation to a common term or standard.

This common term which brings all languages together and which gives all tongues a basic similarity in spite of the diversity of the sounds employed, is none other than the very ideas which these words express, that is, the objects of nature represented by the senses to the human mind and the notions man has formed by distinguishing the different aspects of these objects and by combining them in a thousand ways.

It is this common foundation, essential to all languages independently of all conventions, which allows each language, each system of convention adopted as the symbols of ideas, to be used as a basis of comparison for all the other systems of convention, as one would compare to the actual system of ideas which can be interpreted by each language, that which was originally expressed in any other language, that which can, in short, be translated.

The common term of all measures of length, area or volume is only the actual size, of which the different measures adopted by different peoples are but arbitrary divisions which can in like manner be compared and reduced to one another.

One language is translated into another, one measure is reduced to another. These different expressions indicate two very different operations.

Languages designate ideas through sounds which are in themselves extraneous to those ideas. These sounds, from one language to another, are entirely different, and to explain them, it is necessary to substitute one sound for another; for the sound of the foreign language, the sound which cor-

[1] This paper is presumed to have been written for Morellet's venture of a *Dictionnaire de Commerce* in five volumes, a project which never materialised, though a prospectus was issued in 1769. See Morellet, *Prospectus d'un nouveau Dictionnaire de Commerce*, Paris, 1769, pp. 1–8; and above, 'Introduction', pp. XXVI–XXVII.

responds to it in the language into which it is being translated. Measures on
p. 76 the contrary, measure size only by size itself. Only the choice of the size taken by agreement for the unit of measurement, and the divisions adopted to indicate the different measures are arbitrary and subject to variation. Thus there are no substitutions to make from one thing to another, only quantities to be compared, and proportions to be substituted for other proportions.

The common term to which the *currencies* of all nations are related is the actual *value* of all objects of commerce which they serve to measure. But since this value can only be expressed by the quantity of money to which it corresponds, it follows that *money* can only be *valued* in terms of other *money*, just as sounds from one language can only be interpreted by means of the sounds of another.

Since the moneys of all civilised nations are made of the same materials, and since they, like measures, differ among themselves only with regard to the divisions of these materials and the arbitrary determination of what is regarded as the unit, they are susceptible, in this respect, to being reduced the one to the other, just as the measures employed by the divers nations are.

We shall see below, that this reduction is made in a very convenient manner, by the expression of their weight and their standard.

But this manner of valuing currencies by the statement of their weight and standard is not adequate for an understanding of the language of commerce in relation to money. All the nations of Europe know two types of money. In addition to the real coins, such as the écu, the louis, the crown and the guinea, which are pieces of metal, marked with a known inscription and negotiable under this denomination, each nation has created a kind of fictitious money which is called money of account or numéraire, whose denominations and divisions, without corresponding to any actual coin, form a common scale, to which actual money is related, by being valued in terms of the number of parts of this scale to which they correspond. In France, this is the livre of account or numéraire, composed of twenty sous, which in turn is subdivided into twelve deniers. There is no coin which corresponds to a livre, but an écu is worth three livres, a louis is worth twenty-four livres, and thus this expression of the values of the two coins in terms of the unit of account, establishes the relation between the écu and a louis as one to eight.

p. 77 Since these moneys of account, as we have seen, are only arbitrary denominations, they vary from nation to nation, and, in the same nation, they may vary from one period to the other.

The English thus have their pound sterling, divided into twenty sous or shillings, which again divide into twelve deniers or pennies. The Dutch calculate in florins, whose divisions do not correspond to those of our livre.

We have therefore to show, in commercial geography, not only the real currencies of each nation, and their evaluation by weight and standard, but also the money of account employed by each nation, and furthermore, their relation to the real money negotiable in the nation, and the relations between the moneys of account of different nations. The relation of the money of account to the actual money of each nation is determined by expressing the value of the actual money in terms of the unit of account of the same country; that of ducats in terms of florins, that of the guinea in shillings and pence sterling, of the louis and écu in livres tournois.[2]

As for the mutual relations of the units of account customary among the different nations, the idea which first presents itself is that of deducing them from the relations between the money of account of each nation and the actual money, and from the knowledge of the weight and standard of the latter. Indeed, knowing the weight and standard of an English crown and the weight and standard of a French écu, the relation between a crown and a French écu is known, and knowing how much an écu is worth in terms of deniers tournois, the value of a crown in terms of deniers tournois may be deduced; and as the value of a crown in terms of pence sterling is also known, the equivalent of pence sterling in deniers tournois is known, and hence the relation between the pound sterling and the livre tournois.

This method of valuing the moneys of account of different nations by comparing them with the actual money of each nation, and by the knowledge of the weight and standard of the latter, would not give rise to any difficulty if all the money was made of a single metal, silver for example, or if the relative value of different metals used for this purpose, gold and silver for example, was the same among all commercial nations, that is if a certain weight of pure gold, a marc[3] for example, was worth exactly the same number of grains of pure silver in all nations. But this relative value of gold and silver varies according to the abundance or relative scarcity of these two metals in the different nations. p. 78

If in one nation there is thirteen times more silver than gold, and thus in consequence thirteen marcs of silver exchange for one marc of gold, fourteen marcs of silver will exchange for one marc of gold in another nation where there is fourteen times more silver than gold. It follows from this, that if, in order to determine the value of the money of account of two nations where gold and silver do not have the same relative value, to value, for example, the pound sterling in terms of the livre tournois, gold coin is used as the term of comparison, a different result would be obtained than if silver coin had been used. It is clear that the true measure lies between these two results, but in order to determine it with complete and rigorous precision, it would be necessary to bring into the solution of this problem a multitude of extremely delicate considerations. Meanwhile, the silver trade among nations, all the

[2] The *livre tournois,* as Turgot explains, was the French money of account, and takes its name from the French town of Tours. It has to be differentiated from the *livre Paris,* which was used for circulation.

[3] The marc was a weight of silver or gold, about 8 oz. troy.

negotiations pertaining to that trade, the use of paper credit for money, the operations of the exchanges and of the banks all assume that this problem has been solved.

The word *money*, in its first, original and proper sense, which corresponds exactly to the latin *moneta*, denotes a piece of metal of a specified weight and standard, and guaranteed by the inscription placed on it by the public authority. Stating the name, the inscription, the weight and the standard of each coin of different nations, while converting this weight to marcs, is all that has to be done in order to give a clear idea of money considered from this first point of view.

But usage has given a wider and more abstract meaning to this word *money*. Metals are divided into pieces of a certain weight; the authority guarantees their standard by an inscription, only in order that they may be used in commerce in a satisfactory and safe manner, so that they may serve there both as a measure of value and as a store representing the value of produce; moreover, the idea of dividing and marking the metals in this way, or, in short, of coining money, has been conceived only because these metals were already serving as a measure and a common pledge of all value.

p. 79 Since money has no other use, this name has come to be regarded as designating that very use, and as it is true to say that money is the measure and pledge of value, because everything which acts as measure and pledge of value can take the place of money, the name money in this wide sense has been given to everything used in this way. It is in this sense that cowries are the *currency* of the Maldivian islands, that livestock was the *currency* of the Germanic tribes and the ancient inhabitants of Latium, that gold, silver and copper are the *currency* of civilised people; that these metals were *currency* before the idea of showing their weight and standard by a legal stamp was conceived. It is in this sense that the name *paper currency* is given to letters of credit, which represent money. It is, finally, in this sense that the name of money fits the purely abstract denominations which serve as a basis of mutual comparison for all values, even those of actual moneys, and which are called *money of account, bank money*, etc.

The word money in this sense, is not to be translated by the Latin word, *moneta*, but by that of *pecunia*, to which it corresponds very exactly.

It is in this last sense, that is, as a measure of value and a pledge of value, that we are going to look at *money* when we follow the course of its introduction in commerce and the progress which the art of *measuring* value has made among mankind.

First of all, it is essential to get a clear idea of what ought to be understood here by this word, *value*.

This abstract noun, which corresponds to the verb '*to be worth*' (*valoir*), in Latin *valere*, has in everyday language several meanings, which it is important to distinguish.

The original meaning of this word, in the Latin language, denoted strength, vigour,[4] *valere* also meant *to be in good health*, and we keep this original meaning in French in the derivations *valide* (healthy), *invalide* (invalid), and *convalescence*. From this use of the word *valour* (*valeur*) as denoting strength, its meaning has been diverted to signify military courage, a virtue which the ancients have nearly always designated by the same word meaning physical strength. The word *'valoir'* in French has taken another frequently used meaning, and one which, although different from the sense given in commerce to this word and to the word *value*, forms, however, its original foundation.

It expresses the suitability relative to our needs by which the gifts and the p. 80
goods of nature are regarded as fit for our enjoyment and for the satisfaction of our desires. It is said that a stew is *worthless* if its flavour is bad, that a food is *bad* for the health, that one material is *better* than another, an expression which has no relation to its *commercial value*, and which only signifies that it is more suitable to the use for which it is intended.

The adjectives *bad, mediocre, good, excellent,* describe the different degrees of this type of value. It must be observed, however, that the noun *value* is not nearly as much used in this sense as the verb *to be worth* (*valoir*). But if it is used, it can only be understood to mean the suitability of an object for our enjoyment. Although this suitability is always relative to ourselves, yet we have in view, when explaining the word *value*, a real quality which is intrinsic to the object and through which it is suitable for our use.

This sense of the word *value* would be appropriate to a man in isolation, without any communication with other men.

Let us consider this man as exerting his abilities on a single object only; he will seek after it, avoid it, or treat it with indifference. In the first case, he would undoubtedly have a motive for seeking after this object; he would judge it to be suitable for his enjoyment, he will find it *good,* and this relative goodness could generally speaking be called *value,* it would not be susceptible to measurement, and the thing which has *value* would not be *evaluated.*

If the same man can choose between several objects suitable to his use, he will be able to prefer one to the other, find an orange more agreeable than chestnuts, a fur better for keeping out the cold than a cotton garment; he will regard one as *worth more* than another; he will compare them in his mind, he will appraise their *worth.* He will consequently decide to undertake those things which he prefers, and leave the others.

The savage has killed a calf, which he takes to his hut; on his way he finds a roe; he kills it and takes it instead of the calf in the expectation of eating a more delicious meat. In the same way a child, who had first filled his pockets with chestnuts, empties them in order to make room for some sugared

[4] There is here a slight difference between the texts. Schelle (*Oeuvres,* III, p. 84) has, in translation: "In the original meaning which this word had in the Latin language, it denoted strength, vigour; . . .".

almonds which have been given to him.

p. 81 This, then, is a comparison of *value*, an evaluation of the different objects in the judgements of this savage and this child; but these *appraisals* are not permanent, they change continually with the need of the person. When the savage is hungry, he values a piece of game more than the best bearskin; but let his appetite be satisfied and let him be cold, and it will be the bearskin that becomes valuable to him.

As often as not, the savage confined his desires to the satisfaction of his immediate needs, and no matter what the quantity is of the objects for which he has no use, as soon as he has taken what he needs, he leaves the remainder, which is of no use to him.

Experience, however, teaches our savage that among the objects suitable for his enjoyment, there are some whose nature makes them capable of being kept for some time, and which he may accumulate for future needs: these keep their value even when the immediate need has been satisfied. He seeks to appropriate them, i.e. to put them in a safe place where he can hide or guard them. It may be seen that the number of considerations which enter into the estimation of this *value, relative* solely *to the man* who enjoys and desires, increases greatly through this new perspective which foresight adds to the original feeling of need. When this feeling, which at first was only transitory, assumes the character of permanence, the man begins to compare his needs, to adapt his quest for objects no longer to the swift impulse of the immediate need alone, but in accordance to the necessity and usefulness (utilité) of the different needs.

As for the other considerations by which this ranking of more or less pressing usefulness is weighed up or modified, one of the first which suggests itself is the suitability of the object, or its relative capacity to satisfy the type of need for which it is sought. It must be admitted that this degree of suitability, with regard to the estimation which results from it, falls to some extent within the order of usefulness since the pleasure of the keener enjoyment produced by this degree of suitability is itself an advantage which a man compares with the more urgent necessity of those objects whose abundance he prefers to the suitability of a single one.

A third consideration is the degree of difficulty which a man meets in
p. 82 procuring the object of his desires; for it is quite clear that of two things of equal usefulness and quality, he would regard that which cost him more toil to obtain as the more precious, and he will take much more care and effort to obtain it. It is for this reason that water, in spite of its necessity and the multitude of pleasures which it provides for man, is not regarded as a precious thing in a well-watered country; that man does not seek to gain its possession, since the abundance of this element allows him to find it all around him. But in the sandy deserts it would command an infinite price.[5]

[5] This last sentence was added by Du Pont. See Schelle, *Oeuvres*, III, p. 86.

We have not yet begun to discuss exchange, and already we have touched upon scarcity, one of the elements in the process of *valuation*. It must be pointed out,[6] that the esteem attached to scarcity is still founded on a particular type of usefulness, for it is because it is more useful to accumulate a thing difficult to find, that it is more sought after and that a man puts more effort into acquiring it.

It is possible to deduce from these three considerations all those that enter into the determination of the type of *value* relating to man in isolation; they are the three elements which combine to determine it. To give it an appropriate name we shall call it *esteem value* (*valeur estimative*), because it is in fact the expression of the degree of esteem which a man attaches to the different objects of his desire.

It seems useful to stress this notion and to analyse what is meant by this degree of esteem which man attaches to his different wants; what is the essence of this valuation, or the expression of the unit to which the value of each particular object is compared, what is the notation of this scale of comparison and what is its unit of measurement.[7]

Reflecting upon this, we find that the totality of things necessary for the subsistence and well-being of man[8] form, if I may use the expression, a *sum of needs* which is fairly limited in spite of all their range and variety.

To obtain the satisfaction of these wants, man has only an even more limited quantity of strength and resources. Each particular object of enjoyment costs him trouble, hardship, labour, and, at the very least, time. It is this use of his resources applied to the quest for each object which provides the offset to his enjoyment, and forms as it were the cost of the thing. The man is still isolated, nature alone supplies his wants, and already he has made a first *bargain* with her, in which she supplies nothing unless he pays for it by his p. 83
labour, the use of his resources and his time.

His capital, in this kind of exchange[9] is confined within narrow limits; he must adjust the sum of his enjoyments to it. He must make a choice in the tremendous store house of nature, and he must divide this *cost* of which he

[6] There is a slight variation in the text at this point. Du Pont (*Oeuvres*, III, p. 271) has: "Il faut remarquer que cette estime . . .", while Schelle (*Oeuvres*, III, p. 86) has: "Mais il faut dire que cette estime . . .".

[7] Du Pont (*Oeuvres*, III, p. 271) has made some minor alterations in this paragraph, thereby distorting its meaning. After "valuation" (évaluation), his text reads: "ou le terme moyen auquel les *valeurs* de chaque objet en particulier sont comparées; quelle est la numération de cette échelle de comparaison; quelle est l'utilité". Schelle (*Oeuvres*, III, p. 87) has what is undoubtedly the correct version: "ou le terme unite auquel les *valeurs* de chaque objet en particulier sont comparées; quelle est la numération de cette échelle de comparaison; quelle est l'unité".

[8] Du Pont (*Oeuvres*, III, p. 272) has made a further alteration at this point. After "well-being of man" (bien être de l'homme), his text reads: "correspond à une *somme de besoins* que . . .". Schelle (*Oeuvres*, III, p. 87) has: "forme, si j'ose ainsi parler, une *somme de besoins* que . . .".

[9] Schelle (*Oeuvres*, III, p. 87) does not have "of exchange" ("de commerce") in his text.

can dispose among the different objects which are agreeable to him, he must *appraise* them on the basis of their *importance* to his subsistence and well being. And what is this appraisal, other than the account he renders to himself of the portion of his toil and time, or, to express these two things in a single word, the portion of his resources which he can use to acquire an evaluated object without thereby sacrificing the quest for other objects of equal or greater importance?

What then is his measure of value here? What is his scale of comparison? It is clear that he has no other than his actual resources. The total sum of these resources is the only unit of this scale, the only fixed point of departure, and the values which he attributes to each object are the proportional parts of this scale. It follows from this that the *esteem value* (*valeur estimative*) of an object, for the man in isolation, is precisely that portion of his total resources which corresponds to the desire he has for this object, or what he is willing to use to satisfy this desire. It might be said, in other words, that it is the relation of this proportional part to the total of the man's resources, a relation expressed by a fraction, whose numerator was the unit and whose denominator the number of values or equal proportional parts which the total of the man's resources contained.

We cannot but pause for a further reflection. We have not yet seen the emergence of exchange, we have not yet brought together two individuals, and already from this first step in our enquiries we touch on one of the newest and most profound truths which the general theory of value contains. It is this truth which l'Abbé Galiani stated twenty years ago in his treatise *Della Moneta* with so much clarity and vigour, but almost without further development, when he said that the *common measure of all value is man.*[10] It is plausible that this same truth, half grasped by the author of a work which has just appeared under the title *Essai analytique sur la richesse et l'impôt* has given rise to the doctrine of a constant and unique value which is always
p. 84 expressed by this unit and of which all individual values are only proportional parts, a doctrine which in that book is a blending of truth and falsity, and which for this reason has appeared rather obscure to the majority of its readers.[11]

This is not the place in which to develop for our readers[12] the obscurities in the short statement we have just made of a proposition which merits being discussed at a length commensurate with its importance; even less should we enumerate its numerous consequences at this moment.

[10] See Galiani, *Della Moneta,* Milan 1831, I, pp. 58–59 for Galiani's text of the sentence referred to by Turgot. For an English translation of this passage, see A.E. Monroe, *Early Economic Thought,* esp. pp. 289–290. Galiani's book was first published in 1750.

[11] See Graslin, *Essai analytique sur la richesse et l'impôt,* loc. cit., Part I, chapter II, esp. p. 33, note (a). For Turgot's other comments on Graslin's work, see above, pp. 123–132.

[12] This phrase, "for our readers", occurs in Schelle, *Oeuvres,* III, p. 88 but not in Du Pont (*Oeuvres,* III, p. 274).

Let us take up the thread of the argument which has guided us so far; let us extend our original assumptions. Instead of considering only one man, let us take two; let each one have in his possession something suitable for his use, but let these things be different and suited to different wants. Suppose, for example, that on a desert island, in the middle of the northern seas, two savages land on different sides, one bringing fish with him in his boat,[13] more than he can consume himself, the other carrying hides beyond what he can use to clothe himself and to make himself a tent. The one bringing fish is cold, the one bringing hides is hungry. It will eventuate that the latter will ask the owner of the fish for part of his provisions, and will offer to give him in return some of his hides: the other will accept. Here is exchange, here is commerce.

Let us pause for a while to consider what happens in this exchange. It is obvious from the first that the man, who, having taken from his catch enough to feed himself for a few days beyond which time those fishes would decay, would have to throw away the remainder as useless, begins to value them when he sees that these fish may be used (by means of exchange) to obtain for him hides which he needs to clothe himself. This superfluous fish acquires in his eyes a value which it did not have before. The owner of the hides will reason likewise and will himself learn to *value* those hides for which personally he has no need. It is likely that in this first case, where we assume that our two men are each provided more than abundantly with the thing they possess, and are accustomed to attach no price to the surplus, the discussion on the conditions of exchange will not be very animated; each would let the other take, one all the fish, the other all the hides, which he himself does not need. But let us vary the assumptions a little: let us give each of these two men an p. 85 interest in keeping their surplus, a motive to attach some value to it. Let us suppose that instead of fish, one had brought corn, which may be preserved for a very long time; that the other, instead of hides, had brought firewood, and that the island produced neither grain nor wood. One of our two savages has his subsistence, the other his firing for several months; they can only replenish their provisions by going back to the continent, from which they were perhaps driven away by the fear of wild beasts or a hostile nation; they can only do so in the stormy season by exposing themselves to the almost inevitable dangers of the sea. It stands to reason that the stock of corn and wood becomes very precious to the two owners, that it has great value for them; but the wood which the one can consume in a month will become quite useless to him, if in the meantime he dies of hunger for want of corn, and the owner of the corn will be no better off if he is in danger of perishing for want of wood. They will thus make an exchange, in order that each of them may have both wood and corn until the time when the season will permit them to

[13] This phrase, "in his boat", occurs in Schelle, *Oeuvres*, III, p. 89, but not in Du Pont (*Oeuvres*, III, p. 275).

put to sea in order to get more corn and wood on the continent. In[14] these circumstances both would obviously be less generous; each will scrupulously weigh all the considerations which may council him to prefer a certain amount of the commodity which he does not have to a certain amount of that which he has; that is, he will calculate the intensity of the two needs, of the two interests which he balances, one against the other, to wit, the interest of keeping corn and that of acquiring wood, or of keeping wood and acquiring corn. In short, he will very precisely determine their esteem value relative to himself. This esteem value is proportional to the interest he has in obtaining the two things; and the comparison of the two *values* is obviously only the comparison of the two *interests*. But each makes his own calculations, and the results may be different: the one would exchange three measures of corn for six armfuls of wood, the other would give him six armfuls of wood only for nine measures of corn. Independently of this kind of mental evaluation by which each of them compares the interest he has of keeping to that of acquiring, both are also animated by a general interest independent of all comparisons, that is the interest of keeping as much of their own commodity
p. 86 as they can, and of acquiring as much as they can of that of the other. With this in mind, each will keep secret the mental comparison which he has made of his two interests, of the two values which he attached to the commodities for exchange, and he will sound out the owner of the commodity he desires by lower offers and higher demands. Since the other will follow the same procedure, they will discuss the conditions of the exchange, and as they both have a great interest in coming to an agreement, they will finally do so. Slowly each of them will increase his offers and reduce his demands, until they finally agree to give a certain quantity of corn for a certain quantity of wood. At the moment of exchange the one who, for example, gives four measures of corn for five armfuls of wood, without doubt prefers these five armfuls of wood to the four measures of corn; he will give them a higher esteem value. But for his part, the one who receives the four measures of corn also prefers them to the five armfuls of wood. This superiority of the esteem value attributed by the acquirer to the thing he acquires over the thing he gives up is essential to the exchange, for it is the sole motive for it. Each would remain as he was, if he did not find an interest, a personal profit, in exchange; if, in his own mind, he did not consider what he receives worth more than what he gives.

But this difference in esteem value is reciprocal and precisely equal on each side; for if it was not equal, one of them would be less desirous of the exchange and he would force the other to come closer to his price by a better offer. It is thus always exactly true that each gives equal value to *receive equal value*. If four measures of corn are given for five armfuls of wood, five armfuls

[14] Schelle (*Oeuvres*, III, p. 90) has "dans" instead of the misprint "sans" (without) which occurs in Du Pont (*Oeuvres*, III, p. 277) and which was faithfully copied in Daire (*Oeuvres*, I, p. 85).

of wood are also given for four measures of corn, and consequently, four measures of corn are equivalent to five armfuls of wood in this particular exchange. These things thus have equal exchange value.

Let us pause again. Let us see exactly what is meant by this *exchange value*, whose equality is the necessary condition of free exchange; let us not depart from the simplicity of our assumptions, where we have only two contracting parties and only two objects of exchange to consider. This *exchange value* is not exactly the same as the *esteem value,*[15] or, in other words, the interest which each of the two separately attached to the two desired objects, whose
p. 87 possession he compares in order to determine what he must give up of the one to acquire some of the other, since the result of the comparison might not be the same in the minds of the two contracting parties. This first value, to which we have given the name *esteem value*, is arrived at through the comparison which each separately makes between the two interests that contend with one another in his case; it exists only in the interest of each of the two taken separately. *Exchange* value on the contrary, is adopted by both the contracting parties, who recognise its equality and who make it the condition of the exchange. In the determination of *esteem* value, each man, taken separately, has compared only two interests, attached by him to the object he has and to the one he desires to have. In the determination of *exchange value*, there are two men who compare, and four interests (which are) compared by them; but the two individual interests of each of the two contracting parties have first been compared between themselves separately, and it is the two results which are then compared together, or rather, discussed by the two contracting parties, in order to form one *average esteem value*, which becomes precisely the *exchange value*, to which we believe we must give the name of *appreciative value* (valeur appréciative) because it determines the *price* or the condition of exchange.

It can be seen from what we have just said, that the *appreciative value*, this value which is equal for the two objects exchanged, is essentially of the same nature as the *esteem value*. It differs from it only in so far as it is the *average* esteem value. We have seen, above, that for each of the contracting parties the esteem value of the thing received is higher than that of the thing given up, and that this difference is exactly equal on each side; by taking half of this difference in order to subtract it from the higher value and to add it to the lower value, they are made *equal*. We have seen that this perfect equality is precisely the characteristic of appreciative value in the exchange. Thus the appreciative value is evidently none other than the *average* of the esteem values which the two contracting parties attach to each object.

[15] There is a slight difference in the text at this point. Schelle (*Oeuvres*, III, p. 91) has: "Ce n'est pas précisement, la *valeur estimative* ou . . ."; Du Pont (*Oeuvres*, III, p. 280) has: "Cette *valeur échangeable* n'est pas précisement la *valeur estimative*, ou, . . .".

We have proved that the esteem value of an object, for the man in isolation, is none other than the relation between that part of his resources which a man can devote to the quest for this object and the totality of his resources; thus the appreciative value in the exchange between two men is the relation between the sum of the parts of their resources which they would be prepared
p. 88 to devote to the quest for each of the objects exchanged and the sum of the resources of those two men. It is worth noting here that the introduction of exchange between our two men increases the wealth of both of them, that is, it gives them both a greater quantity of satisfaction in return for the same resources. I assume in the example of our two savages that the shore which produces corn and the shore which produces wood, are remote from each other; a single savage would be obliged to make two journeys to obtain his provisions of corn and wood; he would consequently lose much time and hard work in navigating. If on the contrary there are two of them, they would use the time and effort that would have been put into the second journey, the one to cut wood, the other to obtain corn. The total sum of corn and wood gathered would be much bigger and so consequently, the share of each man.

Let us retrace our steps. It follows from our definition of *appreciative value* that it is not the relation between two things exchanged or between the *price* and the thing sold, as some people have been tempted to think. This expression would be absolutely inappropriate in the comparison of the two values, of the two terms of exchange. It implies a relation of equality, and this relation of equality assumes two things already equal; now, those two equal things are not the two things compared, but rather the value of the things exchanged. Thus, the *values* which have a relation of equality may not be confused with this relation of equality which assumes that two values have been compared. There is without doubt a sense in which the *values* have a relation, and we have explained it above in a careful study of esteem value; we have even said that this relation, like all relations, could be expressed as a fraction. It is precisely the equality of these two fractions that constitutes the essential condition of the exchange, an equality which is achieved by fixing the *appreciative* value at half the difference between the two esteem values.

In commercial language, *price* is often confused with *value* without causing inconvenience, because in effect the stating of a price always involves the stating of a value. They are, however, different concepts which it is important to distinguish. The price is the thing which is given in exchange for an object. From this definition it follows that this other object is also the price of the first. When exchange is under discussion, it is almost superfluous to make this
p. 89 remark, and as all commerce consists of exchange, it is obvious that this expression (*price*) always fits both things traded, which are equally each other's price. The price and the thing bought or, if you like the two prices, are of equal value: the price is worth as much as the purchase, and the purchase as much as the price. But the name value, strictly speaking, is no more

applicable to one of these two terms of exchange than to the other. Why then do we use these terms for one another? Here is the reason; and its explanation will enable us to take a further step in the theory of *value.*

This reason is the impossibility of expressing value in terms of itself. It is easy to be convinced of this impossibility if only one reflects on what we have just said and demonstrated about the nature of value.

Indeed, how do we find the expression of a fraction whose first term, the numerator, the fundamental unit, is an inestimable object, which is defined in the vaguest possible manner? How can the value of an object be expressed as corresponding to the two-hundredth part of a man's resources, and of what resources are we talking? It is essential to introduce the consideration of time in the calculation of these resources, but what interval will be chosen? Will it be a life time, or a year, a month, a day? Nothing of the sort to be sure; for man, with respect to each object he needs, must, in order to obtain it, inevitably employ his resources for periods of vastly different duration. How to estimate these intervals of time which, passing at one and the same time for all types of man's needs, must yet only enter in unequal lengths into the calculation relative to each particular type of need. How to evaluate these imaginery parts of one continuous span of time, which flows, if I may put it in this way, along an indivisible line. And what thread could be a guide in such a labyrinth of calculations, of which all the elements are indeterminate? It is thus impossible to express *value* in itself; and all that human language can express in this regard is that the value of one thing equals the *value* of another. The benefit evaluated, or rather, felt by two men, establishes this equation in each particular case, without any one ever thinking of *summing*
p. 90 the resources of man in order to compare its total to each needed object. Interest always determines the result of this comparison, but it has never actually made the comparison, nor could it do so.

The only means of expressing value is then, as we have said, to express that one thing is equal in value to another; or, if you like, in other words to present one value as equal to a required value. Value, like size, has no other measure than itself, and if values are measured by comparison with other values, as length is measured by comparison with other lengths, then, in both means of comparison, there is no *fundamental unit* given by nature, there is only an *arbitrary unit* given by convention. Since in all exchange there are two equal values and since the measure of one can be given in terms of the other, there must be agreement about the arbitrary unit which is taken for the foundation of this measure, or, if you like, for the unit of notation of the parts which are to compose the scale of comparison for value. Suppose that one of the two contracting parties in the exchange wishes to express the value of the thing he acquires, he will take for the unit of his scale of value a constant part of what he gives, and he will express in whole numbers and in fractions of this unit the quantity he will give for a fixed quantity of the thing he receives. This quantity expresses the *value* for him, and will be the *price* of what he receives; from whence it can be seen that the price is always the expression of the value, and that thus, for the acquirer, to express the value is to give the price of the thing acquired in terms of the quantity he gives to acquire it. He will thus say indifferently that this quantity is *the value*, or *the price* of what he buys. In employing these two forms of speech he will have the same meaning in mind, and he will put the same meaning into the minds of those who hear him; which explains how the two words *value* and *price*, although expressing fundamentally different ideas, can, without causing inconvenience, be substituted for each other in daily speech, when rigorous precision is not required.

It is rather obvious that if one of the two contracting parties has taken a certain arbitrary part of the thing he gives up, in order to measure the value of the thing he acquires, the other party will have the same right in his turn to take that same thing acquired by his opponent, but given up by himself, in order to measure the value of the thing his opponent has given him, and
p. 91 which served as a measure for the latter. In our example, the one who has given four bags of corn for five armfuls of wood will take a bag of corn for the unit of his scale, and will say: the armful of wood is worth four-fifths of a bag of corn. The one who has given the wood for the corn, on the contrary, will take the armful of wood for his unit and will say: the bag of corn is worth one and a quarter armfuls of wood. This operation is exactly the same as that which takes place between two men who might wish to value reciprocally, the one French ells in terms of Spanish vares, the other Spanish vares in terms of French ells.[16]

In both cases, an aliquot part of the most familiar thing, which serves to evaluate the other, is taken as a fixed and indivisible unit, and the second is evaluated by comparing it with the part arbitrarily taken as the unit. But just as Spanish vares no more measure French ells than French ells measure Spanish vares, the bag of corn does not measure the value of an armful of wood any more than an armful of wood measures the value of a bag of corn.

From this general proposition the inference must be drawn that in all exchanges both terms of exchanges are equally the measure of the value of the other term; for the same reason, in all exchanges, the two terms are both equally representative scales, that is, whosoever has corn can obtain for that corn a quantity of wood equal in value with that corn, just as the person who has wood, can, with that wood, obtain a quantity of corn of equal value.

This is an extremely simple truth, but one that is very fundamental to the theory of value, money and commerce. Obvious as it may be, it is yet frequently misunderstood by the best of minds, and ignorance of its most immediate consequences has often led the administration into the most dis-

[16] The Spanish vare and the French ell were both measures of length; the vare was about 92 cm., the Paris ell about 118 cm.

astrous delusions. It suffices to quote the famous system of Law.[17]

We have dwelt for a very long time on the first hypotheses of the man in isolation, and of the two men exchanging two objects; but we wished to draw from them all the ideas of the theory of value which do not entail more complications. By thus always utilising the simplest possible hypothesis, the ideas which result from it necessarily present themselves to the mind in a neater and more straightforward fashion.

We have only to extend our assumptions, to multiply the number of traders p. 92
and things traded, in order to see the birth of commerce and to complete the sequence of ideas attached to the word 'to be worth' (valoir).

Even for this last objective, it will suffice to multiply the number of men, while still considering only two single objects of exchange.

If we assume there are four men instead of two, to wit, two owners of wood and two owners of corn, it may at first be imagined that two traders meet on the one hand, and two on the other, without any communication between the four; then each exchange will be made separately, as if the two contracting parties were alone in the world. But, the very fact that the exchanges are made separately is no reason why they should be made on the same conditions. In each exchange taken separately, the appreciative value of the two exchanged objects is equal for both parties; but it must not be forgotten that this appreciative value is none other than the averaging of the two esteem values given to the objects of exchange by the contracting parties. Now, it is quite possible that this average result is radically different in the two exchanges settled separately, because the esteem values depend on the way in which each considers the objects of his needs, on the degree of usefulness which he assigns to them among his other needs; they are different for each individual. Consequently, if one only considers the two individuals on the one side and the two individuals on the other, the average result may be very different. It is quite possible that the contracting parties of one of the exchanges are less sensitive to cold than the contracting parties of the other; this circumstance is sufficient to cause them to attach less esteem value to wood and more to corn. Thus while in one of the exchanges four bags of corn and five armfuls of wood will only be equivalent to two bags of corn, which will not prevent that, in each contract, the value of the two objects is exactly equal for the two contracting parties, since one is given for the other.

Let us now bring our four men together, let us enable them to communicate with one another to learn of the conditions offered by each of the owners, either of wood or of corn. It follows that the person who would consent to p. 93
give four bags of corn for five armfuls of wood, will no longer be willing to do so when he finds out that one of the owners of wood consents to give five armfuls of wood for only two bags of corn. But the latter, learning in his turn that four bags of corn may be had for the same quantity of five armfuls of

[17] Cf. 'Letter on Paper-Money', above, p. 2, note 6.

wood, will change his mind too, and will no longer content himself with two. He would be quite prepared to take four, but the owners of corn would no more consent to give them to him than the owners of wood would be willing to content themselves with two. The conditions of the projected exchange will thus be changed and a new *evaluation* will take place, a appreciation of the value of wood and corn. It is immediately clear that this appreciation will be the same in the two exchanges and for the four dealers, that is, that for the same quantity of wood the owners of corn will give neither more nor less corn, and that for the same quantity of corn the owners of wood will give neither more nor less wood. At first glance it can be seen that if one of the owners of corn were to demand less wood than the other for the same quantity of corn, the two owners of wood would address themselves to him in order to profit from this reduction in price. This competition would urge this owner to demand more wood than he first demanded for the same quantity of corn; in his turn, the other owner of corn would lower his demand for wood, or raise his offer of corn, in order to win back the owners of the wood he needs, and this effect would take place until the two owners of corn offered the same quantity of corn for the same quantity of wood.[18]

[18] This paper was never finished. (Note by Du Pont.)

CHAPTER X

1770

EXTRACTS FROM 'PAPER ON LENDING AT INTEREST'[1]

Schelle III 154–202

[Section I–III. *Reasons for the paper and background.* Some months ago a complaint was made to the magistrate at Angoulême against an individual who allegedly had exacted usurious interest rates in credit transactions. This complaint has caused a great deal of consternation as well as further complaints against lenders, and has thrown the whole credit structure of the area into confusion. Because credit has been so widely interrupted, bankruptcies are rapidly increasing. This financial crisis is of such importance, that the Royal Council should be informed. This paper has been written to provide the Council with a resumé of events, and a solution to the problem. pp. 154–7

[In order to appreciate the facts of the case, some background material about the district is provided. Angoulême ought to be a flourishing town, because of its geographical location, but unfortunately scarcity of capital has prevented this. At present, its major commerce is connected with the manufacture of paper, the brandy trade, and some iron works.]

The paper trade, in general has steady prices; the opposite applies to that in brandy: this commodity is subject to huge variations in price. These variations lead to very hazardous speculations, which may either procure immense profits, or entail ruinous losses. The enterprises of the iron masters, p. 157

[1] This paper was written in connection with a lawsuit in Angoulême in 1769 between two debtors and their creditor. Because part of the paper deals with particulars of the lawsuit and with moral arguments against canon law on the subject of usury, only those parts of economic interest have been translated in full. The other sections have been condensed, the condensed parts are placed in square brackets. As indicated in the Introduction (above pp. XXVII–XXIX) there are several versions of this paper. The translation has been made from Schelle, who revised Du Pont's text by utilising *Théorie de l'intérêt de l'argent,* which quotes large sections from Turgot's original manuscript. A manuscript copy of this work, entitled 'Mémoire sur l'usure', the title Turgot used in a letter to Du Pont, 13/11/1770 (in Schelle, *Oeuvres,* III, pp. 392–393) is in the Goldsmith's Library of the University of London (MS 131). It appears to be a copy by an amanuensis, and is bound in red morocco with Turgot's coat of arms embossed in gold on the front cover. A third version, printed from this, or from a very similar manuscript, as is clear from internal evidence, was published in 1789. Textual changes between Schelle, the manuscript version and the 1789 edition will be indicated in footnotes throughout the text.

which supply the navy, require very large and lengthy advances from them, which return to them with profits which are all the more considerable as they return later. To avoid losing the opportunity of a large order, they are forced to obtain money at any price, and they find the greater advantages as, by paying in cash for the ore and the wood, they obtain a very considerable reduction in the price of these raw materials for their enterprises.

IV. *Cause of the High Interest Rate in Angoulême.* It is easy to understand that the combination of a trade which is equally susceptible to large risks and large profits, and an area where capitals are in short supply,[2] as found in the town of Angoulême, must have resulted in a fairly high current rate of interest, and generally higher than it is in other places of commerce. Indeed, it is notorious that for a period of about forty years, most of the financial transactions have been made at the rate of eight or nine per cent per annum, and sometimes at a rate of ten per cent, depending on the size of the demand, and the risk involved.

). 157–61 |Sections V–X. *The Details of the Legal Dispute, and some of its Consequences.* In this type of commercial situation, bankruptcies are frequent. Two of these bankrupts, in collusion with some friends, fraudulently obtained money by issuing bills on each other, which were endorsed by their friends and discounted with the defendant at a fairly high interest rate. When the bills fell due, the two bankrupts, instead of paying, denounced their creditor to the magistrate for charging usurious interest rates. This action has intimidated other lenders, who are now refusing to discount bills until they are sure of the legal position. This has disrupted the whole credit system of Angoulême.|

p. 161 XI. *Disastrous effects of this unrest on the credit and commerce of Angoulême.* As expected, the effect of the lawsuits has been the total loss of credit for the whole trade of Angoulême. The licence given to the dishonesty of the borrowers has closed the purses of all the lenders, whose wealth,
p. 162 moreover, has been severely shaken by this blow. No expired obligations are renewed, all enterprises come to a halt, the manufacturers are exposed to failure through the impossibility of finding credit in expectation of the return of their funds.[3] At the beginning of this paper I already referred to the large number of bills of exchange which have been protested since these disturbances started.

I have been informed that the merchants who deal in cloth for the consumption of the town, having addressed themselves to Lyon, according to their custom, in order to place their orders, have received the reply that no

[2] A slight textual variation should be noted here. The Manuscript version, p. 4, has *très garnie* (well furnished, in good supply) instead of *dégarnie* (in short supply) which is used by the 1789 edition (ibid., p. 6) and by Schelle (*Oeuvres,* III, p. 157). This would seem to be a copying error of the amanuensis who prepared the manuscript copy.

[3] The manuscript version and the 1789 edition start a new paragraph at this point; they do not follow the paragraphing by Schelle, following Du Pont in this section.

transactions will be made with people from Angoulême except on cash terms. This disrepute has even affected the subsistence of the people: since the harvest has failed in the province, they need the resources of trade to fill the gap. It would be expected that the town of Angoulême, being situated on a navigable river, would always be abundantly provided, and that her merchants would be eager to set up stores, not only for local provisions, but even for those of part of the province; but the inability of undertaking any form of speculation, which the general disrepute has brought about, makes this expedient worthless.

[Sections XII–XIII. It is necessary to put an end to these difficulties, but it is not easy to remedy their causes, because of the prejudices contained in the law concerning interest.] pp. 162–3

XIV. *Defects of our Laws on the Subject of Interest; Impossibility of observing them rigorously; Disadvantages of the Arbitrary Limits which have been imposed in Practice.* I will not mince words. The laws recognised in the courts on the subject of the interest of money are poor; our legislation conforms to the extreme prejudice about usury introduced during the era of ignorance by theologians who understood the meaning of Scripture no better than the principles of natural right. The rigorous observation of these laws would mean the destruction of all commerce; consequently, they are not observed rigorously: they forbid all stipulation of interest without the alienation of capital; they prohibit, as illegal, all interest stipulated at a rate higher than that fixed by the ordinances of the Prince. And it is a well known fact that there is no commercial centre on earth where the majority of transactions do not depend on the borrowing of money without the alienation of capital, and where interest rates would not be fixed by convention, according to the relative abundance[4] of money on the spot, and the relative certainty of the solvency of the borrower. The rigidity of the law has yielded to the force of circumstances: jurisprudence has had to moderate in practice its theoretical principles, and has openly come to allow borrowing by bill, by discount, and other types of financial transactions between merchants. This will always happen when the law prohibits what the nature of things requires. However, this situation – where laws are not observed, but continue to exist without being repealed, and are even still partly enforced – entails very great disadvantages. On the one hand, the known disregard of the law reduces the respect which citizens should have for everything which carries its authority; on the other hand, the existence of this law maintains a troublesome prejudice, stigmatises something which is legal in itself, with which society p. 164

[4] Some textual changes between the editions should be noted at this point. The manuscript version and 1789 edition read as follows in translation: ". . . of the Prince, and it is a well known fact that there is no commercial centre on earth where the majority of transactions do not depend on the borrowing of money without the alienation of capital and where interest rates would not be fixed by the single convention, according to the relative abundance . . ." (pp. 13, 18 resp.).

cannot dispense, and which consequently, a large group of citizens should be permitted to do. This class of citizens is degraded by this, and the onset of this degradation in the opinion of the public weakens the restraints imposed by its honour, that valuable support of integrity. The author of "*Esprit des Lois* has aptly stated that: "When the laws prohibit a necessary thing, they only succeed in making dishonest men of those who do it".[5]

pp. 164–7 [The virtual non-observance of this law has meant that it has become most arbitrary, because there is no certainty as to when it will be invoked. The penalties for transgressions of this law are also most severe and include: compensation to the borrower, banishment; and for the second offence, condemnation to the galleys for life, or banishment for life. In the law, no distinction has been made between usury proper or exorbitant interest rates, and acceptable rates of interest. This makes the law even more arbitrary.

[XV. What has happened in Angoulême proves the disadvantages arising from the arbitrariness of the law on interest.

[XVI. This makes it imperative that the Government must settle the matter: either by repealing the law altogether, or by making it more specific.

[XVII. The reform of the law is a difficult matter. It is therefore necessary to have knowledge of the true facts surrounding interest, in order to combat the prejudice of vested interest in this matter.

[XVIII. In order to examine the question in the light of natural right, an extensive discussion is required which will weigh up the evidence for, and against, the taking of interest on loans. I must apologise for setting out this argument at length, since the prejudice surrounding this topic is sufficiently great to warrant such treatment.]

p. 167 XIX. *Proof of the legitimacy of lending at interest, based on its absolute necessity for commerce; development of this necessity.* First of all, the absolute necessity of lending for the prosperity and the maintenance of commerce is a very strong proof against the principles adopted by dogmatic theologians on the subject of lending at interest, for what man who is
p. 168 reasonable and religious at the same time can presume that Providence has forbidden a thing which is absolutely essential for the prosperity of society? Now, the necessity of lending at interest for commerce, and consequently, for civilised society, is proven from the first by the tolerance which the absolute need of commerce has forced to be given to this type of transaction, in spite of rigid prejudices of both theologians and legal experts. Moreover, this necessity is a self-evident thing. There is no commercial centre on earth[6]

[5] See Montesquieu, *De l'Esprit des Lois*, Book XXI, chapter 20, where, in connection with the views of Aristotle and the scholastics on interest, he states: "... car, toutes les fois que l'on défend une chose naturellement permise ou nécessaire, on ne fait que rendre malhonnêtes gens ceux qui le font." (In *Oeuvres de Montesquieu*, I, p. 514). It should be noted that this passage does not occur in the first edition of *De l'Esprit des Lois*.

[6] A slight variation in texts should be noted at this point. Schelle (*Oeuvres*, III, p. 168) has: "Il n'y a pas sur la terre une place de commerce ...". The manuscript version (p. 21) and the

where enterprises do not depend on borrowed money; there is not a single merchant perhaps who has not frequently been obliged to have recourse to the purse of others; even the richest in capitals could not be sure of never needing this expedient except by keeping part of their funds idle, and consequently, by diminishing the extent of their enterprises. It is no less obvious that those outside capitals necessary to all merchants can only be confided to them by their owners to the extent that the latter discover an advantage in it capable of compensating them for the deprivation of money which they could have used, and for the risks attached to all commercial enterprises. If the money lent for uncertain enterprises did not yield an interest higher than that on sound mortgages, people would never lend to merchants. If it was prohibited to draw interest from money which had to be returned on a fixed date, all money for which the owners could foresee a need in a certain time, while not needing it currently, would be lost to commerce during this interval. It would be utterly lost to those who have an urgent need for it. The rigorous enforcement of such a prohibition would remove immense sums from the circulation, which are now made available through the certainty of recovering them in case of need, to the mutual advantage of lenders and borrowers; and the lack of them would necessarily make itself felt by the rise in the rate of interest, and by the cessation of a large part of commercial enterprises.

XX. *Necessity of leaving the determination of interest in commerce to the agreements of the merchants, and to the operation of the different factors which cause it to vary: indication of these factors.* It is thus from absolute necessity, and to maintain confidence and the circulation of money, without which there is no commerce at all, that the lending of money at interest p. 169 without the alienation of capital, and at a rate higher than the interest (le denier)[7] fixed for Government stock, is sanctioned in commerce. It is essential that money is considered in commerce as a genuine commodity whose price depends on agreement and varies, like that of all other commodities, according to the ratio between offer and demand. Interest being the price of loanable funds, it rises when there are more borrowers than lenders; it falls, on the contrary, when there is more money offered than is demanded for borrowing. It is in this way that the normal rate of interest is established, but this normal rate is not the only rule which is followed, nor should it be followed to fix the rate of interest for individual transactions. The risks which the capital may run in the hands of the borrower, the needs of the latter, and the profit which he hopes to draw from the money which he borrows, are the circumstances which, when combined in different ways, and with the normal rate of interest, will often carry the rate to a higher level than it is in the or-

1789 edition (p. 27) have: "J'ai déjà dit qu'il n'y a pas sur la terre une place de Commerce . . .", which refers back to remarks made in section XIV, above p. 151.

[7] For a discussion of the meaning of this expression, see *Reflections*, section 57, and note 33, above p. 68.

dinary course of trade. It is quite obvious that the lender would decide to lend his capital only through the lure of a high profit, and it is no less obvious that the borrower would decide to pay an interest which is all the higher as his needs are more urgent, or as he hopes to draw a greater profit from this money.

XXI. *Inequalities in the rate of interest because of the inequality of risks are no more than just.*[8] What injustice can there be in this? Can it be expected that an owner of money risk his funds without any compensation?

He can refuse to lend, it is said; undoubtedly, and this is just what proves that, when lending, he can expect the profit to be proportionate to his risks. For, why deprive persons who, when they borrow cannot give security of an assistance they most urgently need? Why deprive them of the means too attempt enterprises from which they hope to get rich?

No law, civil or canon, forces anybody to render them gratuitous assistance; why should civil or canon law prohibit them to procure it at a price which they consent to pay for their own benefit?

p. 170 [XXII. *The legitimacy of lending at interest is independent of profit.* Scholars have tried to disprove the legitimacy of interest by arguing that the borrower does not always profit from the loan, while the lender always profits from the interest. This argument is invalid.

[XXIII. *The legitimacy of interest is a direct consequence of the ownership which the lender has in the object he lends.* The legitimacy of lending at interest arises from the inviolable right of private property. The owner of an object can do with it what he likes: he can sell it or let it. The buyer or the lessee voluntarily buys or leases it, and the price he pays will be just, as long
p. 171 as neither of the parties is fraudulent.] Property in money is no less absolute than that in furniture, in a piece of cloth, or in a diamond; the owner is no more bound to dispose of it gratuitously; giving it, lending it gratuitously is a laudable action inspired by generosity, sometimes demanded by charity and humanity, but which is never in the nature of strict law. A person may similarly give or lend all sorts of commodities, and he ought to do so in certain cases. Apart from these circumstances, in which charity demands sacrifices to help the unfortunate, money may be sold, and is sold, in fact, when it is placed in an annuity; it is sold for money when money in one place is given in exchange for the receipt of money in another, the type of transaction known as *foreign exchange*, in which less money is given at one place to receive more of it in another, just as, in a transaction of lending at interest, less money is given at one time in order to receive more at another, because the difference in time, like that in space, causes a real difference in the value of money.[9]

[8] Both the manuscript version (p. 23) and the 1789 edition (p. 30f) have this section in one paragraph.

[9] Cf. Galiani, *Della Moneta,* II, p. 186, and A.E. Monroe, op. cit., p. 302 for an English translation of this passage.

XXIV. *The ownership of money entails the right to sell it and the right to draw a rent from it.* Since money is sold like any other possession, why should it not be let like any other possession? And since interest is only the rent of money lent for a period of time, why would it not be permissible to receive it? By what strange whim does morality or law forbid a free contract between two parties who both derive advantage therefrom? And can it be doubted that they derive such advantage since they have no other motive to p. 172
decide them on it? Why would the borrower offer a rent for this money for a period of time, if during this time, the use of this money were not advantageous to him? And, if it is replied that necessity forces him to submit to these terms, is not the gratification of real need a benefit? Is this not the greatest benefit of all? It is similarly necessity which forces man to fetch bread at the baker's; does the baker have any less right to receive the price of the bread he sells?[10]

|XXV. *False ideas of the scholastics on the alleged sterility of money; false consequences they have drawn from it.* The scholastic theologians, following pp. 172–4
Aristotle,[11] have argued that money is sterile because money does not yield money. But since only the soil and cattle yield natural fruit, have they not forgotten to include other types of personal property such as jewels, furniture, etc.? Have they not forgotten that for individuals money is equivalent to real objects, and that money in this sense is indispensible to all productive enterprises? Have they also not forgotten that those who use money in their enterprises generally draw a profit from it?

[XXVI. Another reason against the legitimacy of interest: the property in money passes to the borrower at the moment of the loan, so that no charge can be made for it. This argument is derived from St. Thomas Aquinas.|[12]

XXVII. *Refutation of this reasoning.* This reasoning is only a web spun of p. 174
errors and misunderstandings which are easily cleared up.

The first proposition, that, in every contract, none of the parties can, without injustice, exact more than he has given, has a true foundation; but the manner in which it is put forward entails a false meaning, which may lead to misunderstanding. In every exchange of value against value (and every agreement, properly so called, or subject to payment, can be regarded as an exchange of this type), there is an interpretation of the word *value*, in which the value is always equal on both sides; but this is not at all through a princi-

[10] Cf. *Reflections*, sections 73 and 74, above, pp. 78–80, for further uses of this bread example. Sections XXV–XXVIII below contain more or less the same theological discussion on interest as sections 73 and 75 of the *Reflections*, see above pp. 78–79, 80–81. For this reason Turgot asked Du Pont to remove the theological discussion from the *Reflections*, as indicated above p. 78, note 51.

[11] See Aristotle, *The Politics*, Bk. I, ch. 10; part of this chapter is reprinted in Monroe, op. cit., see esp. p. 20. Cf. also St. Thomas Aquinas, *Summa Theologica*, Question LXXVIII, reprinted in Monroe, op. cit., pp. 65–77, see esp. pp. 67–69.

[12] See Aquinas, *Summa Theologica*, op. cit., p. 69.

ple of justice, it is because things cannot be otherwise. The exchange, being free on both sides, can only be motivated by the preference of each of the contracting parties for the thing he receives over the thing he gives. This preference presumes that each attributes a greater value to the thing he acquires than to the thing he gives up, relative to his individual use and to the satisfaction of his needs and desires. But this difference in value is equal on both sides; it is this equality which causes the preference to be exactly mutual, and the parties to be in agreement. It follows from this that in the eyes of a third party, the two values exchanged are exactly equal, and that, consequent-
p. 175 ly, in every transaction between men, equal value is always given for equal value. But this value depends solely on the opinion of the two dealers as regards the degree of usefulness of the things exchanged for the satisfaction of their desires or their needs: it does not, in itself, have any reality which may be used as a basis for arguing that one of the parties has wronged the other.[13]

If there are only two *dealers*, the terms of their contract are entirely arbitrary, and unless one of the two has used duress or fraud, the conditions of the exchange do not concern morality in any way. When there are several *traders*, as each is interested in not paying more to one for what another agrees to give him at a lower price, a normal value is established, by the comparison of all the offers and demands, which differs from that established in the exchange between two men only in that it is the mean of the different values which would have resulted from the chaffering of the parties in each exchange considered separately. But, this mean or normal value does not acquire any reality apart from the opinion and comparison of mutual needs; it is continually susceptible to variation, and no obligation can be derived from it to give such and such a good for such and such a price. The owner is always free to keep it, and consequently, to determine the price at which he agrees to part with it.[14]

It is quite true that in a brisk trade, carried on by a multitude of hands, each individual buyer and seller has so little influence on the formation of this general opinion and on the current evaluation which results therefrom, that this evaluation may be regarded as an independent phenomenon. In this sense, common practice permits this normal value to be called the true value of the thing; but since this expression, convenient rather than precise, cannot impair in any way the absolute right which ownership confers to the seller over his merchandise and to the buyer over his money, it cannot be concluded that this value may serve as a basis for any moral rule; and it remains strictly true that the conditions of any exchange cannot be unjust except to the extent that duress and fraud have influenced them.

[13] Cf. 'Value and Money', above pp. 145–146. It should also be noted that both the manuscript version (p. 32) and the 1789 edition (p. 41) do not start a new paragraph at this point.

[14] Cf. *Reflections*, section 74, above pp. 79–80.

[If a young stranger is overcharged in a purchase, the injustice arises from the fact that the trader has taken advantage of his ignorance of the normal value. This transaction is not unjust because the trader has charged more than an 'intrinsic value', since the normal value is not intrinsic in any way. The transaction is unjust because it involved a form of fraud.] p. 176

The conclusion to be drawn from this explanation is that, in every exchange, in every agreement which is based on two reciprocal terms, injustice can only be based on duress, fraud, dishonesty, the abuse of confidence, and never on an alleged metaphysical inequality between the thing sold and its price.[15]

The second proposition in the reasoning which I am attacking is based once more on the gross misunderstanding and on an assumption which is precisely the one in question. "What the lender demands", it is said, "over and above the principal, is something he receives in excess of what he has given, since by receiving the principal alone he receives the exact equivalent of what he has given."[16] It is true that in repaying the principal, the borrower returns exactly the same weight of metal which the lender had given him. But where have our logicians observed that in a loan it is only necessary to consider the weight of the metal lent and repaid, and not the value and the usefulness it has for the lender and the borrower? Where have they observed that to determine this value, it is only necessary to consider the weights of the metal handed over at two different dates, without comparing the difference in usefulness which exists at the date of borrowing between a sum currently owned and an equal sum which is to be received at a distant date? Is not this difference well known, and is not the trivial proverb, *a bird in the hand is better than two in the bush,* a naive expression of this well known fact? Now, if a sum actually owned is worth more, is more useful, is preferable to the assurance of receiving a similar sum in one or several years' time, it is not true that the lender receives as much as he gives when he does not stipulate interest, for he gives the money and receives only an assurance. Now, if he receives less, why should this difference not be compensated by the assurance of an increase in the sum proportioned to the delay? This compensation is precisely the rate of interest. p. 177

[The distinction often made in discussions about the legitimacy of interest between an object hired and consumed during use, and an object which is not consumed during hire, is also invalid. In hiring an object which is not consumed, such as a diamond, usefulness is obtained which must be paid for. pp. 177–78

[15] A slight variation between texts should be noted here. Schelle (*Oeuvres,* III, p. 176) has: ". . . entre la chose vendue et son prix." Both the manuscript version (p. 34) and the 1789 edition (p. 45) have: ". . . entre la chose reçue et la chose donnée." (. . . between the thing received and that given.)

[16] This quotation may have been taken from Robert Joseph Pothier, *Traités des contrats de bienfaisance, selon les règles tant du for de la conscience que du for exterieur,* par l'auteur du *Traité des obligations* (i.e. Pothier), Paris, 1766–67, 2 Vols. This work was cited earlier in section XXV by Turgot. See Schelle, *Oeuvres,* III, p. 173.

[But, it is replied, this usefulness does not have to be paid for, since it is transferred together with the ownership during the period of hire.]

Again, an unfortunate misunderstanding. It is true that the borrower becomes the owner of the money considered physically, as a certain quantity of metal. But is he really the owner of the value of the money? Certainly not, since this value is only confided to him for a time, to be repaid on the expiration of the contract. But, without entering into this discussion which amounts to a real quibble about words, what can be concluded from my alleged
p. 179 ownership of the money. Do I not obtain this ownership from the person who has lent me the money? Is it not by his consent that I have obtained it, and have the conditions of this consent not been settled between him and myself? That is so, the use which I make of this money will be the use of my property, the usefulness which it yields me is an accessory to my ownership. All this will be true, but when? When the money is mine, when this ownership has been transferred to me; and when will this be so? When I have bought it, and paid for it. Now, at what price do I buy this ownership? What do I give in exchange? Is it not clear that it is my commitment to return on a certain date a certain sum, whatever it may be? Is it not also quite clear that in order to determine this equivalent in such a way that our gain will be equal on both sides, we must take account of the usefulness which this ownership I will acquire, but which I do not yet have, will yield me, and the usefulness which this ownership could yield to the lender during the time he is deprived of it? If you like, the reasoning of the legal experts will prove that I do not have to pay for the use of a thing when I already have acquired ownership of it; but it does not prove that I could not, when deciding to acquire this ownership, fix the price in consideration of this use which is attached to the ownership. In short, the object still assumes that which is in question, that is, that the money received today and the money which must be repaid in a year's time are exactly equal. In reasoning in this manner, it is forgotten that it is not the value of the money when it has been repaid that has to be compared with the value of the money when it is lent, but that it is the value of the promise of a sum of money which has to be compared with the value of a sum of money available now. The assumption is that it is the money paid back which is, in a loan contract, the equivalent of the money lent, and this assumption is absurd, for it is at the time of the contract that the respective conditions must be considered, and it is at this time that equality has to be established between them. Now, at the time of lending there certainly only exist a sum of money on the one hand, and a promise on the other. If it is assumed[17] that a thou-
p. 180 sand francs and a promise of a thousand francs are exactly of the same value, an even more absurd assumption is made; if these two things are equivalent,

[17] A slight variation between texts should be noted here. Schelle (*Oeuvres,* III, p. 179) has: "Si on suppose . . ."; the manuscript version (p. 40) and the 1789 edition (p. 51) have: "Si ces messieurs supposent . . .".

why do people borrow?

It is very curious that the principle of the equality of values which must be present in agreements is the starting point for the establishment of a theory according to which the whole of the gain is for one of the parties, and none of it for the other. Surely, nothing is more tangible; for, when at the end of a few years, a sum of money is returned to me which I had lent without interest, it is very clear that I have gained nothing and that, after having been deprived of its use and having risked its loss, I have precisely only what I would have had if I had kept it in my coffers during that time. It is just as clear that the borrower has benefited from this money, since he had no other motive for borrowing than this; I would therefore have given something for nothing, I would have been generous; but if, in my generosity, I gave something real, I accordingly could have sold it without being unjust.

[It is doing unwarranted honour to sophistries like those attacked, to discuss them at such length, but then, they are backed with the authority of education and of the church.

[XXVIII. *Examination and refutation of arguments drawn from Scripture against the legitimacy of interest.* The mistaken arguments discussed above partly derive from misinterpretations of passages from the *Scriptures*: namely, the saying of Jesus in Luke, chapter VI, verse 35, and some passages of the Mosaic Law from the *Old Testament.*[18] These passages are irrelevant to the problem. pp. 180–86

[XXIX. *True origin of the Opinions condemning Interest.* The condemnation of interest arose from the fact that in non-commercial societies, the major class of borrowers was that which borrowed for consumption purposes. In some of these cases, it would have been a charitable act to lend without charging interest. In these societies, the risks of the lender were also greater, which drove interest to exorbitant heights. (In ancient Rome, 12 per cent was considered to be a moderate rate.)[19] Because of high interest rates and the predominance of consumption loans at that time, the Church fathers took such a rigid view of this subject; but this is now completely outdated.]

XXX. *Lessening of the causes which made lending at interest odious to the nations.* The causes[20] which formerly made lending at interest odious, have p. 186

[18] I.e. "But love ye your enemies, and do good, and lend, hoping for nothing again; and your reward shall be great." Luke 6:35; "thou shalt not lend upon usury to thy brothers; usury of money, usury of victuals, usury of any thing that is lent upon usury: Unto a stranger thou mayest lend upon usury; but unto thy brother thou shalt not lend upon usury; . . ." Deut. 23:19,20; "If thou lend money to any of my people that is poor by thee, thou shalt not be to him as a usurer, neither shalt thou lay upon him usury", Exodus 22:25.

[19] Cf. Montesquieu, *l'Esprit des Lois,* Book XXII, chapter 22, where he remarks regarding the rate of interest in ancient Rome: ". . . et je crois que les plus ordinaires étaient de douze per cent. per an." (first edition, II, p. 123).

[20] A slight variation between texts should be noted here. Schelle (*Oeuvres,* III, p. 186) has: "Les causes . . .". The manuscript version (p. 51) and the 1789 edition (p. 65) have: "Cependant les causes . . ." (However, the causes . . .).

ceased to operate with as much force. Since slavery has been abolished among us, insolvency has less cruel consequences; it no longer entails capital punishment or the loss of freedom. Imprisonment (for debt), which we have
p. 187 retained, is in truth a hard and cruel law for the poor; but its harshness has at least been mitigated by many restrictions and limited to a certain type of debt. The suppression of slavery has given an activity to the arts unknown to ancient peoples, among whom each well-to-do individual used to let his slaves manufacture at home nearly everything he needed. Today, the practice of the mechanical arts is an expedient open to every working man. This multitude of works, and the advances they necessarily require, offer profitable employment to money on all sides; the infinitely increasing enterprises of commerce use immense capitals. The poor, who are reduced to absolute misery by their inability to work, find aid in the superfluity of the wealthy and the various charities, which does not appear to have existed among the people of antiquity, and which, indeed, was less necessary there, since in the constitution of societies, the poor, when reduced to the final degree of destitution would naturally fall into slavery. On the other hand, the vastness of the capitals accumulated from century to century by that spirit of thrift which is inseparable from commerce, swollen especially by the abundance of treasure brought from America, has, throughout Europe; caused the rate of interest to fall. All these circumstances together have caused that the borrowing for subsistence by the poor is no more than a fraction of the total of loans; that the majority of loans are made to the rich, or at least to industrious men who hope to obtain large profits from the use of the money they borrow. Consequently, lending at interest inevitably became less odious, since, through commercial activity, it has, on the contrary become a source of profit to the borrower. It has become common in all commercial towns to the extent that the magistrates, and even theologians, have come to tolerate it. The condemnation of lending in itself, or of interest exacted without the alienation of capital, has become a form of speculation left to dogmatic theologians, and in practice, all commercial and financial ventures depend on lending at interest without the alienation of capital.

pp. 187–191 [XXXI. *The stigma attached to the name of usurer is now limited to a few types of usury.* The name of usurer is now reserved for the small money lender who lends to the poor and unfortunate on a weekly basis, and who charges exorbitant rates of interest.

[XXXII. *The usurers whose occupation is to lend to the poor are really harmful to society.* The usurers who lend to the poor are harmful to society, not because they charge interest, but because they take advantage of the pressing needs of others by charging excessive rates. It is because of this that they should be punished.

[XXXIII. *The prohibition of usury is not at all the solution to this particular problem.*

[XXXIV. *Consequences of what has been said on the true causes for the disrepute of lending at interest, and on the changes which have occurred in public opinion in this regard.* The changes in society discussed above have made the general prohibition of interest archaic practice. Only usury proper must be forbidden.

[XXXV. *General consequence: no ground for the prohibition of lending at interest.*]

XXXVI. *Interest is the price of money in commerce, and this price must be left to the course of events, to the competition of commerce.* If the natural order is adhered to,[21] money must be regarded as a commodity which the owner has the right to sell or let; consequently, the law should not demand the alienation of capital in order to allow the stipulation of interest. There is no more reason for the law to fix the rate of this interest. This rate must be determined, like the price of all things in trade, by the chaffering between the dealers and by the relationship between offer and demand. There is no commodity for which the most enlightened, the most meticulously careful, and the most accurate administration can take the responsibility of balancing all the circumstances which must influence the determination of the price, and of setting one which is disadvantageous to neither the seller nor the buyer. Now, the rate of interest is even more difficult to determine than the price of any other kind of commodity, because this rate depends on even more critical and variable circumstances and considerations; that of the time at which the loan is made, that of the date stipulated for its repayment, and above all, that of the risk or the judgement of the risk which the capital is bound to run. This judgement varies continually: a momentary alarm, the occurrence of some bankruptcies, rumours of war, may spread a general concern, which suddenly makes all monetary transaction dearer. The judgement and the reality of the risk vary even more from one man to another, and increase or diminish in every possible degree; therefore, there ought to be as many variations in the rate of interest. A commodity has the same price for everybody, because everybody pays for it with the same money, and commodities in general use, whose production and consumption naturally adjust to each other, have more or less the same price for a long time. But money on loan does not have the same price, either for all men or at all times, because in lending, money is paid for with a *promise*[22] only, and because, if the money of all buyers looks the same, the promises of all the borrowers are not the same. To fix the rate of interest by law, is to deprive someone who cannot offer security proportioned to the lowness of the legal rate of the expedient of borrowing; it is consequently,

p. 191

p. 192

[21] A slight variation between texts should be noted at this point. Schelle (*Oeuvres*, III, p. 191) has: "Si l'on s'en tient à l'ordre naturel . . .". Both the manuscript version (p. 58) and the 1789 edition (p. 75) have: "A s'en tenir à l'ordre naturel . . .". (Adhering to the natural law . . .).

[22] Neither the manuscript version (p. 59) nor the 1789 edition (p. 76) italicise "promesse".

to make a multitude of commercial enterprises, which cannot be carried out without risking capital, impossible.

pp. 192–93 [XXXVII. The only justification for setting a legal rate is to give judges a rule by which to determine whether a loan is usurious or not. Due to the various circumstances which influence particular loan contracts, and the price charged for them, this is impossible.]

XXXVIII. *Advantages which will arise for commerce and for society in general from a law which conforms completely to the principles which have been developed here.* The trade in money should be free, as all trade ought to be. The result of this freedom would be competition, and the effect of this competition would be a low rate of interest: not only because the shame and risks attached to lending at interest are a surcharge which the borrower always pays, just as the buyer of prohibited commodities always pays for the risks of the smuggler, but even more, because a very large quantity of money which lies idle in chests, would enter the circulation when prejudice, no longer consolidated by the authority of law, would slowly give way to reason. Thrift would become all the stronger in accumulating capitals, when the money trade is an outlet which is always open to money. Today, loans can only be placed in large quantities. An artisan is inconvenienced by his small savings; they are sterile for him until they become large enough to be placed on loan. He must keep them, always exposed to the temptation of dissipating them in
p. 194 taverns. If the trade in money were to acquire the degree of activity which would result from complete freedom and the destruction of prejudice, money merchants would start business, and gather small sums; in the towns and in the country they would collect the savings of the working people, to turn them into capitals and to supply them to commercial centres, just as, from village to village, right up to the heart of Normandy, merchants are seen gathering butter and eggs which are produced there, in order to sell them in Paris. This facility of allowing their savings to bear fruit, open to the people, would be for them a most powerful encouragement to thrift and sobriety, and would offer them the only possible means of preventing the misery into which they are thrown by the smallest mishap, by sickness, or, in any case, by old age.

pp. 194–202 [Sections XL–LIII. Concluding remarks. If this proposed change in the law appears to be too sudden, the change could be more gradually introduced. Some proceedings against usurers, for instance, could still be started. A change in the law however, would prevent occurrences like those described at Angoulême happening in the whole of France, and it would therefore safeguard the needs of trade.

[The magistrates, moreover, would not have to admit the charges made at Angoulême. In the new legislation, the type of money lender ought to be immaterial, while a rate of interest greater than six per cent should not be taken as an excuse to start criminal proceedings. Unfortunately, the officers of justice at Angoulême do not hold these principles, so that the Intendant and the Contrôleur-Général will have to interfere. The Royal Council would probably be the best tribunal to settle the matter. It could appoint a special commission to investigate. However, the following ought in any case to be done. The originators of the trouble at Angoulême should be punished for the disruption to commerce which they caused; and a proposal made by the judges in the case should also be examined. They suggested the appointment of a special officer who would investigate this type of case, and who would be able to fix the proper rate of interest. This type of proposal, as has been fully discussed above,[23] has many disadvantages. Final conclusion: In the opinion of the author, the matter should be taken from the hands of the local judges and placed in the hands of a special commission appointed by the Royal Council.|

Written in Limoges, 27 January, 1770.[24]

[23] See especially sections XIX and XXXVI, above pp. 152–153, 161–162.
[24] This sentence occurs only in the manuscript version.

CHAPTER XI

1770

EXTRACTS FROM 'LETTERS TO THE CONTRÔLEUR-GÉNÉRAL (ABBÉ TERRAY) ON THE GRAIN TRADE'[1]

Schelle III pp. 265–369

FIRST LETTER

Limoges, 30 Octobe

pp. 266–274 |The first letter is more or less a preamble to what is to follow. Turgot's argu ment in it can be summarised as follows: I have promised to write you on th advantages of the free trade in grain, and propose to deal with this subject i a considerable amount of detail. You have not given me enough time to repl to your request for advice on this subject, since it deserves to be treated a book length and time is too pressing. However, you owe it to the public, to th King, and to yourself as minister, to treat this matter carefully, since it ha repercussions on the whole country and not just on agriculture. The problen is also controversial; on the one hand, *the economists* have supporte

[1] Turgot's letters to Abbé Terray, who was then Contrôleur-Général, on the subject of th grain trade, which were written at the end of 1770, have been considered to be one of his mo important pieces of economic work. Of the seven letters originally written, only four have su vived, since Turgot was unable to have copies made of the second, third and fourth letter. They were all written while Turgot was on a tour of inspection of his district, and therefo show signs of haste. Turgot himself was quite pleased with them, as he wrote to Du Pont d Nemours, but he feared that Terray would not read them. (Turgot to Du Pont, 14/12/1770, i Schelle, *Oeuvres*, III, p. 394.) Terray, however, after having received them is supposed to hav said that among all the Intendants, only Turgot had "genuine understanding, enlightenme and merit". (See Du Pont to the Margrave of Baden, 1/1/1783, in Knies (ed.), *Carl Friedrich von Baden brieflicher Verkehr mit Mirabeau und Du Pont*, II, p. 345.)

Since the letters are long (over 150 pages of small handwriting, as Turgot wrote to Du Pon 14/12/1770, in Schelle, *Oeuvres*, III, p. 394), only selections with theoretical interest have bee translated. To give some continuity to the text, part of Turgot's argument has been sum marised. These summaries have been placed in square brackets in the text.

There are several versions of this paper. The translation has been made from Schelle's te who revised the Du Pont version (*Oeuvres*, VI, pp. 120–291) by utilising the manuscript copie at the Château de Lantheuil. The last three letters were published first in pamphlet form as *Le tres sur les grains, écrites à M. l'Abbé Terray . . . par M. Turgot*, presumably in Paris in eithe 1788 or 1789. (See 'Introduction' above p. xxxii, n. 117.) This version will be referred to as the 178 edition.

freedom of the grain trade;[2] while on the other, many reputable writers have opposed this policy.][3]

SECOND, THIRD, AND FOURTH LETTERS

Tulle, 8 November; Egletons, 10 November; Bort, 13 November pp. 274–285

[These letters have unfortunately been lost, and only Du Pont's summaries have been preserved. These are reproduced by Daire and Schelle, but will not be summarised here. The second letter deals with the "interests of the cultivator", the third with the possibility of establishing grain stores, and the fourth with a statistical analysis of the average price of grain, and some further conclusions on grain stores.]

FIFTH LETTER

Saint-Angel, 14 November

Sir, at the end of the letter which I had the honour of writing you from Bort yesterday on the freedom of the grain trade, I promised you a fifth letter, intended to discuss the arguments with which you presented me at Compiègne, and with which you then appeared to be greatly taken. p. 285

"Three types of people", you said, "are interested in the selection of a plan for the policy of grain: the proprietors of landed estates, the cultivators, and the consumers.

I agree that the system of freedom is immensely favourable to the proprietors.

In connection with the cultivators, the advantage of such a system for them is purely a temporary one, since on the expiration of the leases, the proprietors are well versed in appropriating the whole of this advantage for themselves by increasing their rents.

[2] For the years 1768–1770, Higgs in his *Bibliography of Economics*, lists well over twenty books and pamphlets by the Physiocrats (or economists) on the subject of free trade in grain. The most important of these are: Baudeau, *Lettres sur les émeutes populaires qui cause la cherté des bléds et sur les précautions du moment*, Paris, 1768; Le Trosne, *Lettres à un ami sur les avantages de la liberté du commerce des grains et le danger des prohibitions*, Amsterdam and Paris, 1768; Baudeau, *Lettres à M. l'Abbé G[aliani] sur les Dialogues anti-économiques*, Paris, 1769; Du Pont de Nemours, *Observations et réponses sur le commerce des grains et des farines*, Amsterdam and Paris, 1769; and Morellet, *Réfutation de l'ouvrage qui a pour titre 'Dialogues sur le commerce des bléds'*, London, 1770.

[3] Higgs, op. cit., also mentions many works against the Physiocratic policy, among which Galiani's *Dialogues sur le commerce des bléds* was by far the most famous. As shown in note 2 above, it was replied to by both Baudeau and Morellet, and Turgot himself was most annoyed with it, since it was so cleverly written. See his letters to Du Pont (30/1/1770, 2/2/1770 in Schelle, *Oeuvres*, III, pp. 372–374); to Mlle de Lespinasse (26/1/1770 in ibid., pp. 420–421) and to Morellet (17/1/1770, in ibid., pp. 419–420). See also 'Letter to l'Abbé Terray on the "Marque des Fers" ', below p. 187.

Finally, the consumers obviously suffer the greatest harm from t freedom, which raises the prices to a level which no longer has any relation their means of subsistence, and which increases all their expenses."

You even added on that occasion "that, in the last few years, it had cost t King several million for the excess value of bread which it was necessary grant the troops".

You concluded from this that "the policy of freedom was favourable on to a very small number of subjects; that it is immaterial to the cultivators, ai that it is most harmful by far to the greatest number of the King's subjects'

p. 286 I do not think I am mistaken in the exposition of your arguments; allow r now, sir, to take up its three aspects in succession.

You agree, first of all, that *the policy of freedom is very advantageous to t proprietors, whose revenues it increases*. We are certainly very much in agre ment on this conclusion; but I doubt whether we are as much in agreement the principles from which we derive it, and, as these principles are very impo tant, I will stop to discuss them.

First of all, however, I want to point out all the advantages you granted r by admitting that the policy of freedom increases the revenue of t proprietors.

This revenue, sir, is the security for all the mortgaged income from land property.

It is the source of the greater part of the wages, which enable the people live, for the people, the day-labourer, the artisan, have nothing by themselve they live on the produce of the soil; they obtain this produce only by buying with their labour, and can buy it only from those who gather it and who p them for their work with that produce or with the money which represents It is therefore the sum of subsistence goods or rather, the mass of valu produced annually by the soil which forms the fund of the wages for distrib tion to all classes of society. The cultivator immediately consumes what necessary for his subsistence; the rest is divided between him and t proprietor; and both, by their expenses, whether these have as objective t continuation or the improvement of cultivation, or whether they are limited the satisfaction of their needs, distribute this remainder in wages to all t other members of society as the price of their labour. The values which t latter have received return to the hands of the cultivators through t purchases of commodities they consume, to leave them again by a circulati the continuity of which is essential to the life of the body politic, just as t circulation of the blood is essential to the life of the animal body. Anythi

[4] The 1789 edition (p. 2) has "of consumers" instead of "of the King's subjects", the phr used by Schelle, and also by Du Pont (*Oeuvres*, VI, p. 156). In connection with Turgot's su mary of Terray's argument (above, pp. 165–166) the 1789 text appears to be more appropria

that increases the sum of values produced by the soil increases, therefore, the sum of wages to be distributed among the other classes of society.

Finally sir, the revenues of the proprietors are the only source from which the State can draw its revenue. No matter in what manner the taxes are levied, and in what form they are collected, in the final analysis they are always paid by the proprietors of landed estates, either through the increase p. 287
of their expenses, or through the decrease of their receipts.

The self-evidence of this truth is very easily shown, for it is quite clear that every tax imposed on consumption will be paid forthwith, in part by the proprietors, in part by the cultivators, in part by the stipendiary class, since these three classes consume and since every consumer is included in one of these three classes.

There is no problem with respect to the portion which the proprietor pays on his own consumption.

The part paid by the cultivator is evidently an increase in the costs of cultivation, since these costs consist of the whole of the cultivator's expenditure, they must return to him every year, with a profit, in order that he may be able to continue his cultivation, and he must necessarily deduct the whole of these costs from the products before determining the portion of the proprietor, or *the rent*, which is reduced accordingly. The proprietor therefore still pays this portion of the tax through the reduction of the revenue.

The part which the wage earners pay on their consumption thus remains; but it is very clear that if the competition of workmen on the one hand, and those who spend, on the other, had fixed the daily wage at 10 *sous*, and the wage earner lived on those 10 *sous* (it is well known that the wage of a man who has only his arms is ordinarily reduced to what is necessary for the subsistence of himself and his family); if, I say, it is then assumed that a new tax on his consumption increases his expenses by 2 *sous*, it is necessary that his day's work be paid more dearly, or that he reduce his consumption. It is obvious that if he is paid more for his day's work, this is at the expense of the proprietor or the cultivator, since they alone have the wherewithal to pay, and when it is the cultivator who pays, it is still at the expense of the proprietor, as I have shown above; but the less well off the labourer, the less domineering he can be, and the proprietor will at first not give in easily to the increase in wages. It will be necessary for the wage earner to reduce his consumption and to suffer. Now, this decrease in consumption will diminish the demand for commodities in proportion, and in the final analysis, always that for subsistence goods. These goods, consequently, will decrease in value; now, this decrease in value, on whom does it fall? On the seller of the commodity, on the cultivator, who, deriving less from his cultivation, will give proportion- p. 288
ately less to his proprietor in rent. The latter therefore pays all in every case.

In reality, this forced reduction in the consumption of the day labourer could not be permanent, because it puts him in a state of penury. Before the

tax, wages were on a level with the customary price of commodities, and this level, which is the result of a multitude of causes combined and balanced with each other, must tend to re-establish itself. It is certain that competition, by causing wages to be at a lower level, reduce those of the simple unskilled workers to what is necessary to their subsistence. It should not be thought, however, that this necessity is thus reduced to the essentials for avoiding starvation to such an extent, that nothing remains outside it, which these men may have at their command either to obtain some little luxuries, or, if they are thrifty, to create a little movable fund which becomes their resort in unforeseen cases of sickness, or times of high prices, or unemployment. When the objects of their expenditure increase in price, they first begin to cut down on this little superfluity and the enjoyments it can procure for them. But it is of this type of *luxury* especially, that it can be said that it is *a most necessary thing*;[5] it is essential that there is a little of it, just as it is necessary that there is *some play* in every machine. A watch of which all the wheels would work into each other with mathematical precision and without the smallest gap, would soon cease to go. If by an unexpected decrease in wages or increase in expenses, the worker can put up with being reduced to strict essentials, the same causes which had forced wages to rise a little above the necessary of yesterday, continue to operate and cause them to rise once more until they attain a higher level, in the same proportion with the necessary of today. If an absence of the ability to pay stands in the way of this return to the natural proportion, if the decrease of the revenue of the proprietors persuaded them to resist this increase in wages, the worker would go elsewhere to look for the competency without which he cannot exist; population would diminish up to the point where the decrease in the number of workers, by curtailing their competition, enables them to lay down the law and to force the proprietors to raise wages. I admit, if the lowness of the price of produce caused by the decrease in consumption continued, the increase in wages would be less con-
p. 289 siderable; but this lowness of the price of commodities having diminished the profits of the cultivator, would force him to diminish his productive expenditure, and consequently, production: now, from the smaller production an increase in price must result. If each of these effects occurred to the fullest extent, the loss resulting from the new tax would fall on the proprietors in several different ways, since he would have less revenue and would not be able to obtain the same objects of enjoyment with the same revenue, which would cause a double loss. But there is reason to believe that the one compensates the other, without it being possible to determine just how they compensate, and if they balance completely. In whatever way this compensation occurs, and even supposing it to be complete, it follows at least that the

[5] A reference to Voltaire's epigram, "Le superflu, chose très nécessaire" (Luxury, a most essential thing), which appeared as a motto on Isaac de Pinto's *Essai sur le Luxe, considéré relativement à la population et à l'économie,* Amsterdam, 1762.

proprietor always bears the whole of the new tax, either in the increase of his expenses, or in the decrease in his revenue.

[The question of who pays import duties must also be considered. In a large State, foreign trade is small as compared with domestic trade, because objects of foreign trade are usually luxuries. There are some exceptions to this, like the trade with the American colonies, which is a trade in necessities. The only enduring type of trade is that trade where imports and exports balance in the long run, and where the balance of trade is therefore small compared with the volume of trade. In such trade, import duties will reduce the volume of trade and raise the price of imported commodities, which increase is ultimately borne by the revenue of the proprietors.] pp. 289–291

Be that as it may, the principle that the whole of the tax is paid by the proprietors and from the revenue of the soil, must be regarded as unchangeable. And it is very essential that the revenue of the soil, that is, the part of the produce which remains after the deduction of the expenses of cultivation, the wages and profit of the cultivator, pays the whole of the tax; for everything else, whether produce from the soil, or profit of any type whatsoever, is destined for the reproduction and the continuation of work of every kind, on which the whole edifice of society depends. In the world, there is only land and human labour: it is by labour that the land produces; it is the produce of the soil which pays the wages of labour, and, generally, all the labour which is required in the service of society, and which occupies the different classes of men. p. 291

From the produce of the soil, the cultivator must first deduct his subsistence, and that of his family, since this is the indispensable wage of his labour, and the motive which induces him to cultivate; next, the interest on his advances, and this interest must be sufficiently high for him to discover an appreciable advantage in placing his capitals in agricultural enterprises, rather than in any other form. Without these two conditions, agriculture would lack advances, and advances are no less necessary there than human labour. The cultivator must also appropriate the wherewithal to meet all the expenses which the continuation of his cultivation requires, for without these expenses, the reproduction of the following year would cease.

This then is the share of the cultivator; it is inviolable, and tyranny could encroach upon it only at the risk of stopping the reproduction, and of damaging the source of taxation. In vain the cultivator is taxed personally; he must either be able to pass on the tax to the proprietor, or reduce his cultivation. p. 292

The surplus produce, that which remains after the portion of the cultivator has been deducted, is the *net product* or the revenue of the soil. It is this net product which the cultivator is able to hand over, and which indeed he does hand over to the proprietor in order to obtain permission from him to cultivate. It is also from this net product, at the expense of the revenue of the proprietor, that all the charges on the land are taken: the tithe of the Clergy, the rent of the lord, and the tax levied on behalf of the King. And it is very essential that all this is taken from the net product, for only this net product is disposable; only this portion of the fruits of the earth is not absolutely necessary for the reproduction of the following year. The remainder is the share of the cultivator, an inviolable share as has been said, which cannot be encroached upon without stopping all activity in the political system.

All the *wages* of the workmen, all the *profits* of the entrepreneurs in every type of manufacture and trade, are paid, partly by the cultivator, namely, for the expenditure required by the satisfaction of their needs, or by the work of their cultivation; partly by the proprietors and the other partakers of the net product, such as the clergy, the fund holder, the sovereign, for the expenses they pay from this net product to obtain all the objects of pleasure, or usefulness, whether individual or public. All these wages, all these profits, are no more disposable than the share of the cultivators in the fruits of the earth; competition necessarily limits them to what is essential for the subsistence of the simple working man, to that interest on the advances of all manufacturing and commercial enterprises, and to that indispensable profit of the entrepreneurs, without which they would prefer other uses of their money, which would entail neither the same risk nor the same effort. I have demonstrated above how the whole part of the tax which, it might be imagined, they could be made to pay, would, in the final analysis, always fall on the proprietor alone.

pp. 292–295 [This digression is longer than I had intended, but the importance of the revenue to the kingdom had to be demonstrated to you. I will now return to the major objective of this letter, that is, the discussion of the three points put forward by you.[6]

[Your arguments rest on your erroneous assumption that the effect of the policy of freedom will be *dearer* grain. This is not necessarily true, as the statistics of average grain prices show. The assumption, so often put forward, that a large part of the harvest will be exported when the policy of free trade is adopted, similarly does not necessarily follow. The English, in spite of their encouragement of exports, do not export a great deal of grain.]

p. 295 There are, on the contrary, some very strong reasons to believe that the average price will fall. I have pointed out above that the price is determined by a comparison between demand and total production. It must therefore fall when total production increases at a faster rate than total requirements. Now, this increase in production is more than likely. If the extension of cultivation is a consequence of the increase in the profits of the cultivator, as soon as the earth produces more, it must follow, at least until the number of consumers is
p. 296 increased, that the commodity falls in price. This fall is assured as long as it does not conflict with the profit of the cultivator.

[6] See above, pp. 165–166.

Recall, sir, what I had the honour to explain at length in my letter written Thursday last from Tulle,[7] on the difference between the average price to the producer and the average price to the consumer. I think I showed there that the mere equalisation of the prices, true aim and unfailing effect of the policy of freedom, without raising the price for the consumer to any extent, and simply by bringing this price together with that of the producer-seller, assures the latter of a tremendous profit. This profit is sufficiently large for much of it still to remain even when it decreases a little by the lowering of the price to the advantage of the consumer. Now, if there is still some profit for the cultivators when the price falls, the competition among the cultivators will cause it to fall. Perhaps, subsequently, the increase in the revenues, by increasing the sum total of wages, will cause an increase in demand; those who used to eat only buck wheat porridge will then eat bread; those who used to be limited to rye bread will add some wheat. The increase in public affluence will increase the population and by this increase in wants a slender increase in price will be generated; fresh encouragement to cultivation which, through the increase in production, will again cause its value to fall. It is by these alternating, small fluctuations in price that the whole nation will slowly progress to the highest state of cultivation, affluence and population which it is able to enjoy relative to the size of its territory. The revenues and the public wealth will increase without involving an increase in the average price for the consumer; this price may even fall a little.

|All this can be shown from the experience of free trade at various points of time both in France and England, and by a comparison between England and France at the present time. These statistics prove that freedom of the grain trade will not necessarily increase the average price of grain.|[8] pp. 296–301

SIXTH LETTER

Angoulême, 27 November

|In my last letter I stated that I would answer your three points on the benefits for the three classes which are affected by a policy of free trade in grain. I have already discussed the interest of the proprietors and now turn to that of the cultivators who, contrary to your assumption,[9] would not be in- pp. 301–302

[7] This is a reference to the second letter, written at Tulle, 8 November. A summary of this letter was included by Du Pont (*Oeuvres*, VI, pp. 136–137), and was reprinted by Daire (*Oeuvres*, I, p. 168) and by Schelle (*Oeuvres*, III, pp. 274–275). It is not included here. See above p. 165.

[8] Turgot had been interested in English grain price statistics for some time, as is shown in his letter to Josiah Tucker, 10/12/1773, in Schelle, *Oeuvres*, III, pp. 614–617. He also illustrated several of the earlier letters to Terray with statistical information drawn from French and English experience. See Schelle, *Oeuvres*, III, pp. 277–285.

[9] See above, pp. 165–166.

different to it. The reason you gave for this assumption is that their gains are short lived, and that they will lose them on the renewal of their leases. Even if we assume that this is the case, there is still a great deal of advantage in the temporary increase in the wealth of the farmers.]

p. 302 Now, this increase in wealth for the class of farmer-cultivators represents a tremendous benefit for them and for the State. If it is assumed that the real increase in the produce of the land is one sixth of the rents, which is not far from the truth, and probably an underestimate, this sixth, accumulated over six years to the profit of the cultivators, forms for them a capital equal to the revenue of the rented lands. I say a capital, for the profits of the cultivators are not squandered on luxuries. If it is assumed that they place it in the national debt, in order to draw interest from it, this would certainly be a net profit for them, and it cannot be denied that they will be the richer for it: but
p. 303 they are not so stupid, and they have a much more lucrative use for their funds. This use is to pour them back into their agricultural enterprises, to increase the sum total of their advances with them, to buy cattle and agricultural implements, to increase all kinds of manures and fertilisers, and to plant and marl the estates, if they can obtain a second lease on these terms from their proprietors.

All these advances have as their immediate objective to increase the amount of produce, to the benefit of the entire State, and to give the cultivators an annual profit. It is essential that this profit is greater than the ordinary interest of loan money, for otherwise, the owner of the capital would prefer to lend it. It is also necessary that this profit is kept completely for the farmer-cultivator, without him yielding the least part to the proprietor: for if this profit was not entirely for the farmer, he would prefer to invest his money in another manner, so as not to share the interest with anyone else. Here then a permanent increase in wealth, to the advantage of the cultivators, equal at least to the interest of the annual revenue of all the leases, converted into capital. This is surely a great deal.

This item is altogether unrelated to the increase in the leases which causes the gain for the proprietor; it only makes the revenue more secure by further assuring the solvency of the farmer.

But this is not all; this capital and this interest, firmly assured to the farmer-cultivator, and steadfastly used by him to swell the advances of cultivation, must, following the present course of events, increase the produce in a much greater proportion than the interest of these new advances. Undoubtedly, the cultivator will in time agree to yield the proprietor his share in this increase in profit; but this will always happen only after he has wholly benefited from it himself up to the time of expiry of the lease: the argument I have put forward as regards the initial profit resulting directly from the policy of freedom is applicable to the second profit, and also to that resulting from this second increase in wealth. Hence, there results a progressive increase in

the wealth of the cultivators, in the advances in agriculture, in the total produce and the values gathered annually from the soil. This progression may be fast or slow: but if the outlets continually raise sales, either by regular exportation, or by an increase in population, it will have no other limit than p. 304
the physical one of the fertility of the soil.

[This happy picture must be contrasted with the unhappy results of the pp. 304–306
curtailing of the freedom of the grain trade. In this case, the value of the produce of the soil will decline, and the cultivators will be impoverished.

[You have also argued that on the expiration of the leases, the proprietors appropriate all the profit of the farmers. This assumption is a lot further from the truth than you suppose. It is, of course, essential that the proprietors can appropriate the whole of the net product over and above the necessary advances of cultivation, but the tenant has the interest of these advances for the further accumulation of new capitals. The proprietors cannot risk appropriating either the advances or the interest on these advances, for that would cause the decline of cultivation and produce. It is true, however, that at the end of the lease, competition will ensure that the new rent is equal to the net product of cultivation, after all costs have been met.]

No sir, it is not at all in this sense that it must be, or has been, said, that the p. 306
freedom of the grain trade is of tremendous benefit to the cultivators. The situation of the cultivators taken individually must be improved by it; but this p. 307
result is but a trifle compared to the immense advantage which must result from it for cultivation in general, through the growth of the capitals used for drawing the produce from the soil, and from the increase in the number of cultivators.

I must insist on this observation, because it attacks directly the major flaw in the arguments which you have permitted me to criticise. As soon as the raising of rents has as its sole cause the competition among a great number of agricultural entrepreneurs, when each of them, individually, would not gain any more, would not draw a better share than previously from his capital and labour, it would still remain true that the number of labourers and agricultural entrepreneurs would be greater, that the sum of capitals employed in agriculture, and consequently the produce, would be greatly increased. Now, that is what really interests the State as a whole.

[The benefits of large advances in agriculture are seen in the provinces of pp. 307–313
Flanders, Picardy, Normandy, etc., where the land is exploited by wealthy tenant farmers who can afford to pay large rents. If these farmers were deprived of a market, or if their market were diminished, their enterprises would decline, and the prosperity would disappear from these districts.

[In the poorer provinces, land has a much smaller value. This is not caused by the different fertility of the soil; it is caused by the less capital intensive cultivation. It is to be hoped that all provinces will follow the more capital intensive methods in the future, to the ultimate benefit of the whole of the

State.[10] On the calculation of M. Dupré de St. Maur,[11] these poor provinces are more than four sevenths of the whole nation. Freedom of the grain trade should greatly diminish this proportion.

[Do not believe, sir, that this will be harmful to the *consumers*. In my next letter, I will deal with the interest of this class of people in the policy of a free trade in grain.]

SEVENTH LETTER

p. 313 *Limoges, 2 December*

Sir, in my last letters, written from Saint-Angel and from Angoulême,[12] I dealt with the interest of the *proprietors* and that of the cultivators in the freedom of the grain trade. To complete the reply to your objections against this freedom, I have to discuss the interest of the *consumers*, whom you believe to be injured by the suppression of the constraints of the old regulations.

As for me, sir, I together with many others, am thoroughly convinced that the policy of freedom is no less advantageous, and that it is even more necessary, for the consumers than it is for the cultivators and the proprietors. I even dare to feel sure I can convince you of this, if you will be so good as to consider my arguments carefully.

Two things are necessary for the livelihood of the consumer: firstly, the existence of the produce; secondly, that it is within his reach, and that he has sufficient means to obtain it. How then could his interest be opposed to that of the cultivator and the proprietor of the land, since it is from them that he receives both the produce and the wage with which to purchase the produce?

Consumption first of all implies production: thus, the livelihood of men is no less based on cultivation than is the revenue of the soil. Now cultivation
p. 314 only takes place because it is profitable to cultivate, and if the cessation of that profit destroys the revenue, it also destroys cultivation and the livelihood of men.

The profits of the cultivator, divided between him and the proprietor, form, through the expenses they pay from them to procure the different objects of their wants, the unique wages-fund of all the other classes of society. These wages are the price of labour and of industry, but labour and industry have only as much value as there is the wherewithal to pay for them, that is, as much as agriculture has generated in consumable produce suitable for the enjoyment of man, over and above what is necessary for the subsistence of the cultivator; the consumer there is doubly dependent on agriculture; he has

[10] The argument in the above paragraph is derived largely from Quesnay's article, 'Fermiers', which appeared in the *Encyclopédie* in 1756. See esp. 'Fermiers', op. cit., pp. 427–458.

[11] Dupré de St. Maur, *Essai sur les monnoies*, Paris, 1746. This work was referred to in a note to Quesnay's article 'Fermiers', op. cit., p. 449, n. 2.

[12] Above, pp. 165–174.

a double interest in its prosperity, both in order that his livelihood exists, and in order that he, as a consumer, has the means to buy it by selling his labour. He has an interest in selling his labour at a price high enough to enable him to pay for the commodities he needs with the price he receives for it, and he must pay for these commodities at a price high enough for those who sell them to draw from this price the means to generate an equal quantity of produce in the following year, as well as the means to continue to buy his labour. Without this exact proportion, either the cultivator would cease to make the earth produce commodities and revenue, or the wage earner would cease to labour, or rather, these two things would occur at the same time, because cultivator and wage-earner, wages and labour, being necessarily correlated, and equally dependent on one another, must either exist, or be destroyed, together. Consequently, if this proportion did not exist, population would diminish and society would destroy itself. Let us not forget to observe that this reduction in the number of men would begin with the class of consuming wage-earners. If less subsistence is produced, someone must starve, and that will not be the cultivator, for before sharing his harvest with anyone else, he begins by taking what he needs himself. If there is only enough grain for himself, he will not give any of it to his shoemaker to pay for a pair of shoes: he will go barefoot and survive. If the production decreases to the point where it yields only just the necessary subsistence for the cultivator, the last grain of corn will be for him, and the proprietor will be forced to cultivate for himself to avoid starvation.[13]

It can, therefore, be said that in a sense the consumer is more interested in p. 315
the extension of cultivation than the cultivator and the proprietor. For the latter two, the question is only that of being more or less wealthy, of living more or less comfortably; but for the wage-earning consumer, existence is at stake; it is a matter of life or death.[14]

If every man consumes three *setiers* of corn or other equivalent subsistence, as many men must be deducted as the number of times three *setiers* of corn are taken from the annual production. And these men who are deducted will be taken from the class of the wage-earning consumers, or, as they are called, the *labouring poor*.

For the existence of society it is essential that the necessary proportion between the price of commodities and the price of labour exists normally. But this proportion does not consist of a point so precise and indivisible that it cannot vary and gradually move away from the equilibrium which is most just and advantageous for the two classes. In that case, either one or the other suffers more or less, and both of them a little. Between health and death there is the middle state of sickness; there are even a thousand degrees of weakness between sickness and health. The proportion can be disturbed for shorter or

[13] The 1789 edition does not start a new paragraph here.
[14] Ibid.

longer intervals in such a way that a great number of men experience all the excess of misery, and that societies are in a state either of crisis and convulsion or weariness and decline. What ought to be desired? Two things: firstly, that this proportion between the price of wages and the price of commodities is the fairest, the closest to equilibrium, the most advantageous possible for the cultivators and the proprietor on the one hand, and the wage-earner on the other; the most suitable, in short, to procure for the whole of society the greatest amount of production, of enjoyment, of wealth and of strength; secondly, that the disturbances occasioned by natural causes are as rare, as short-lived, and as light as possible.

There, sir, is the true end of legislation on the matter of subsistence. All that is required now is to examine what means lead to this end in the best way, whether freedom, or prohibitions and regulations. I venture to say that this way of stating the nature of the question decides it, for the right price and
p. 316 the constant price both result necessarily from free trade, and can only result from free trade. I will not develop this idea any further here as it would lead me too far afield, and would cause me to digress from the particular aim of this letter. It is sufficient to have indicated at the outset the source of the wages of the consumer, and the manner in which his interest is linked with that of agriculture. I will now turn to an enumeration of the advantages which the consumers must derive from the free trade in subsistence goods.

[The consumers certainly gain from the increase and improvement in cultivation which is caused by the policy of free trade. They also gain from the increase in produce brought to market as a result of free trade, because this raises the value of grain by extending the market, and makes the long term storage of grain more profitable, thereby preventing the use of grain for alternative employments.]

p. 317 There are two methods of restoring prices to their level, despite the unevenness of harvests. The one consists in transporting grain from provinces where the harvest is good to those where it is bad; the other is to store it up in abundant years for use in famine years. These two methods entail costs, and free trade will always choose that which, all told, entails the least cost. Barring special circumstances, this is usually transportation, since, on the one hand, the return of the funds is speedier, and, on the other, the waste product is less considerable, the grain being consumed the sooner. But if the government, by placing obstacles in the way of transportation, leaves no other alternative
p. 318 than storage, it is evident that it increases the share of the rats and weevils to no purpose; it increases it even more by prohibiting storage by the merchants, who, having no other occupation nor any other interest than to preserve their grain, are a great deal more attentive and skilled in this than the farmers, whose true occupation is to grow it, and who need all their attention for this.

pp. 318–320 [There are several ways of overcoming these difficulties in the storing of grain; they have been described and practised on previous occasions by people concerned with this matter. But to continue with the question at hand, production is proportioned to consumption, and as consumption increases, so will production. The problem of famine can therefore best be solved by encouraging consumption, including foreign consumption by exportation. The stimulus to production and capital formation given by the policy of free trade will increase the sum of produce in the nation, and therefore the fund from which everyone can consume. The increase and improvement of cultivation will also increase the possibilities for employment, thereby making it easier for the people to earn their living.]

But these advantages are not confined to finding work more easily; for, p. 320
from the very fact that labour is more sought after, wages must rise by degrees, because labourers will become scarce relative to the wages offered. It is a well known fact that in the last few years, while the building trade has been brisk in Paris, masons have been given higher wages. This increase is inevitable as long as the number of labourers does not increase in proportion to the new values put into the wages fund for distribution. The greater quantity of wages offered, and the affluence of the people, increase the population: but p. 321
this increase, following the natural order, is much less speedy than that of production. The year after a field has been cleared, manured, and sown, it returns the wherewithal to feed a man; but, before a man is brought up, twenty years are necessary, and before these twenty years have passed, production would have had time to increase more and more if its progress were not hampered and restrained by the limits of consumption. Workmen coming from abroad can also prevent the increase of wages: however, men are too strongly attached to their native country for this immigration ever to be too large. But whether the increase in population comes from the influx of foreigners, or from the multiplication of the species, it will always be the result of the affluence of the people, and will always presuppose it. Here then, in the increase in values brought about by the policy of free trade, is an obvious advantage for the class of wage-earning consumers, since it causes a greater wages fund to be available for distribution, which produces: firstly, a greater certainty of finding work, and, for each labourer, a greater number of useful working days; secondly, an actual increase in the price of wages, through the competition of cultivators and proprietors, who will raise it in emulation of one another to attract workmen; thirdly, an increase in population, consequence of the greater affluence of the people.

[The equalisation of prices is another advantage of the policy of freedom. pp. 321–336
This results from the process of distributing grain evenly between provinces in times of harvest failure by allowing free transportation. It can also result from a policy of public granaries which distributes the grain more evenly over good and bad years. This has been done in various small states, and also in France on several occasions. It will of course require capital formation, but this

should not be a difficulty. The people will also have to be convinced of the wisdom of the procedure.[15] The profit made by these public granaries will, however, be an offsetting advantage to the treasury. This policy of purchasing in abundant years and selling in lean years will have the desirable result of greatly stabilising grain prices.]

p. 336 One of the great disadvantages of the inequality of the price for the consumer is based on the fact that the proportion which is established between the price of subsistence goods and the price of a day's work, does not follow the average price exactly, but constantly remains below it, to the detriment of the day labourer; so that, if the prices of dear, average and cheap years were distributed in such a way that they were more or less equal every year, wages would be higher, to the advantage of the consumer, than they are when wages vary a lot. This is easy to demonstrate. The daily wage, like the price of every thing else, is determined by the relationship between offer and demand, that is, by the reciprocal need of those who give work and those who have to live by working. Wage-earning people, in good and bad years alike, have no other means to live than by working; they will, therefore, offer their labour, and competition will force them to settle for the wage necessary for their subsistence. They will not foresee and forecast the possibility of a dearth in order to force those who pay them to raise their wages; for, whatever this distant future may be, they must live at the present time, and if they make themselves too hard to please, their neighbour would take the work at a lower price. It is, therefore, on the customary rate that the price of wages will settle itself; it will even fall below this proportion in years of low prices, because, if on the one hand, this low price makes the people lazy and reduces the competition among the labourers, on the other hand, it deprives the cultivators, and, by
p. 337 repercussion, the proprietors, of the means of giving work. Then again, the increase in prices in dear years does not only fail to be considered in the determination of wages, but tends, rather to decrease them. Indeed, the misery of the people banishes idleness, and makes work so necessary for them, that they give it at a lower price. All those among the proprietors who have a fixed revenue, and even, in the case of excessive dearth, all those who are in a situation of giving employment, themselves suffer by the increase of their expenses, and are not compensated for this by the increase in their revenue (for it cannot be repeated too often that only the equality of prices causes the increase of the revenue of the cultivators, and that they are not compensated by a high price in the years of dearth, for the low prices of the years of abundance, because the quantity which they sell is proportionately far less than the rise in the price). They are themselves, therefore, in no situation to give employment;

[15] Turgot himself attempted to convince the people of the wisdom of this measure in the preamble to the decree of the Royal Council of August 1774 which restored the freedom of the grain trade. (See Schelle, *Oeuvres,* IV, pp. 201–210). This was one of his first acts after being appointed Contrôleur-Général.

most often, they decide to do so only from motives of charity, and by profiting from the readiness of the workers to lower their wages. Thus, not only do the wage-earners fail to share in any way in the jolt which the transitory dearth gives to the price, but they do not even participate to the extent that the transitory dearth increases average prices. Yet it is mainly the years of dearth which raise average prices, even in the countries where the absence of free trade maintains a customary, rather low price, which is far below the mean price. It follows from this that, without the mean price of subsistence goods rising to the loss of the consumer, the price of wages will rise to his benefit by the simple equalisation of the mean price between abundant and unfruitful years, because then the mean price will coincide with the customary price, and it is always to the customary price that the price of wages is related.

I cannot deny myself a reflection here. In my letter written from Tulle,[16] and in even more detail in that from Bort,[17] I showed you that the policy of free trade and the equalisation of prices alone – the mean price remaining the
p. 338 same for the consumers – must assure the cultivators, the proprietors and the State of an immense increase in profits and revenues. I believe I showed you in this letter that, with the mean price still remaining the same for the consumers, by the mere effect of the equalisation of prices and the policy of freedom, the consumers will gain by being remunerated in a proportion which is more advantageous for them, since their current wage is determined by its proportion with a price lower than the mean price, and since it will then be proportioned to the mean price, that is, to their real expenses. It appears to me that the combination of these two truths ought to inspire a great deal of confidence in the results of the policy of freedom.

I add that the advantage to the consumers will still be very great even when the mean price of consumption goods would rise, and that the welfare which would be procured for wage-earners by the re-establishment of the proportion between their wage and their expenses will always be equally real, even if the mean price were to rise, provided that it was always constant, or almost invariable.

I further add that the observation which has been developed here, completely refutes the objection which the adversaries of the freedom of the grain trade are so often heard to repeat. Experience shows, they say, that the price of wages does not rise with the price of grain, and, as they always assume that freedom increases the price of grain, they conclude from this that freedom is fatal to the consumers.

[16] This refers to Turgot's second letter which has been lost. A summary of its contents prepared by Du Pont (*Oeuvres*, VI, pp. 136–137) has been reprinted by Daire (*Oeuvres*, I, p. 168) and Schelle (*Oeuvres*, III, 274–275).

[17] This refers to Turgot's fourth letter which has been lost. A summary of its contents prepared by Du Pont (*Oeuvres*, VI, pp. 140–155) has been reprinted by Daire (*Oeuvres*, I, pp. 170–182) and by Schelle (*Oeuvres*, III. pp. 277–285).

I believe to have shown, on the contrary, that even when the momentary dearth failed to increase the price of wages, and even when it lowered it below its natural proportion, it must be concluded that the evil lies in the momentary dearth, and, in order to remedy this, it is necessary to establish a price as constant and equal as possible, that is, to give trade complete freedom.

pp. 338–354 [This can be shown by statistical data from England and France. Examples can be given which show the difference in the behaviour of the average price over periods when there was free trade and when there was not. Forbidding the trade in grain between districts makes the people liable to the harmful effects of harvest failure and high prices. From free trade, as I have shown, only good results can follow.

[I would also like to mention some specific dues which ought to be abolished: that of the *droits de ménage et de péage,* of the *maîtrisse des boulangers,* and of the *banalité des moulins.*[18] These three raise the price of bread unnecessarily.]

p. 354 I cannot help making some reflections on the danger of some remarks in the preface to your plan, which perhaps I have already made, but to whose repetition there can be no objection.

To announce to the people that the dearth which they experience is the *result of scheming* and not of the disturbance of the seasons, to tell them that they *suffer dearth amidst plenty*, this is to sanction all the *past, present, and future* slanders to which they themselves resort but too readily, and to which many people are eager to rouse them, against the administration and administrators of every rank. This is, at the same time, to become accountable for the dearths which may continue, or occur in the future, it is to undertake personally to provide them with *abundance,* whatever may happen: now, it is essential to be very sure about your facts before making such a promise. I admit that no plan for regulation would inspire me with such confidence. I would prefer to base my security on physical necessity and on justice. The people are well aware of the fact that the Government cannot command the seasons, and they must understand that it has no right to violate the property of the husbandmen and the grain merchants. It is a sign of strength, even in the eyes of the people, when they can be told: *What you ask of me is an injustice.* Those who are not satisfied with this reasoning, will never be satisfied with any, and will always slander the government, no matter what measures it

[18] *Droits de ménage et de péage:* These were seigneurial toll rights dating back to feudal times. Many were abolished during the reign of Louis XIV, but there were plenty of them left in the eighteenth century. See Alexis de Tocqueville, *The Old Regime and the French Revolution,* New York, 1955, p. 293 f. *La Maîtrisse des boulangers:* master craftsmanship in the bakers guild which was difficult and costly to obtain, and therefore raised the price of bread. *La banalité des moulins:* the feudal right of the seigneur to force peasants to hire his mill for the grinding of their grain. This was generally very expensive for the peasants; de Tocqueville, op. cit., p. 292, states that there were no banal rights in Paris, and in the rich provinces of Artois, Flanders and Hainault. Turgot abolished many of these toll rights in the first year of his finance ministry, and attempted to abolish the guilds in 1776.

takes to please them; for it will not gratify them seeing that it is impossible for the government to procure cheap grain for the people when the harvests have failed, and that there is no possible means of obtaining it at a lower price than that which would result from complete freedom, that is, from the observance of rigorous justice.

CHAPTER XII

1773

LETTER TO L'ABBÉ TERRAY ON THE 'MARQUE DES FERS'[1]

D.D. I 376–388

Limoges, 24 December 1773

I am honoured to report to you on the state of the ironworks and mills in the Generality of Limoges which are engaged in the manufacture of iron articles.[2]

You have requested this account of me several times; I would have liked to have been able to send it to you more promptly, and, above all, in a more finished state; but in spite of the trouble to which I went to obtain as detailed an account on each of the ironworks as you seem to require, you will observe that there still remains a great deal of uncertainty about the output of iron
p. 377 from these different works. You will also notice that this uncertainty derives largely from the purely physical circumstances which cause variations in the output, such as the shortage or abundance of water in the different factories. The variations in the market and in the wealth of the entrepreneurs also have an influence on the fluctuations in output, almost as great as the physical causes.

As for the observations you seem to require on the means of instilling more life into this branch of industry, or of restoring to it that which it is said to have lost, I have few to offer. I know of no means whatever of stimulating any trade or industry other than that of giving it the greatest freedom, and freeing it from all those burdens which the mistaken interest of the treasury has inordinately increased upon all kinds of commodities, and particularly upon the manufactures of iron.

[1] Turgot's letter on the 'marque des fers' was written in response to a request by l'Abbé Terray in connection with a project to raise a new duty on iron, which he had apparently foreshadowed in 1771. The 'marque des fers' or 'le droit de marque des fers' was a duty on iron and iron commodities first established in the seventeenth century during the reign of Henry IV.

The letter was first published in Paris in 1789 in *Mémoires sur le prêt à intérêt et sur le commerce des fers*, Paris, 1789; it was included under the title used here in Du Pont's edition of the works (VI, pp. 438–453), from which it was reprinted in Daire, and in Schelle (*Oeuvres*, III, pp. 617–626).

[2] The 1789 edition has this and the following paragraph as one single paragraph.

I cannot conceal from you that one of the chief causes of my delay in responding to your inquiries, has been the rumour which is circulating to the p. 378
effect that their object was the imposition of new duties, or the extension of old ones. The opinion, founded on too many precedents, that the investigations of the government have for their sole object the discovery of p. 379
ways of extracting more money from the people, has given rise to a general distrust, and the majority of those to whom inquiries are directed do not reply, or seek to mislead by replies sometimes false and sometimes in- p. 380
complete. I cannot believe, sir, that you would intend to impose new burdens on a trade which, to the contrary, you say you want to encourage. If I had thought this, I confess I would congratulate myself on the involuntary delay in my furnishing you with the information you have requested, and I would regret not being able to prolong the delay even more.

If, after complete liberty has been obtained by the relief from all taxes on the manufacturing, transportation, sale and consumption of commodities, anything remains to be done by the government to encourage a branch of trade, it can only be by means of education, that is, by encouraging the research of men of science and craftsmen who tend to perfect the craft, and, above all, by extending the knowledge of the practical processes which greed seeks to keep as so many secrets. It would be useful for the government to incur some expenses in sending young men to foreign countries in order to learn processes of manufacture unknown in France, and to publish the results of these researches. These means are good; but freedom of commerce and deliverance from taxes are much more efficient and much more necessary.

You appear, in the letters with which you have honoured me on this subject, to believe that certain obstacles which might be placed on the importation of foreign iron would act as an encouragement to our national trade. You intimate even that you have received repeated representations from different provinces as regards the favour which these iron articles from abroad obtain, to the prejudice of the commerce and manufacture of native iron commodities. I believe, indeed, that iron masters, who know only about their own iron, imagine that they would earn more if they had fewer competitors. There is no merchant who would not like to be the sole seller of his commodity. There is no branch of trade in which those who are engaged in it do not seek to ward off competition, and do not find some sophisms to make people believe that it is in the State's interest to prevent at least the competition from abroad, which they most easily represent as the enemy of the national commerce. If we listen to them, and we have listened to them but too often, all branches of commerce will be infected by this kind of monopoly. These fools do not see that this same monopoly which they practice, not, as they would have the government believe, against foreigners, but against their own fellow-citizens, consumers of the commodity, is returned to them by these fellow p. 381
citizens, who are sellers in their turn, in all the other branches of commerce

where the first in their turn become buyers. They do not see that all these associations of men engaged in a particular trade will not fail to arm themselves with the same pretexts in order to obtain from the misled government the same exclusion of foreigners; they do not see that in this balance of annoyance and injustice between all kinds of industry, in which the artisans and the merchants of each kind oppress each other as sellers, and are oppressed as buyers, there is no advantage to any party; but there is a real loss to the whole of national commerce, or rather, a loss to the State, which buying less from abroad, similarly will sell less to them. This forced increase in price for all buyers necessarily diminishes the sum total of enjoyment, the amount of disposable revenues, the wealth of the proprietors and of the
p. 382 sovereign, and the amount of wages to be distributed to the people. This loss is doubled again, because in this war of reciprocal oppression, in which the government lends its authority to all against all, the only sector of industry excepted, is that of the tilling of the soil, which is oppressed by everybody in concert through these national monopolies, and which, far from being able to oppress anyone, cannot even take advantage of the natural right to sell its commodity either to foreigners or to those of its fellow-citizens who would buy it, so that from all the classes of working citizens, only the small farmer
p. 383 suffers from monopoly as buyer, and at the same time as seller. He alone cannot freely buy from abroad any of the things he requires; he alone cannot freely sell abroad the commodity he produces, while the cloth merchant or any other, buys as much wheat as he wants from the foreigner and sells him as much as he can of his cloth. Whatever sophisms are collected by the self-interest of a few merchants, the truth is that all branches of commerce ought to be free, equally free, and entirely free; that the system of some modern politicians who fancy that they encourage national commerce by prohibiting the importation of foreign merchandise is plain delusion; that this system results only in setting all branches of commerce as enemies against one another, in nourishing among nations a germ of hatred and of war, of which even the lightest effects are a thousand times more costly to the people, more destructive of wealth, population and happiness, than all those paltry mercantile profits which people fancy they will ensure, benefit the nations which allow themselves to be misled. The truth is that in wishing to hurt others, we only hurt ourselves, not only because the retaliation to these prohibitions is so easy to devise that other nations do not fail to think of it in their turn, but also because we deprive our own nation of the incalculable advantages of a free commerce; advantages so great that, if a great State like France were willing to experience them, the rapid advancement of her commerce and industry would soon compel the other nations to imitate her in order not to be impoverished by the total loss of their own commerce.

But supposing these principles not to be, as I am quite convinced they will be, clearly proven, supposing even that we admit the expediency of prohibition in some branches of commerce, then I would be so bold as to say that iron should be excepted for an incontrovertible reason, which is also peculiar to it.

This reason is that iron is not merely a consumption good useful for the different purposes of life: the iron used in household goods, in ornaments, in weapons, is not the largest part of the metal produced and sold. Above all, it p. 384
is as an implement necessary in the execution of all crafts, without exception, that this metal is so important and so valuable in commerce. It is, in this respect, the raw material of all the crafts, manufactures, of agriculture even, to which it furnishes the greater part of its implements. For this reason it is a commodity of the first necessity. For this reason, even if we were to adopt the idea of encouraging manufactures by prohibitions, iron ought never to be subject to them, because these prohibitions, in the opinion even of those who support them, ought to be placed only on goods manufactured for consumption, and not on commodities used in manufacture, such as the raw materials and the implements required in production; since, according to this system, the buyer of iron implements used in his manufacture or in the cultivation of his land ought to enjoy all the advantages which the principles of this system give to the seller over the ordinary consumer.

To prohibit the importation of foreign iron, therefore, is to favour the iron master not only at the expense of the domestic consumers, as in the ordinary cases of prohibition, it is to favour them at the expense of all manufacturers, of all branches of industry, and at the expense of agriculture, and the production of all foodstuffs, in a special and even more direct manner than the effect of all other prohibitions by which, it must be admitted, it is still constrained.

I am persuaded that this thought, which no doubt has occurred to you, will prevent you from complying with the inconsiderate entreaties of the iron masters and of all those who can only consider this branch of commerce by itself and as isolated from all other branches with whom it has relations of the first necessity.

I will add here two further considerations which, in my opinion, deserve your full attention.

Firstly, many crafts not only need iron, but iron of various qualities, and adapted to the nature of each work. For some, relatively soft iron is needed, for others, more brittle iron. The most important manufactures employ steel, and steel again varies in quality; that of Germany is suited for certain pur- p. 385
poses, that of England, which is more valuable, for others. Now there are certain kinds of iron which our Kingdom does not supply, and which must be obtained abroad. With regard to steel, it is well known that very little of it is produced in France, that this kind of production is only just in the experimental stage, and that, however successful the trials may have been, it may take half a century perhaps before enough steel can be produced in France to supply a reasonable part of the use made of it by manufactures, during which time it will be necessary to obtain from abroad ready made tools, because

they cannot be made in France with the necessary precision, and because the products would lose too much of their value and price if they were made with imperfect instruments. Thus, to prohibit the importation of foreign types of iron would be to ruin our own manufacture; it would mean destroying those in which steel is employed, and all those which need special quality iron. To charge these types of iron with excessive duties would be to lead these manufactures to an inevitable decay, in time; it would mean sacrificing a large part of our national commerce to the very mistaken self-interest of the iron masters.

It seems to me that the first consideration proves that in the current state of trade in manufactures and the domestic iron industry, it would be imprudent to restrain the importation of foreign iron. What remains to be discussed will prove that this importation will never cease to be necessary, and that, on the contrary, the need for it will probably never cease to grow with the passing of time.

Indeed, it is sufficient to consider the tremendous quantity of charcoal which is consumed by the smelting of the ore and by its reduction into metal, and the equally large quantity which is consumed by the ironworks where the metal is refined, in order to be convinced that, however abundant the ore may be, it can only be developed to the extent that it is situated in the neighbourhood of a very large quantity of cheap wood. However plentiful a forest situated near a river flowing to Paris may be, the establishment of an ironworks would certainly never be found expedient there, because the wood has a value there which could never be recovered from the sale of the iron which is manufactured with it. Moreover, the principal benefit expected from
p. 386 the establishment of an ironworks is that of giving a value and a market to forests which did not have any before. It follows from this that as the woods become scarce, as they acquire value through new markets, through the opening of roads and navigable canals, through the increase in agriculture and population, the smelting and production of iron articles must become less profitable and gradually decline. It follows from this that the longer nations have been developed, relative to the progress they have made towards wealth and prosperity, they must manufacture less iron, and obtain more from abroad. It is for this reason that England, which, of all nations in Europe, is the most advanced in this regard, obtains only a small amount of crude iron domestically, and buys a great deal of it in Germany and in the Baltic, which she increases in value by converting it into steel and hardware. The trade in iron is assigned by nature to new peoples, to people who possess vast virgin forests, far removed from all markets, where there is still profit in burning very large quantities of wood just for the sake of the value of the salts which are extracted by washing the ashes. This trade, declining in England, still quite flourishing in France, much more so in Germany, and in the Baltic countries, must, in the natural order of things, proceed to Russia, to Siberia,

and to the American colonies, until these countries become populated in turn, and, all nations being more or less in balance in this regard, the increase in the price of iron will become sufficiently great for the advantage in manufacturing it to be restored even in the country where its production had been abandoned, for want of the ability to maintain a competitive position with the poor nations. If this decline of ironworks resulting from the increase in wealth, population and the multiplication of markets for trade generally was a misfortune, it would be an inevitable misfortune, which it would be useless to attempt to prevent. But it is not a misfortune at all if this trade declines only to be replaced by more profitable ones. It is necessary to reason about France relative to other nations, just as it is necessary to reason about the provinces supplying Paris with consumption goods relative to the provinces of the interior; the proprietors in the neighbourhood of the Seine certainly do not regret that their woods have too high a value to enable the establishment of ironworks in that area, and they resign themselves quite happily to purchasing, with the revenue from their wood, the iron which other provinces p. 387
sell to them.

To persist in opposing this necessary result, from a narrow-minded political viewpoint which thinks it is possible to grow everything at home, would be to act just like the proprietors of Brie who thought themselves thrifty by drinking the bad wine from their own vineyards, which really cost them more in the sacrifice of land suitable for good wheat, than they could have bought from the proceeds of their wheat. It would be to sacrifice a large profit in order to retain a smaller one.

Thus our policy should surrender itself to the course of nature, and the course of commerce, which is no less necessary and no less irresistible than the course of nature, without seeking to direct this course. For, in order to guide it without disturbing it, and without injuring ourselves, it would be necessary for us to be able to follow all the changes in the needs, the interests, and the industry of mankind. It would be necessary to know these in such detail as would be physical impossible to obtain, and in which even the most skilful, the most active and the most painstaking government will risk always to be wrong in half the cases, as is observed or acknowledged by Abbé Galiani in a work[3] in which he nevertheless vindicates with the greatest zeal the system of prohibitions just on the type of trade where they are most disastrous, to wit, the grain trade. I add that, even if we had for all these particulars the mass of knowledge which is impossible to gather, the result would only be to let things go precisely as they would have gone by themselves, by the simple action of the self interest of man, enlivened and held in check by a free competition.

[3] I.e. Ferdinando Galiani, *Dialogues sur le commerce des blèds*, Paris, 1770. For other comments by Turgot on this work see 'Letters on the Grain Trade', above p. 165, n. 3 and the references there cited.

But, if we ought not to drive away the foreign iron which we need, it does not follow that we should burden our own iron with duties, or rather, taxes, on their manufacture, or on their transport. Quite the contrary, the manufacture and transport of French iron should be left perfectly free, in order that they may draw the greatest advantage from our mines and forests, as long as the entrepreneurs find it profitable, and that, by their competition, they may help to supply our agriculture and our crafts with the implements that they require at the lowest possible price.

p. 388 For my own conscience's sake, sir, I felt it my duty to communicate to you all the thoughts which were prompted by a fear that you might yield to proposals which I consider dangerous, and which would injure the trade which you desire to encourage. I know that you do not disapprove of the boldness with which I have openly expressed what I believe to be the truth.

I am, etc.

INDEX

Accise, 97
Accumulation of capital, 64–65, 84–85, 94–95, 115–116
Act of Navigation, 11
Advances, 73, 76, 126, 160
  annual, XXIII, 103, 109
  in agriculture, 66, 71, 172–173
  in iron industry, 149–150
  in manufacturing, 69–70
  original, 103
  origin of, 66, 116–117
  see also Capital
Aguesseau, Comte de, 1
Aide, 97
Alembert, J. L. R. d', XIV, XV
Angelescue, D., XII
Appreciative value, 144, 147–148
  see also Value
Aquinas, St. Thomas, 155
Aristotle, 155
Arnouville, M. Machault de, 23
Ashley, W. J., X, XIX, 62, 89, 95
Auguillon, Duc de, 35

Baden, Carl Friedrich von, 164
Balance of Trade,
  attack on, 28
Banalité des moulins, 180
Barbier, XXIX
Bastiat, X
Batbie, XVIII
Baudeau, Abbé N., 165
Bentham, J., XXIX
Bertin, Contrôleur-Général, XXI, XXII, 96
Bills, 2, 3, 6, 7, 8, 150
Blervache, Simon Cliquot de, 33
Blondel, Mme, XXVIII
Böhm-Bawerk, E. von, XXIX–XXX
Boisguilbert, P. le P. de, 104
Bonaparte, Napoleon, XX, 110
Burton, J. H., XXII
Butel-Dumont, 9, 33

Caillard, M., XXI
  correspondence with Turgot, XII, XVIII, XXI, XXXII, 76, 78
Cannan, E., 16
Cantillon, R., XII
Capital, XVIII, XXVII, 2, 29, 30, 56, 69–70, 76, 88–89, 103, 149, 172–173
  employments of, 69–70, 71, 73–74, 77, 85–86, 87, 116–117
  see also accumulation of capital, advances
Cavour, X
Chevalier, M., X
Child, Sir Josiah, XIV, 22, 33, 38
  New Discourse of Trade, XIII, 9–12
Cicé, l'Abbé de, XI, 1
Class analysis, 45, 46, 49–50, 70–71, 72, 90–94, 123–124
Cobden, R., X
Colbert, J. B., 40, 110
Commerce,
  science of, 11, 21, 22
Comparative advantage, XXXIII
Competition, XIV, 14, 15, 16, 29, 30, 32, 187
Condorcet, Marquis de, XXI, XXIX
  Vie de M. Turgot, X, XI, XVI, XXIX, XXXIII
Corporations, XXI, 12, 24

Corvée, 97
Credit, xxvii, xxviii, 2–3, 5, 149–150
Culpeper, Sir Thomas, 9, 33

Dakin, D., ix, xi, xiii, xxx, xxxi, xxxii, xxxiii, 34, 97
Davenant, Charles, 26
Debasement of money, 4
Diderot, xv, 14
Diminishing returns, xxiv
Distribution theory, xxv, xxxii
Division of labour, 44–46, 64
Droits de ménage et de péage, 180
Du Pont de Nemours, P. S., xiii, xv, xxix, xxx, xxxii, 1, 164–165
  correspondence with Turgot, xvii, xviii, xix, xx, xxi, xxiii, xxiv, xxviii, xxix, xxx, xxxi, xxxii, 14, 50, 52, 67, 73, 78, 83, 164, 165
  Mémoires sur la vie . . . de Turgot, xi, xxvi, xxxiii
Du Tot, xii, 1, 2

Edgeworth, F. Y., xxiv
Eloge de Gournay, x, xvi–xvii, xxxiv, 18, 20–42, 98
Encyclopédie, xiv–xv, xviii, xxvi, xxxiv, 14, 16, 17, 125, 174
Ephémérides du Citoyen, xix, xxviii, xxxv, 52–53, 56, 75, 76, 77, 89, 93
Equilibrium, xxiv, 87, 175–176
Esteem value, 139–140, 143–144
  see also value
Exchange theory, xxvi, 43–44, 57–58, 141–143, 147–148
Exchange value, xxv, 4, 103, 128
  see also value

Fairs, xvi, 14, 16–19
Fairs and Markets, xiv–xv, xxxiv, 14–19, 125, 129
Faure, E., ix
Foncin, P., ix
Fondation, x, xv
Forbonnais, F. V. de, 17, 33
Freedom, of trade, 26, 32, 165–166
  to work, 29, 127
Free trade, xiv, xvi, xxviii, xxxii, 16, 28, 36, 124, 177, 183
  in grain, xxx, xxxi, xxxii, 10, 171, 174, 176
  in iron industry, xxxiii, 188
  in loan market, 162

Galiani, l'Abbé F.,
  Della Moneta, xxv, 140, 154
  Dialogues sur le commerce des blêds, xxx, 165, 187
Gee, Joshua, xiii
Geoffrin, Mme Marie, 20
Gold and silver, 5, 56, 62–64, 118–119
Goudar, Ange, 33
Gournay, Vincent de, xiii, xiv, xv
  as translator of Child, xiii, 9–13, 18
  Turgot's acquaintance with, xiii, xiv
  see also Eloge de Gournay
Gouttes, Abbé J. L., xxix, 149
Grande culture, 55–56, 72, 107, 108, 111
Graslin, J. J. L., xxiii, xxiv–xxv, xxvi, 110, 123, 140
  Essai analytique, 123–125, 127–129, 131–132, 140

Hanotaux, P., 8
Hanse towns, 29
Hayek, F. A. von, xxx
Hecht, Jacqueline, xxxiv
Heckscher, E. F., 16, 24
Hennings, K., xxx
Henry IV, King of France, 126, 182
Herbert, C. J., 29
Higgs, H.,
  Bibliography of Economics, xxix, xxxii, 165
Hoarding, xxiv, 9, 69
Hodgson, W. B., ix, xviii
Houdon, xxi
Hughes, Gustave d', ix
Hume, David, xii, 100
  correspondence with Turgot, xxii–xxiii, xxiv
  Essays, xiv, 100
  History of England, 107
  Turgot's alleged translation of, xiv

Interest, xii, xiv, xxvii, xxviii, 2, 3, 10, 11, 30, 56, 77–81, 87–88, 149–163
  as price of capital, 113

Interest (*contd*)
  and profits, 153–154
  determined by supply and demand, 11, 81, 153–154, 161
  effects of high, 9, 29
  legal regulation of, 113–114, 151–152
  theological arguments on, XIX, XXVIII, 11, 78–79, 80–81, 155–160

Jaucourt, 17
Johnson, Samuel, 16

Knies, K., XXIX, 164
Ko and Yang, XVIII

Labour, productive and unproductive, XXV
  see also class analysis
Laissez-faire, IX, X, XVII, XXVIII, XXXIII
  Origin of, 40
Land,
  division of, 43–44
  ownership of, 47–48
  value of, 67–68, 72
Land tax, XXI, XXII, 104, 106
  see also taxes
Laverdy, Contrôleur-Général, XXX
Law, John, XII, 3
  his financial system, 1, 2, 4, 147
  Money and Trade Considered, 2, 3, 4, 5, 7
Law of gravity, 21
Laws of nature, 21
Laws of returns, 111–113
Legendre, F., 40
Lespinasse, Mlle de, XXX, 165
Le Trosne, G. F., 165
Letter on Marque de fers, X, XXIX, XXXIII–XXXIV, 16, 182–188
Letter on Paper Money, X, XI–XIII, XXXIV, 1–8, 147
Letters on the Grain Trade, XXX–XXXIII, XXXIV–XXXV, 46, 65, 127, 164–181, 187
Liberty, 29, 30, 183
  see also freedom, free trade
Locke, John, XII, 4, 11, 47
Louis XIV, King of France, 110
Louis XVI, King of France, IX, 22
Luke, gospel of, 78, 80, 159
Lundberg, I. C., XIX, XXI, XXXV, 44
Luxury, 9, 29, 84–85, 168

McCulloch, J. R., X
Maîtrisse des boulangers, 180
Markets, XVI, 14–15, 130–131
  see also fairs
Marking, of commodities, 12, 16, 27, 182–188
Marmontel, J. F., XVI, 20, 29
Marshall, A., XXX
Maurepas, J. F. R., Comte de, 22, 23
Measure of value, XXVI, 4, 58–59, 140
  see also value
Meek, R. L., X, XXXIV
  Turgot on Progress, X, XVIII, XX, XXI, XXXVI
Melon, J. F., XII
Métayage, 54–55
Mirabeau, V. de R., Comte de, 108, 123, 164
  Ami des hommes, 123
  Philosophie rurale, XXII, XXIII, 106, 118, 123
  Théorie de l'impôt, XXII, 106, 107, 108, 123
Mizuta, H., XXVI
Money, XII, XXIV, XXVI, 3, 4, 11, 59–60, 60–61, 133–136
  circulation of, 7, 9, 75–76, 95, 115–122, 128, 153
  value of, XXVII, 81–84
  see also gold and silver, quantity theory, paper money
Money of account, XXVII, 134–135
Monopoly, 25, 183, 184
Monroe, A. E., 140, 154, 155
Montesquieu, C. S. de,
  L'Esprit des Lois, XII, 152, 159
  Lettres persanes, XII
Morellet, l'Abbé de, XXVI–XXVII, XXX, 165
  Dictionaire de commerce, XXVI–XXVII, 133
  Mémoires de, XIV, XV, XXVI
  Turgot's correspondence with, XXX, 165
Morley, J., IX
Moses, 11, 159
Moveable wealth, 65–66, 67, 94
  see also advances, capital

Natural liberty, 26
 see also freedom, free trade, liberty
Net product, XXV, 48–49, 71, 102–103, 126, 127, 169
Net revenue, 28
Neymark, A., x, XVIII
Notes on the translation of Child, XIII–XIV, XXXIV, 9–13, 29, 31

Observations on Graslin, XXIV–XXV, 46, 110, 123–132, 140
Observations on Saint-Péravy, XXIII–XXIV, 109–122, 126
Oncken, A., 40
Origin of towns, 15–16

Palgrave,
 Dictionary of Political Economy, 33, 35, 40
Paper money, 3–4, 5
 see also money
Paper on Lending at Interest, XIX, XXVII–XXIX, XXXIII, XXXIV, 80, 149–163
Pâris-Duverney, J., XII
Peel, Robert, x
Physiocrats, XX, XXIII, XXV
Pinto, Isaac de, 168
Plan d'un ouvrage sur le commerce, XIII
Plan for a Paper on Taxation, XXI–XXII, 96–108
Police, 16
Pothier, R. J., 157
Price, XXX, XXXII, 15, 26, 145–146, 175–176, 178–179
 of grain, 170–171, 176
 see also value
Privileges, 16, 17
Profit, 2, 9, 10, 14, 26, 29, 69–70, 74, 76, 80, 87, 94, 115, 149–150, 153–154, 168, 170, 171, 174, 187

Quantity theory of money, XII, 4, 5–7, 81–84
Quesnay, F., x, XIII, XIV, XXII, 72, 102, 103, 110, 117, 118
 Analyse du formule arithmétique, 103, 109
 Dialogue sur le commerce, 118
 Explication, 103
 Fermier, 17, 103, 125, 174
 Grains, 29, 103, 125
 Hommes, 117
 Impôt, XV, 102, 103, 104, 108, 114
 Intérêt de l'argent, XV
 Maximes générales, 103
 Philosophie rurale, XXIII, 103, 106
 Tableau économique, XVII, XXIII, 89
Questions sur le Chine, XVII–XVIII

Reflections on the Formation ... of Wealth, x, XI, XVII–XXI, XXV, XXVI, XXVIII, XXIX, XXXII, 43–95, 153, 155, 156
 1788 edition, XX, XXXV, 62, 74, 75, 77, 78, 92
 tirage-à-part, XVII, XX, XXXV, 62, 75, 76, 77, 78, 92
Rentes constituées, 1
Rentier, 9, 113
Revenue, XXII, XXV, 3, 8, 18, 27, 30, 48–49, 50, 56, 98, 102–104, 123, 124–125, 166–167, 171
Ricardo, D., x
Risk, 26, 154, 161
Rivière, Mercier de la, 114
Roberts, H. van Dyke, 104
Robineau, G., XIX
Rossi, P. L. E., x
Rousseau, J. J., 17, 97

Saint-Maur, Dupré de, 174
Saint-Péravy, G. de, XXIII, XXIV, 109–110, 126
 Mémoire sur ... l'impôt indirect, 109–110, 113–115
Saving-investment analysis, XXIV, 95, 121–122
Say, J. B., x, XX
Say, Léon, XV
Say's Law, XIV
Schelle, G., XIII, XVII, XXXV–XXXVI
 Pourquoi les Réflexions ..., XIX, XX, 50
 Premiers travaux économiques ..., XI
 Turgot, XI
 Vincent de Gournay, XIII, XV, XVII, 20, 40
Schumpeter, J. A., XVIII, XXIV
Sée, H., 12
Self interest, 16, 25–26, 29, 40, 187
Shepherd, R. P., IX

Silhouette, M. de, Contrôleur-Général, 37
Slavery, 51–53, 60, 67, 160
Smith, A., x, xviii, xxvi, 16, 95
Smuggling, 29, 30, 31, 114–115
Specie mechanism, 118–119
Stark, W., xxix
Stephens, W. W., ix, x, xvi, xxxiv
Sully, M. le duc de, 126

Taille, 30, 99, 106, 108
Tariffs, 30
Taxation, xii, xxi, xxv, 7, 17, 93, 96–108
  Direct, xxii, 97–99
  Indirect, xxii, xxiii, xxiv, xxv, 97–98, 100–102, 110
Taxes, 10, 16, 17, 18, 129–132
  and disposable wealth, 124–125
  and inflationary finance, 7
  as obstacles to industry, 30
  on consumption, 97–99, 114–115, 132, 167
  on house rent, xxiii, 114
  on interest, 113–114
  on luxury goods, xxiii, 114–115, 132
  paid by landowner, 31, 169
  see also accise, aide, corvée, landtax, *taille, vingtième*
Tax-farm, xxiv, 30–31, 115–116
Terrasson, l'Abbé J., xii
  Lettres sur le nouveau système . . ., 1, 2, 3, 4, 5, 6, 7
Terray, l'Abbé, Contrôleur-Général, xxxi–xxxiii, 16, 164–165
Tirage-à-part,
  see Reflections on the Formation . . . of Wealth
Tithe, 93, 104–105
Tocqueville, A. de, 180
Tolls, 17
Thrift, 9, 69, 84–85, 94, 160
Trudaine, D. C., xiii, 33
Trudaine, J. C., xiii, 33
Tucker, Josiah, xiii, xiv, xviii, xxxii, 171
Tull, Jethro, 111
Turgot, A. R. J.
  and Adam Smith, x, xviii, xxvi, 95
  and Gournay, xiii, xvi–xvii
  and Morellet, xxvi–xxvii
  and Quesnay, x, xiii
  as economist, x–xi
  as contributor to *Encyclopédie*, xiv, xv, xviii, xxvi, 14
  as translator, xiv, xv

Usury, 11, 149–150, 160
  see also interest
Utrecht, Treaty of, 23

Value, xxv, xxvi, 21, 57–58, 120, 124–125, 136–139
  and time, xxvii, 155–157, 158–159
  see also appreciative value, esteem value, exchange value, price
Value and Money, x, xxv–xxvii, 133–148, 156
Vattierlle, E., xxiv
Vauban, S. le Prestre de, xxii, 104
Verduc, C., 37
Véri, l'Abbé de, 1, 22
Vigreux, P. B., xii, xxvi
Villebarre, M. J. de, 23
Vingtième, 106, 107
Virgil, xxi
Voltaire, F. M. A. de, xv, xxi, 168
  Siècle de Louis XIV, 2, 68

Wages, xxv, 45–46, 65, 104, 126–127, 131, 167–168, 170, 171, 175–176, 177, 178–179
Wages fund, 174
Wealth, 5, 21, 27, 28, 88–89, 123, 172
  definition of, xiii, xxv
  disposable, 91–94, 125
  Turgot's *piece* on, xix, 43–95
Wicksell, K., xxx
Wit, Johan de, 22, 38

Yomakawa, Y., xxiv

APPENDIX

Notes to Appendix: Concordance to various editions of the Reflections

Because the *Reflections* is the work by Turgot most frequently referred to by commentators who have used the variety of editions in which this work was published over the last two hundred years, a concordance of the present edition of the *Reflections* with other frequently used editions will be found useful. This is all the more useful because the numbering of the sections of the *Reflections* is not uniform in these editions: for example, section 38 of the present edition is the equivalent of section 40 (XL) in the widely used Daire edition.

In order of their appearance, the following editions have been included in the concordance:

(1) the *tirage-à-part*, prepared for Turgot by Du Pont de Nemours in 1770;
(2) the version printed by Du Pont de Nemours in the *Ephémérides du Citoyen* in serial form in the issues of November and December, 1769 and January, 1770;
(3) the edition published in 1788, from which the present translation has been made;
(4) the 1793 English translation, as reprinted in J. R. McCulloch (editor), *A Select Collection of Scarce and Valuable Economical Tracts*, published in 1859;
(5) the version included by Du Pont in his edition of *Oeuvres de Turgot*, Vol. V;
(6) the Du Pont version reprinted by E. Daire in his edition of *Oeuvres de Turgot*, Vol. I, published in 1844;
(7) the Ashley translation published in the Macmillan reprints of Economic Classics series in 1898;
(8) the version published by G. Schelle in his edition of *Oeuvres de Turgot*, Vol. II.

The first column indicates the section numbering of the present edition together with the opening words of the section title. For each of the above-mentioned editions, the following information is provided:
(i) the number under which that section appears in that edition;
(ii) the number of paragraphs contained in the section in that edition;
(iii) the page reference to the section in that edition.
For the version printed in the *Ephémérides*, there is a fourth column which indicates the part of the journal in which the section appeared, Parts I, II, III referring to November, December 1769 and January 1770 respectively. An asterisk behind the page reference to the version printed in Du Pont's edition of *Oeuvres de Turgot* indicates that Du Pont inserted a note to that section written by himself.

APPENDIX—A CONCORDANCE TO VARIOUS EDITIONS OF THE REFLECTIONS

Present Edition		*Tirage-à-part*			*Ephémérides*				*1788*			*1795*			*Du Pont, Oeuvres V*			*Daire I*			*Ashley*			*Schelle II*		
Sect.	*Title*	*Sect.*	*No. of Paras.*	*pp.*	*Sect.*	*Part of Journal*	*No. of Paras.*	*pp.*	*Sect.*	*No. of Paras.*	*pp.*	*Sect.*	*No. of Paras.*	*pp.*	*Sect.*	*No. of Paras.*	*pp.*	*Sect.*	*No. of Paras.*	*pp.*	*Sect.*	*No. of Paras.*	*pp.*	*Sect.*	*No. of Paras.*	*pp.*
1	The impossibility of . . .	I	1	3–4	I	I	1	14	I	1	5–6	1	1	243	I	1	1	I	1	7	I	1	3	I	1	534
2	The above hypothesis . . .	II	3	4–6	II	I	3	15–16	II	3	6–7	2	3	243–244	II	3	2–3	II	3	7–8	II	3	3–4	II	3	534–535
3	The products of the earth	III	1	6–8	III	I	1	17–19	III	1	7–9	3	1	244–245	III	1	3–4	III	1	8–9	III	1	5–6	III	1	535–536
4	The necessity of . . .	IV	1	8–9	IV	I	1	19–20	IV	1	9–10	4	1	245–246	IV	2	5	IV	2	9	IV	1	6	IV	2	536
5	Pre-eminence of . . .	V	1	10–12	V	I	1	20–22	V	1	10–11	5	1	246–247	V	1	6–7	V	1	9–10	V	1	7–8	V	1	536–537
6	The wages of . . .	VI	1	12–13	VI	I	1	23	VI	1	12	6	1	247	VI	1	7–8	VI	1	10	VI	1	8	VI	1	537
7	The Husbandman is . . .	VII	1	13–14	VII	I	1	24–25	VII	1	12–13	7	1	248	VII	1	8–9	VII	1	10–11	VII	1	9	VII	1	538
8	First division of . . .	VIII	1	14–15	VIII	I	1	25–26	VIII	1	14	8	1	248–249	VIII	1	9–10	VIII	1	11–12	VIII	1	10	VIII	1	538
9	In Ancient times . . .	IX	1	15–17	IX	I	1	26–27	IX	1	14–15	9	1	249	IX	1	10–11	IX	1	12	IX	1	10–11	IX	1	539
10	Progress of society . . .	X	1	17	X	I	1	28	X	1	15–16	10	1	249–250	X	1	11	X	1	12	X	1	11	X	1	539
11	The Proprietors begin . . .	XI	1	18	XI	I	1	28–29	XI	1	16	11	1	250	XI	1	11–12	XI	1	13	XI	1	12	XI	1	539–540
12	Inequality in . . .	XII	1	18–21	XII	I	1	29–31	XII	1	17–18	12	1	250–251	XII	4	12–13*	XII	5	13–14	XII	1	12–13	XII	5	540–541
13	Consequence of . . .	XIII	1	21	XIII	I	1	32	XIII	1	18–19	13	1	251–252	XIII	1	14	XIII	1	14	XIII	1	13–14	XIII	1	541
14	Division of the produce . . .	XIV	1	22	XIV	I	1	33	XIV	1	19–20	14	1	252	XIV	1	14–15	XIV	1	14	XIV	1	14	XIV	1	541
15	A new division of . . .	XV	1	23–24	XV	I	1	34–35	XV	1	20	15	1	252	XV	1	15–16	XV	1	14–15	XV	1	14–15	XV	1	541–542
16	Resemblance between . . .	XVI	1	24–25	XVI	I	1	35–36	XVI	1	21	16	1	253	XVI	1	16	XVI	1	15	XVI	1	15	XVI	1	542
17	Essential difference . . .	XVII	2	25–27	XVII	I	2	36–38	XVII	2	21–23	17	2	253–254	XVII	4	16–18	XVII	4	15–16	XVII	2	16–17	XVII	4	542–543
18	This difference . . .	XVIII	1	27	XVIII	I	1	38	XVIII	1	23	18	1	254	XVIII	1	18	XVIII	1	16	XVIII	1	17	XVIII	1	543
19	How the Proprietors . . .	XIX	1	28	XIX	I	1	39	XIX	1	24	19	1	254–255	XIX	1	19	XIX	1	16	XIX	1	17	XIX	1	543
20	First method . . .	XX	1	28–29	XX	I	2	39–41	XX	1	24–25	20	1	255	XX	4	19–20	XX	4	16–17	XX	1	18	XX	4	544
21	Second method . . .	XXI	4	29–32	XXI–XXIII	I	3	41–45	XXI	4	25–27	21	4	255–256	XXI–XXIII	—	20–24	XXI–XXIII	—	17–18	XXI	4	19–20	XXI	4	544–547
22	Cultivation by slaves . . .	XXII	1	32–33	XXIV	I	1	46	XXII	1	27–28	22	1	257	XXIV	1	24–25	XXIV	1	19	XXII	1	20	XXII	1	547–548
23	Bondage to the soil . . .	XXIII	1	33–34	XXV	I	1	47	XXIII	1	28–29	23	1	257	XXV	2	25	XXV	2	19	XXIII	1	20–21	XXIII	2	548
24	Vassalage succeeds . . .	XXIV	1	34–35	XXVI	I	1	48–49	XXIV	1	29–30	24	1	257–258	XXVI	1	26	XXVI	1	19–20	XXIV	1	21–22	XXIV	1	548
25	Fourth Method . . .	XXV	1	35–37	XXVII	I	1	49–51	XXV	1	30–31	25	1	258–259	XXVII	1	27–28	XXVII	1	20–21	XXV	1	22–23	XXV	1	549
26	Fifth Method . . .	XXVI	1	38–39	XXVIII	I	1	51–53	XXVI	1	31–32	26	1	259–260	XXVIII	1	28–29	XXVIII	1	21	XXVI	1	23–24	XXVI	1	549–550
27	The last method . . .	XXVII	2	39–40	XXIX	I	2	53–54	XXVII	2	33	27	2	260	XXIX	2	29–30	XXIX	2	21	XXVII	2	24	XXVII	2	550
28	Recapitulation . . .	XXVIII	8	40–42	XXX	I	8	54–55	XXVIII	8	33–35	28	8	260–261	XXX	3	30–31	XXX	3	22	XXVIII	8	25	XXVIII	3	550–551
29	Of Capitals in general . . .	XXIX	1	42–43	XXXI	II	1	31	XXIX	1	35	29	1	261	XXXI	1	31–32	XXXI	1	22	XXIX	1	27	XXIX	1	551
30	Of the use of . . .	XXX	1	43	XXXII	II	1	32	XXX	1	35–36	30	1	261	XXXII	1	32	XXXII	1	22–23	XXX	1	27	XXX	1	551
31	Rise of Commerce	XXXI	1	43–46	XXXIII	II	1	32–35	XXXI	1	36–38	31	1	262–263	XXXIII	1	32–34	XXXIII	1	23	XXXI	1	28–29	XXXI	1	552
32	How current value . . .	XXXII	1	46–48	XXXIV	II	1	35–36	XXXII	1	38–39	32	1	263	XXXIV	1	34–36	XXXIV	1	24	XXXII	1	29–30	XXXII	1	553
33	Commerce gives . . .	XXXIII	1	48–49	XXXV	II	1	37–38	XXXIII	1	39–40	33	1	264	XXXV	1	36	XXXV	1	24	XXXIII	1	30–31	XXXIII	1	553–554
34	Each commodity may . . .	XXXIV	2	49–51	XXXVI	II	2	38–40	XXXIV	2	40–41	34	2	265	XXXVI	3	37–38	XXXVI	3	25	XXXIV	2	31–32	XXXIV	3	554
35	Every commodity does . . .	XXXV	1	51–52	XXXVII	II	1	40–41	XXXV	1	42–43	35	1	265–266	XXXVII	4	38–39	XXXVII	4	25–26	XXXV	1	32–33	XXXV	4	555
36	For want of . . .	XXXVI	1	53–54	XXXVIII	II	1	42–43	XXXVI	1	43–44	36	1	266	XXXVIII	2	40–41	XXXVIII	2	26	XXXVI	1	33–34	XXXVI	2	555–556
37	Examples of . . .	XXXVII	2	55–56	XXXIX	II	2	44–45	XXXVII	2	44–45	37	2	266–267	XXXIX	4	41–42	XXXIX	4	27	XXXVII	2	34–35	XXXVII	4	556–557
38	Every commodity is . . .	XXXVIII	1	57–58	XL	II	1	46–47	XXXVIII	1	46–47	38	1	267–268	XL	3	43	XL	3	27–28	XXXVIII	1	35–36	XXXVIII	3	557
39	Every commodity has . . .	XXXIX	1	58–59	XLI	II	1	47–48	XXXIX	1	47–48	39	1	268	XLI	1	44	XLI	1	28	XXXIX	1	36	XXXIX	1	557–558
40	Reciprocally . . .	XL	1	59	XLII	II	1	48	XL	1	48	40	1	268	XLII	1	45	XLII	1	28	XL	1	36	XL	1	558
41	Different substances . . .	XLI	1	60–61	XLIII	II	1	49–50	XLI	1	48–49	41	1	269	XLIII	1	45–46	XLIII	1	28–29	XLI	1	37	XLI	1	558
42	Metals, and . . .	XLII	2	61–63	XLIV	II	2	50–52	XLII	2	49–50	42	2	269–270	XLIV	2	46–48	XLIV	2	29–30	XLII	2	37–39	XLII	2	558–559
43	By the nature of . . .	XLIII	1	64–65	XLV	II	1	53–54	XLIII	1	51	43	1	270–271	XLV	2	48–49	XLV	2	30	XLIII	1	39	XLIII	2	559–560
44	The employment of . . .	XLIV	1	65	XLVI	II	1	54	XLIV	1	52–53	44	1	271	XLVI	3	49	XLVI	3	30	XLIV	1	39–40	XLIV	3	560
45	The use of gold and . . .	XLV	1	66	XLVII	II	1	55	XLV	1	53	45	1	271	XLVII	1	50	XLVII	1	30	XLV	1	40	XLV	1	560
46	Variations in . . .	XLVI	2	66–68	XLVIII	II	2	55–57	XLVI	2	53–55	46	3	271–272	XLVIII	4	50–52	XLVIII	4	31	XLVI	2	40–41	XLVI	4	560–561
47	The practice of paying . . .	XLVII	1	69	XLIX	II	1	58	XLVII	1	55–56	47	1	273	XLIX	2	52	XLIX	2	31–32	XLVII	1	41	XLVII	2	561–562
48	The use of money . . .	XLVIII	1	70	L	II	1	59	XLVIII	1	56	48	1	273	L	1	53	L	1	32	XLVIII	1	42	XLVIII	1	562
49	Concerning the storing . . .	XLIX	1	70–71	LI	II	1	59–60	XLIX	1	56–57	49	1	273–274	LI	1	53–54	LI	1	32	XLIX	1	43	XLIX	1	562
50	Moveable wealth . . .	L	1	71–73	LII	II	1	60–62	L	1	57–58	50	1	274–275	LII	1	54–55*	LII	1	32–33	L	1	43–44	L	1	562–563
51	Moveable wealth is . . .	LI	1	73–74	LIII	II	1	62–63	LI	1	59	51	1	275	LIII	1	56	LIII	1	33	LI	1	44–45	LI	1	563
52	Necessity of advances . . .	LII	1	74–75	LIV	II	1	63–64	LII	1	59–60	52	1	275	LIV	1	56–57	LIV	1	34	LII	1	45	LII	1	563–564
53	First advances . . .	LIII	1	75–76	LV	II	1	64–65	LIII	1	60–61	53	1	276	LV	1	57–58	LV	1	34	LIII	1	46	LIII	1	564
54	Cattle, moveable wealth . . .	LIV	1	77–78	LVI	II	1	66–67	LIV	1	61–62	54	1	276–277	LVI	3	58–59	LVI	3	35	LIV	1	47	LIV	3	564–565
55	Another kind . . .	LV	1	78–79	—	—	—	—	LV	1	63	55	1	277	—	—	—	—	—	—	LV	1	47–48	LV	2	565
56	Moveable wealth has . . .	LVI	1	79–80	LVII	II	2	67–69	LVI	1	63–64	56	1	278	LVII	2	59–61	LVII	2	35–36	LVI	1	48–49	LVI	1	565–566
57	Valuation of lands	LVII	1	80–82	LVIII	II	1	69–70	LVII	1	65–66	57	1	278–279	LVIII	1	61–62	LVIII	1	36	LVII	1	49–50	LVII	1	566–567
58	Every money capital	LVIII	1	82–84	LIX	II	1	71–73	LVIII	1	66–68	58	1	279–280	LIX	1	62–63	LIX	1	36–37	LVIII	1	50–51	LVIII	1	567
59	Another employment . . .	LIX	1	84–85	LX	II	1	73–74	LIX	1	68–69	59	1	280	LX	1	64	LX	1	37–38	LIX	1	51–52	LIX	1	567–568
60	Further explanations . . .	LX	1	85–89	LXI	II	1	74–78	LX	1	69–72	60	1	280–282	LXI	1	65–67	LXI	1	38–39	LX	1	52–54	LX	1	568–589
61	Subdivision of . . .	LXI	1	89–90	LXII	II	1	78–79	LXI	1	72–73	61	1	282	LXII	1	67–68	LXII	1	39	LXI	1	54	LXI	1	569–570
62	Another employment . . .	LXII	1	90–92	LXIII	II	1	79–81	LXII	1	73–75	62	1	283–284	LXIII	2	68–70	LXIII	2	39–40	LXII	1	54–56	LXII	2	570–571
63	The competition . . .	LXIII	1	93	LXIV	II	1	82	LXIII	1	75–76	63	1	284	LXIV	2	70–71	LXIV	2	40	LXIII	1	56	LXIII	2	571
64	The lack of capitalist . . .	LXIV	1	94–95	LXV	II	1	83–84	LXIV	1	76–77	64	1	284–285	LXV	4	71–72	LXV	4	40–41	LXIV	1	57	LXIV	4	571–572
65	Subdivision of the class . . .	LXV	1	95–96	LXVI	II	1	84–85	LXV	1	77–78	65	1	285	LXVI	1	72	LXVI	1	41	LXV	1	58	LXV	1	572
66	Fourth employment . . .	LXVI	1	96–99	LXVII	II	1	85–88	LXVI	2	78–81	66	2	285–287	LXVII	8	73–75	LXVII	8	41–42	LXVI	2	58–60	LXVI	8	572–573
67	Different orders . . .	LXVI	1	100–103	LXVIII	II	2	89–92	LXVI	2	81–84	67	1	287–289	LXVIII	2	76–80*	LXVIII	2	43–45	LXVII	2	60–62	LXVII	2	573–575
68	The true idea of . . .	LXVII	1	103–105	LXIX	II	1	92–94	LXVII	1	84–85	68	1	289	LXIX	1	80–82	LXIX	1	45	LXVIII	1	62–63	LXVIII	1	575
69	All enterprises . . .	LXVIII	1	105–106	LXX	II	1	94–95	LXVIII	1	86–87	69	1	290	LXX	1	82–83	LXX	1	45–46	LXIX	1	63–64	LXIX	1	575–576
70	Capitals being . . .	LXIX	1	107–108	LXXI	II	1	96	LXIX	1	87–88	70	1	290–291	LXXI	1	83	LXXI	1	46	LXX	1	64–65	LXX	1	576
71	Fifth employment of . . .	LXX	1	108–109	LXXII	II	1	97–98	LXX	1	88–89	71	1	291	LXXII	2	84	LXXII	2	46	LXXI	1	65	LXXI	2	576–577
72	False ideas about . . .	LXXII	1	109–110	LXXIII	III	1	114–115	LXXI	1	89–90	72	1	291–292	LXXIII	2	85	LXXIII	2	47	LXXII	1	67	LXXII	2	577
73	Errors of the . . .	LXXIII	2	110–115	—	—	—	—	LXXII	2	90–94	73	2	292–294	— —	—	—	—	—	—	LXXIII	2	68–70	LXXIII	3	577–579
74	True foundation of . . .	LXXIV	1	115–117	LXXIV	III	1	115–117	LXXIII	1	94–96	74	1	294–295	LXXIV	1	86–87	LXXIV	1	47–48	LXXIV	1	71–72	LXXIV	1	579–580
75	Reply to an objection . . .	LXXV	1	117–121	—	—	—	—	LXXIV	1	96–99	75	2	295–297	— —	—	—	—	—	—	LXXV	1	72–73	—	—	—
76	The rate of interest . . .	LXXVI	1	121–122	LXXV	III	1	117–118	LXXV	1	99–100	76	1	297	LXXV	1	87–88	LXXV	1	48	LXXVI	1	74	LXXV	1	580–581
77	Money has two . . .	LXXVII	1	123–124	LXXVI	III	1	119–120	LXXVI	1	100–101	77	1	298	LXXVI	3	88–89	LXXVI	3	48	LXXVII	1	74–75	LXXVI	3	581
78	These two valuations . . .	LXXVIII	4	124–128	LXXVII	III	2	120–134	LXXVII	4	101–104	78	4	298–300	LXXVII	7	89–100*	LXXVII	7	49–53	LXXVIII	4	75–77	LXXVII	7	581–586
79	In the valuation of . . .	LXXIX	1	128–129	LXXVIII	III	1	134–135	LXXVIII	1	105–106	79	1	300–301	LXXVIII	1	101–102	LXXVIII	1	54	LXXIX	1	77–78	LXXVIII	1	587
80	The price of interest . . .	LXXX	1	130–132	LXXIX	III	1	136–138	LXXIX	1	106–108	80	1	301–302	LXXIX	3	102–103	LXXIX	3	54–55	LXXX	1	78–79	LXXIX	3	587–588
81	The spirit of thrift . . .	LXXXI	1	132–133	LXXX	III	1	138–139	LXXX	1	108	81	1	302	LXXX	1	104*	LXXX	1	55	LXXXI	1	79–80	LXXX	1	588
82	The fall in the rate . . .	LXXXII	1	133–134	LXXXI	III	1	139–140	LXXXI	1	109–110	82	1	302–303	LXXXI	1	104–105	LXXXI	1	55–56	LXXXII	1	80	LXXXI	1	588–589
83	Recapitulation of . . .	LXXXIII	6	134–135	LXXXII	III	6	141–142	LXXXII	6	110–111	83	6	303	LXXXII	6	105–106	LXXXII	6	56	LXXXIII	6	81	LXXXII	6	589
84	The influence which . . .	LXXXIV	1	135	LXXXIII	III	1	142	LXXXIII	1	111	84	1	303	LXXXIII	1	106	LXXXIII	1	56	LXXXIV	1	81	LXXXIII	1	589–590
85	Money invested in land . . .	LXXXV	1	136	LXXXIV	III	1	142–143	LXXXIV	1	111–112	85	1	303–304	LXXXIV	1	107	LXXXIV	1	56	LXXXV	1	82	LXXXIV	1	590
86	Money placed on loan . . .	LXXXVI	1	136–137	LXXV	III	1	143	LXXXV	1	112	86	1	304	LXXXV	3	107–108*	LXXXV	3	56–57	LXXXVI	1	82	LXXXV	3	590
87	Money invested in . . .	LXXXVII	1	137–138	LXXXVI	III	1	144–146	LXXXVI	1	113	87	1	304–305	LXXXVI	1	108–109	LXXXVI	1	57	LXXXVII	1	83	LXXXVI	1	591
88	However, the product . . .	LXXXVIII	2	138–141	LXXXVII	III	2	146–148	LXXXVII	2	114–116	88	2	305–306	LXXXVII	2	109–111	LXXXVII	2	57–58	LXXXVIII	2	83–85	LXXXVII	2	591–592
89	The current interest . . .	LXXXIX	1	141–143	LXXXVIII	III	1	149–150	LXXXIII	1	116–117	89	1	306–307	LXXXVIII	3	111–113	LXXXVIII	3	58–59	LXXXIX	1	85–86	LXXXVIII	3	592–593
90	Influence of the rate . . .	XC	1	143–144	LXXXIX	III	1	151–152	LXXXIX	1	118	90	1	307	LXXXIX	1	113	LXXXIX	1	59	XC	1	86	LXXXIX	1	593
91	The total wealth	XCI	1	144–146	XC	III	1	152–154	XC	1	119–120	91	1	307–308	XC	2	114–115	XC	2	59–60	XCI	1	86–88	XC	3	593–594
92	The sum of capitals . . .	XCII	3	146–150	XCI	III	3	155–158	XCI	3	121–124	92	3	308–310	XCI	3	115–118	XCI	3	60–61	XCII	3	88–90	XCI	3	594–596
93	In which of the three . . .	XCIII	1	150–151	XCII	III	1	159	XCII	1	124	93	1	310	XCII	1	118–119	XCII	1	62	XCIII	1	90	XCII	1	596
94	The capitalist lender . . .	XCIV	1	151–153	XCIII	III	1	159–161	XCIII	1	125–126	94	2	310–311	XCIII	1	119–120	XCIII	1	62	XCIV	1	90–91	XCIII	1	596–597
95	The interest drawn . . .	XCV	1	153–154	XCIV	III	1	161–162	XCIV	1	126	95	1	311–312	XCIV	2	120–121	XCIV	2	62–63	XCV	1	92	XCIV	2	597
96	The interest of money . . .	XCVI	2	154–157	XCV	III	2	162–165	XCV	2	127–129	96	3	312–313	XCV	3	121–123	XCV	3	63–64	XCVI	2	92–94	XCV	3	597–598
97	Objection	XCVII	1	157	XCVI	III	1	165–166	XCVI	1	130	97	1	313	XCVI	1	123–124	XCVI	1	64	XCVII	1	94	XCVI	1	598
98	Answer to the objection . . .	XCVIII	2	157–159	XCVII	III	2	166–167	XCVII	2	130–131	98	2	313–314	XCVII	2	124–125*	XCVII	2	64	XCVIII	2	94–95	XCVII	2	599
99	There exists no truly . . .	XCIX	2	159–161	XCVIII	III	2	167–169	XCVIII	2	131–133	99	3	314–315	XCVIII	4	125–126	XCVIII	4	65	XCIX	2	95–96	XCVIII	4	599–600
100	The land has also . . .	C	1	161–163	XCIX	III	1	169–172	XCIX	1	133–135	100	3	315–316	XCIX	1	127–129	XCIX	1	65–66	C	1	96–98	XCIX	1	600–601
101	Although money is . . .	CI	1	164–165	C	III	1	172–173	C	1	135–136	101	1	316–317	C	1	129–130	C	1	66–67	CI	1	98–99	C	1	601